Rational
Exuberance

Rational Exuberance

The Influence of Generation X on the New American Economy

MEREDITH BAGBY

A DUTTON BOOK

DUTTON
Published by the Penguin Group
Penguin Putnam Inc., 375 Hudson Street, New York, New York 10014, U.S.A.
Penguin Books Ltd, 27 Wrights Lane, London W8 5TZ, England
Penguin Books Australia Ltd, Ringwood, Victoria, Australia
Penguin Books Canada Ltd, 10 Alcorn Avenue, Toronto, Ontario, Canada M4V 3B2
Penguin Books (N.Z.) Ltd, 182–190 Wairau Road, Auckland 10, New Zealand

Penguin Books Ltd, Registered Offices: Harmondsworth, Middlesex, England

First published by Dutton, an imprint of Dutton NAL, a member of Penguin Putnam Inc.

First Printing, September, 1998
10 9 8 7 6 5 4 3 2 1

 REGISTERED TRADEMARK—MARCA REGISTRADA

LIBRARY OF CONGRESS CATALOGING-IN-PUBLICATION DATA:
Bagby, Meredith E.
    Rational exuberance : the influence of generation X on the new American economy / Meredith Bagby.
    p. cm.
    ISBN 0-525-94408-7
    1. Generation X—United States—Attitudes.   2. Generation X—United States—Economic conditions.   3. Young consumers—United States.   4. United States—Economic conditions—1981–
I. Title.
HQ799.7.B34   1998
305.235—dc21   98-7453
                                                                              CIP

Printed in the United States of America
Set in Times New Roman

This book is printed on acid-free paper ∞

The Lilies of the Field

O star on the breast of the river,
O marvel of bloom and grace,
Did you fall straight down from heaven,
Out of the sweetest place?

"Nay, nay, I fell not out of heaven,
None gave me my saintly white:
It slowly grew from the blackness
Down in the dreary night.
From the ooze of the silent river
I won my glory and grace:
White souls fall not, O my poet,
They rise to the sweetest place."

—Anonymous

In memory of my grandmother, Ila Paunee Rigsby Bagby.

CONTENTS

ACKNOWLEDGMENTS

Many thanks to my editor, Kari Paschall, at Dutton Plume for the impetus to write this book and for her constant help and guidance.

Much appreciation to Nicole Davis, Katie McKaskie, Ann Arkush, John Coletti, and Erin Ortiz for their excellent research and input.

To the many young adults who were interviewed for this book—your examples show that we are anything but a doomed generation.

INTRODUCTION

Every generation has defining characteristics. My generation, strangely known as Generation X, is still in its formative stages. However, those of our population born after 1964, the end of the Baby Boomer age, have already grown features that markedly set us apart from any generation that has come before.

We have been determined by the negatives and positives of an American era that saw moms transformed into full-time workers, become masters of their own reproductive systems, and engineer elections through platforms they supported. We watched too many dads leave their kids behind in reckless abandon and shrink into the masses of downsized victims. We learned to view the government as a bottomless pit of corruption.

Enter Generation X. With caution—and on little cat feet—wary, worn before wear, fearful, and suspicious. Still, and in seeming contradiction, we came wrapped in the passions of newness and with the relentless energy that birth always spawns. Most significantly, we observed and set into our consciousness the lessons of the past—a rare and powerful trait that many generations have found foreign.

Listening and watching, we decided to turn the voices and strengths within ourselves to write our own destinies, and this has become our saving shield. We are above all self-reliant and self-defining. We start our own companies at a staggering rate. We take enormous personal and business risks. We explore. We invent. We question. We go our own way. The plusses of this behavior are legion as we lead our nation and our world into truly global, color-blind, nonideological, and border-less, thought, action, and production.

If there is one major flaw in us, it is our current inability to unify and marshal our beliefs into a cohesive political power. In order to change anything, and we see many changes that must be made in our world, we must work with reason and logic (our style anyway) and within the framework that we have inherited.

You will not see us march much on the streets. But we are lining up now in Washington, in state capitals and local courthouses, on Wall Street, Main Street, and Madison Avenue to see that reforms grow out of methodical transcendency and applied practicality.

Where is our idealism? Where are our stars? Where are our heavens? We have them and they are showing through, but perhaps in quieter and more subtle ways. We do not need to run people over or burn up civilization to change it. We approach the world scene with our own big stick—the click of our keyboards—and with our own special burst of passion delivered, not in emotionally charged demagoguery, but in rational exuberance.

Rational
Exuberance

CHAPTER I

"To a New Generation ..."

Setting the Record Straight

It is time for a new generation of leadership to cope with new problems and new opportunities. For this is a new world to be won. —John F. Kennedy

On January 20, 1961, President John F. Kennedy addressed a nation brimming with hope. In his inaugural address he told his listeners, "The torch has been passed to a new generation of Americans." His speech echoed the symbolic moment in the medieval tale of King Arthur. Arthur, on the eve of losing his kingdom, tells the story of Camelot to a country boy, Thomas of Warwick. He tells young Tom to keep the dream of Camelot alive, if only in his own thoughts. The message for Thomas and for us is clear. To each new generation falls the burden of carrying forward the lessons and the hopes of the last.

Whether at Arthur's court, in the Elysian fields, or on the Lost Horizon, we imagine for ourselves a happier time, a brighter tomorrow, a place where it never rains till after sundown. This vision is as old as human society itself. Whether driven by the logic of nature, our own hubris, or the spirituality of the undiscovered country, we are programmed with the optimism that all history leads to some end, that each human life is important, that every generation will do better than the last.

Our outlook ebbs and flows with the tides of human events. Some years make us hopeful; others bring despair. Yet even in our worst moments that optimism never perishes. In times of depression, war, tyranny, a people look to their young for the regeneration of the spirit, for the elixir of their ills, as the marvels of the future. Who can doubt the importance of youth in igniting the passion of the French Revolution, the resistance at Tiananmen Square, the arrogance of Nazi Germany, or the social upheaval in our own cultural revolution of the 1960s? For good or for evil, youth is a powerful marshaling force. As Joseph Conrad wrote, "Youth is the flame that lures us on to joys, to perils, to love, to vain effort. . . . It is the heat of life in the handful of dust."

America has always been a nation of youthful exuberance. We relish the story of the prodigy, the journey of the frontiersman. And yet in recent years we seem to be losing faith in our future. According to a *Washington Post*/ABC News polls, 70 percent of Americans believe that America's best years are behind us. *Newsweek* reported that almost 40 percent of us don't even believe that America will exist as one nation a hundred years from today. A survey conducted by the Public Agenda Group found that seven out of ten parents have a negative view of today's kids. The study reports that "regardless of racial or ethnic background, parents concur with the general public: they do not expect the current generation of children or teens to fulfill or redeem hopes for a better world."

The press reflects America's feelings about the next generation. Young adults have been dubbed the Doofus Generation, the New Lost, Grungers, New Petulants, Boomerang (poverty-stricken, we return to our parents), Generation P (poor and pissed off), the Scarce, Busters, 13ers (the thirteenth generation born in America), and the name that will never go away—Generation X. With the names came the comments . . . *Atlantic Monthly* called us "reckless bicycle messengers, hustlers, and McJobbers in the low wage/low benefit service economy." *Psychology Today* described us as "not knowing how to do an honest day's work." *Futurist* pinpointed our core traits as "lack of respect for authority, cynicism, materialism and selfishness." *U.S.*

News and World Report said we are nothing but "flesh and blood Bart Simpsons, so poorly educated that we can't find Vietnam on a map or date the Civil War within fifty years. With our MTV-rotted minds and sound-bite attention spans, we are a whiny cohort with the moral compass of a street gang." What's happening here? Why do Americans have such a negative view of their young?

As a culture, we were innocent in the fifties. Then came political assassinations, sexual and moral revolutions, an overthrow of the old stability. Peter Collier and David Horowitz, coauthors of *Destructive Generation*, said our parents' generation "was a time when the System—that collection of values that provide guidelines for societies as well as individuals—was assaulted and mauled. But while we wanted a revolution, we didn't have a plan. The decade ended with a big bang that made society into a collection of splintered groups, special interest organizations, and newly mined minorities, whose only common belief was that America was guilty and untrustworthy."

Generation X, never afforded the luxury of innocence, sorts through the debris. Our role in American history seems clear: If our parents' generation was about dismantling the status quo, our generation will be about building new institutions, moral codes, families, churches, corporations. As the demographer and marketing executive Karen Ritchie, the author of *Marketing to Generation X*, writes, "If the Boomers, as a group, tested every institution they encountered, dismantling in the process much of the foundation of the 1950s society, the task for Generation X will be the renovation of these institutions." Our job is to make order out of the chaos—to resurrect America from the ashes of burning crosses, draft cards, and bras, from the humiliation of public betrayals, from the rubble of riots from Kent State to Rodney King, from the shells of cities rotted by crime and despair, from the wreckage of broken homes. If our parents were the revolutionaries, then let us be the rebuilders.

Compared to the dimensions of the universe, the course of a human generation is but a breath in time. But measured by the challenges of the day a generation can change the course of human history. Think of the single generations that brought us the high art of the Renaissance, the philosophy of the Enlightenment, the religion of the Reformation, the poetry of the Romantics. In our own country, one generation had the vision to forge American independence, and another brought us through the Civil War. Other generations have given us the power of industry, the defense of liberty, the extension of civil rights. Our generation must be visionaries, too. We must reconstruct a society whose institutions have been torn asunder. And there is an urgency to our mission.

We have come of age in what appears to be a time of peace and prosperity. We are a generation that has not known wars, the hunger of depression, the fear of atomic destruction. But behind what the Czech president, Vaclav Havel, calls "civilization's thin veneer" there are the stirrings of future conflicts. Social, demographic, and economic whirlwinds are gathering force beneath the calm of today that, if ignored, could erupt during our lifetimes. The overextension of our government, growing economic inequality, increasing ethnic rumblings, deteriorating education systems, apathy from our citizenry, and an oversimplification of our problems by media and politicians threaten the health of our republic. At the heart of this book is the desire to present some of those challenges and how we, the next generation, will face them.

Don't Call Us Generation X

On second thought, if you are a politician, advertising or marketing director, credit card pusher, or spin doctor, don't call us—period. Most twenty-somethings recoil at the idea of being called Generation X, regarding it as a media ploy to get them to buy something.

The journalist Susan Faludi provides some insights into how the media came up with this handle and the myths it spreads about us. She explains that the media work like a game of "telephone." First a newspaper or magazine issues a trend story, then others pick it up and repeat it. America is consumed by trend stories, which show three characteristics: the absence of data, generalizations, and a "reliance on words like 'increasingly' and 'more and more.' " Trend spotting is a practice journalists use to take a stab at guessing where our culture might be heading. The trend spotters looked at the new crop of young adults and took a guess about what we were like, and gave their guess a label: Generation X.

In the media and advertising industry's game of "telephone," one of the first to spot us was *Time*, in the article "Proceeding with Caution" (July 1990). *Time*'s writers said we were whiners; they made the overarching claim, "The 20-something generation is balking at work, marriage, and Baby-Boomer values." Other magazines and papers soon followed, "assessing that guess," as Alex Abrams, the coauthor of *Late Bloomers*, notes. Television news, hungry for the new information, picked up on the images. Soon the entertainment industry jumped on the bandwagon with films like *Slackers* or *Reality Bites*, or the failed ABC sitcom, *Home Free*, about a young man who returns home to live with his parents. "A guess is reported, repeated, and finally returned to the country as truth because it has proved itself by appearing in so many venues," Abrams writes.

Advertising executives then needed to determine the character of their audience to clarify whom they were targeting. The generation to whom they direct their marketing must have a name and personality. Unfortunately, our generation has turned out to be so difficult to define that marketers have been left to draw straws for a way to pigeonhole us. With higher percentages of African-Americans, Latinos, and Asians, our generation is more ethnically diverse than the population at large—so diverse that advertisers have shifted their focus from demographics to "psychographics," a new science that categorizes people "by lifestyle and values rather than age." Likewise, pollsters need to identify a generation in order to predict its preferences in political parties and candidates.

Karen Ritchie contends that phrases like " 'Generation X' . . . become the essential building blocks for headline writers and million-dollar anchors." Television, especially, "relies on catchy phrases to pique the public interest and quickly and simply convey complex information and images. Trends and information become oversimplified. . . . Details get lost in broad brush strokes." What has been lost in these broad brush strokes is our ethnic diversity, complex political views (combining aspects of liberal and conservative), and the many facets of our multiple cultures and backgrounds.

Researchers and pollsters have discovered that we are a tricky market not easily conned by advertisers. We are not the apathetic "slackers" referred to by politicians. We cannot be typified by one distinctive personality type. We are an age group adaptable to an increasingly complex world. We are more tolerant than previous generations of deviations from the norm simply because there is no norm for us.

Considering the shoddy treatment of our age group by the media, I understand why so many people in it do not want to be identified by or slotted into any generational label. *American Demographic* reports that only 15 percent of young adults say they associate with a generation at all. The independent nature of this generation makes its members reluctant to cling to any group or institution. As John Coletti, the founder of Nylon, a web design company, put it, "I don't associate with any generation. I don't like labels. They are limiting." The Director of President Clinton's Medicare Commission, Bobby Jindal, says, "My generational affiliation is but one of many ways, and not even the most important one, to differentiate and identify myself."

Even so, most young adults realize the importance of "defining a generation." Society needs to make demographic assumptions about people in order to sell them goods, collect taxes, and dole out government benefits. How do you administer affirmative action if you don't define race? How do you mail Social Security checks if you can't measure seniority? How do you open a business if you can't define your market? Even though Anna Marie Nieves-Bryant, the executive director of the New York City office of Do Something, a national community service organization, doesn't like the term "Generation X," she realizes its potency. "Sometimes you have to use these terms to get your point across."

Photo Courtesy of Kellyanne Fitzpatrick

KELLYANNE FITZPATRICK
Founder, The Polling Company

POLLSTER, REPUBLICAN VOICE

In 1995, Kellyanne Fitzpatrick launched The Polling Company, a consulting and research firm that works with Republican candidates, conservative public-interest groups, and private companies. Speaker of the House Newt Gingrich calls her "an extraordinary political analyst" whose "insights ... are helping shape the national discussion." She is so effective at communicating the cause that she won a weekly slot on CNN's *Inside Politics* during the 1996 campaign. In her view, the biggest challenge for our generation is "providing our own children with what we didn't have: fathers, time, attention, security."

She says that it is a myth that young people don't want to be involved in politics. In fact, she says, technology could allow this generation to be more involved than any previous one. "We are going to be using the Net and new media as sources of news and information much more often and much more efficiently as one way to tear down institutional barriers toward more fluid voting."

Perhaps the biggest problem, though, with this label is that others created it. A Columbia University student, Nicole Davis, writes, "Only a handful of people born in this age group call themselves Generation X. What the media have effectively done is to create an identity for a group who does not tune in to these mainstream projections of news and trends. A vacuum is left in its place, an empty hole where members of our generation dare not venture. As long as we shrink from this generated name which represents us, our voices will not be heard." With their definitions, politicians, marketers, and spin doctors not only try to win our attention, they also shape the perception—and to a degree the reality—of our personalities, our views of ourselves, and our world. When we choose not to represent ourselves, the government and the media will do it for us.

Bigger Than You Thought

The media often present Generation X as a small demographic cohort sandwiched in between the huge Boomer generation and what many are now calling the "second baby boom," also called the boomlet. But the media have not told us the birth years of Generation X. Indeed, depending on the dates you choose, this generation could be anywhere from 30 million people to 80 million. If this generation extends for twenty years (the same size time frame attributed to the baby boom), Generation X is actually *larger* than the baby boom. So what is the right definition?

The baby boom started after the end of World War II. Between 1946 and 1964 75 million babies were born in America; adjusting for immigration and deaths there are presently 73 million Boomers representing about 29 percent of today's estimated 270 million Americans. Boomers have often been described by demographers as the pig in the python. They are also called the "tidal wave" because they are the largest sea of population ever to roll over the country. Our institutions and citizens must continually stretch and be reconfigured to accommodate the sheer size of the Boomer generation, willingly or not.

What no one could predict was that several forces would collide in the 1960s and 1970s to drive birthrates and family size down; this shaped the "baby bust" or Generation X experience and outlook. Between 1946 and 1957 births reached or surpassed 4 million each year. In 1965 the birthrate began to drop. This drop is what most historians point to as the natural end of the baby boom and the beginning of the next generation. By 1973 births had dropped 27 percent. During the baby boom, working dads and homemaker moms averaged 3.7 children, stretched over a decade or more. By the mid-1970s the average couple had fewer than 2 children.

Divorce, birth control, women's liberation, abortion, and a changing economy during the sixties and seventies account for the decline in the birthrate. During this time, divorce laws were liberalized and many marriages dissolved. By the 1970s the United States had the world's highest divorce rate. Empowered by new forms of birth control, legalization of abortion, the civil rights movement, and women's liberation, women were able to take control of their bodies. They could plan parenthood, pursue their education, and launch their careers. In addition, the strong economy of the 1960s and early 1970s provided better job opportunities for women. The economy's later downturn during the Carter administration made it imperative for some women to work. With fewer marriages holding together long enough to produce children and with the opportunity for more women to pursue careers, birthrates dropped. A new smaller generation was spawned in the seventies.

While most historians agree on a general starting point for Generation X, there is much contention on what marks the end of this generation. One camp put the end of the baby bust at 1976, when births started to pick up again as more Baby Boomers began to have children. Some call this generation the "baby boomlet," or even "Generation Y," and predict that it will be as large as and even may surpass the baby boom. Thus, Generation X, about 45 million people born between 1965 and 1976, is considerably smaller than the generations that flank it.

Are these the right definitions? How do you define a generation? Is it a decade? Two decades? Historians William Strauss and Neil Howe argue that a generation "mirrors the length of a phase in human life," which they take to be roughly twenty-one years. The boom was twenty years long. According to Strauss and Howe and some others, Generation X is much larger than the media represent. Their birth years extend from 1963 to 1982, making Generation X a remarkably large segment of the population. According to these estimates there are nearly 80 million people in the United States aged 15 to 35 as of 1997, outnumbering the baby boomers and making up 50 percent of the population aged 18 to 54. If Ritchie's estimates are in the ballpark, Generation X will be rewriting history books while revising the way its members are perceived by the media and politicians, owing to sheer numbers.

Slackers We're Not

Once the media appropriated the term "Generation X" to describe the generation that followed the Boomers, they had to come up with an image to go with the label. The prototypical GenXer became a "slacker." William Safire, in his weekly *New York Times Magazine* column, "On Language," put the word "slacker" under the microscope. It is defined as "one who avoids work or physical exercise; a shirker." The word was used during both world wars and Vietnam to denote draft dodgers, but in its present usage, "slacker" is closer to its original definition: lazy discontented youths content to watch reruns of the *Brady Bunch* on their parents' couch.

"Slacker" connotes a twenty-something who either chooses not to work or cannot find work. For whatever reason, it implies nonparticipation in the work system. Richard Linklater's 1991 film, *Slackers*, depicts a young bunch in Austin, Texas, out of college and not doing the work for which they were trained. Unwilling to reduce themselves to unfulfilling careers in telemarketing or fast food, the ensemble just hangs out, philosophizing over topics from politics to the cultural significance of the Big Gulp. The slacker myth implies that we can afford not to work. As the story goes, we are living in our parents' basements, glued to MTV, and using our college degrees as coasters.

There is no doubt that some slackers exist, but as *Late Bloomers* coauthor David Lipsky explains, "There's always a group that chooses not to join the dominant middle-class culture. In the fifties, it was the beats. In the sixties, it was the hippies. The media just rediscover the chameleon every ten years." The media make the lifestyle of a handful of people the stereotype for an entire generation. But the facts belie this picture. Most reports and numbers show that twenty-somethings work hard. Fact: According to the U.S. Census Bureau, people aged 24 to 35 work 3.6 percent longer each week than the national average. Lawrence Rifkin, 26, is a securities analyst in New York City by day and the owner of a pharmaceuticals company by night—which he runs from his one-bedroom apartment. He told *Forbes* magazine (May 8, 1995), "I'm up on weekends until three in the morning working on this." Rifkin is not atypical. "The so-called Generation X is the most entrepreneurial generation in American history," said *Forbes* magazine. Opinion Research Corporation confirmed the claim with a poll showing that 54 percent of 18-to-24-year-olds are highly interested in starting businesses, compared with 36 percent of 35-to-64-year-olds.

One reason for the misperceptions may be that young adults have a different work pattern than other generations. Distrustful of corporations who downsized our parents and more desirous of giving our children family time, which we never really had, we are reevaluating the "work ethic." In addition, our job prospects are often limited. According to Labor Department data, young adults have suffered an unemployment rate twice the national average for most of the 1990s.

Our generation faces the unavoidable fact that many jobs that previously required a high-school diploma now require a college degree. The Bureau of Labor Statistics predicts that the underemployment of young adults (for example, college graduates holding low-paying, low-responsibility positions) is likely to continue into the year 2005. Not coincidentally, the National Opinion Research Center at the University of Chicago found that job satisfaction is lowest among young adults. People aged 18 to 24 are most likely to say they are dissatisfied with their work. Behind this dissatisfaction is the fact that many young adults are in low-paying entry-level jobs. "I think we start in the basement then work to the bottom," quips a young woman in *The Baby Bust: A Generation Come of Age*, by William Dunn.

Aside from dissatisfaction with the job market, there is a desire to have a balanced life. Many of us growing up in the sixties and seventies either were children of divorce or had parents who worked. As a result, "quality time" for parents and children was sacrificed. According to the Families and Work Institute, 60 percent of men and women under age twenty-five with children would make "a lot" of sacrifices in money and career advancement in order to spend more time with their families (versus 34 percent of young workers overall). Unlike the Boomers, fewer of us measure our lives by our career status. A 1993 Roper Poll found that only 46 percent of our generation identified their jobs as an "expression of themselves," 10 percent less than Baby Boomers. *Time* said our generation was "planning its escape from the 9-to-5 routine."

Perhaps, that is why so many of us are attracted by the entrepreneurial lifestyle. A recent college grad, John Coletti, preferred to start his own Web site business to joining the ranks of corporate America. He says, "Our ethic is not one that pervaded the culture of the . . . post–World War II generation. We combine a belief in sixties idealism with social and economic pragmatism. Our ethic puts personal freedom, happiness, and lifestyle choice above the house in the suburbs, the new car, and the many other status symbols that characterize the 'work ethic' of past generations. For us, it is autonomy at all costs." This generation isn't lazy. It is just reevaluating the choices between career and other aspects of life.

Not Just White and Suburban

Who is in Generation X? Until now, the projected image has been primarily white and middle-class. As a result, minorities have been excluded from the attention Generation X has received. "Generation X doesn't mean much to many twenty-somethings of color," Allen Hughes, codirector of the film *Menace II Society*, said. "Our film had the same demographics as *Reality Bites*, but they didn't call it a Generation X film; they called it a damn gangster film. Call it racist, or whatever, but we don't count when it comes to Generation X." Considering the actual racial and cultural diversity of young adults, the stereotype of Generation X as white and middle-class is exceedingly narrow. As Karen Ritchie points out, "The white American of European descent, who was assumed to be the majority of the baby boom generation, may well be a minority in Generation X. And since so-called minorities comprise more than half of the population in six of the largest metropolitan areas in the U.S., who can realistically claim that Generation X applies to the white kids living in suburbia?"

Diversity is the name of the game for this generation. We have the highest percentage of naturalized citizens of any generation born in the twentieth century. White non-Hispanics are now 75 percent of the population and this percentage is expected to decline to 64 percent by the year 2020. The Census Bureau predicts that birthrates will be dramatically lower for white Americans than Hispanics, African-Americans, and Asians. By the year 2020, the average age of whites will be 42. That's 10 and 12 years older than that of blacks and Hispanics, respectively.

The popular media have largely ignored this ethnic diversity in their formulation of the image of our generation. David Mays, the founder and publisher of *The Source*, a hip-hop magazine, says, "The

Photo Courtesy of David Mays

DAVID MAYS
Founder, editor-in-chief, The Source

HIP-HOPSTER, FUTURE MEDIA MOGUL

He is the editor of *The Source*, the magazine of hip-hop music, culture, and politics, which is the biggest and fastest-growing newsstand title in America. His newsstand sales are more than those of *Rolling Stone*, *Spin*, and *Vibe* and the magazine had advertising revenues of more than $15 million in 1997 and total circulation of more than 350,000. Not bad for a guy who started a single-page newsletter in college with a $250 publishing budget. His secret to success? Hard work and perseverance. "I had times when we were just broke and the whole staff pretty much walked out. You have got to just stick with it and pull things through, when you really believe in something."

term 'Generation X' has little to do with us. There is an entire diverse generation growing up in America which is being ignored by the mainstream media." Already outnumbering African-Americans in our age group, Hispanics will be the largest minority in our country by 2010 and yet get little notice in mainstream media. The Hispanic recording artist Selena was all but ignored by the mainstream media until her murder revealed the groundswell of her fans. How many have heard of Luis Miguel? In 1996 he was one of the top-selling musical artists in the world and is quickly on his way to becoming Latin America's next Julio Iglesias.

Diversity isn't just ethnic: Consider the single mother. There are more than 8 million single-mother families in this demographic, yet how many of us think of the young mother as a representative of, or even as part of, "Generation X"?

Of course, these "oversights" reflect deeper problems in our society. How do we create a fair society when 25 percent of young black males are in prison? How do we communicate with each other when fewer and fewer of us speak English? How do we define race when more of us belong to many ethnicities? And when 2030 rolls around, how do we ask a poorer generation of Americans to pay for the retirement of older, whiter, richer folks? These are just some of the many questions that will confront us in the decades ahead. One thing is for sure—having a generational definition that leaves out entire portions of our population does not make finding answers easier.

Yes, We Have a Political Agenda

"Okay, we weren't at Woodstock, and we don't march for political events every six months, but we are there at Lollapalooza and we've had a few marches of our own," high school senior Erin Ortiz says of her generation. When she was just thirteen she participated in her first political event. It was a citywide school walkout to protest budget cuts in New York City's public schools. "We were tired of having to share textbooks with two other people. We were tired of having to stand in overcrowded classrooms because there weren't enough seats to go around and of simply never having enough teachers." As Erin tells it, it is not that young people don't care; it is just that the battles are different from those of generations past. The injustices tend to be economic and tend to be less visible than earlier ones simply because they don't have the visceral appeal of a slogan like "Make love, not war." Our battle cries are "Down with the deficit" or "Education first." Instead of burning bras, we plant trees. Let's face it, the photo op is just not there.

Even though you don't see us in the media as much as you saw our parents, we are still active community participants. A survey of almost nine thousand young people conducted by the Josephson Institute of Ethics based in Los Angeles found that nearly six in ten college students feel an ethical obligation to give to charity. Three fourths say that making a difference in the lives of others is very important. More than half say that doing volunteer work for a worthy cause is important. In fact, 68 percent of high school students and 73 percent of college students had done charity volunteer work at least once in the previous twelve months. The study shows that Generation X volunteers more than any other generation in America.

Kim Mowery took a year off from Brown University to serve as national director of the Sierra Student Coalition. "Whether it's mentoring kids or planting trees, people can directly do and see that they're making a difference. Volunteer work gives people instant gratification," she said. Or how about Kathryn McKell, who at age 20 is program manager for the AIDS Council of Manatee County, Florida. "People with AIDS get insulated from the community, fired from jobs, separated from their peer groups," says this GenXer who has worked with the National Civilian Community Corps as well as other volunteer efforts. You will also find young adults "being political" in the media as young commentators for CNN or MSNBC (a network that is a joint venture between Microsoft and NBC), as writers for political magazines like *The Weekly Standard* or *The New Republic*, or in political action groups like Third Millennium and 2030.

Despite these efforts to become involved, we remain almost invisible around election time. Only 20 percent of 18-to-24-year-olds voted in the 1992 and 1994 congressional elections, and only roughly one third voted in the 1996 presidential election. That compares to 45 percent and 60 percent of the entire voting-age population in the 1992 and 1994 congressional elections, respectively. Why? One reason,

Photo Courtesy of Sean Hartgrove

JEFF SHESOL
*Special Assistant to the President and presidential
speech writer*

HISTORIAN, PRESIDENTIAL SPEECH WRITER

He first won acclaim by poking fun at political correctness in his syndicated comic strip *Thatch*, which runs daily in over one hundred newspapers such as the *Boston Globe* and the *New York Daily News*. He created the strip while in high school in Denver, and by the time he graduated from Brown it had appeared in the *Wall Street Journal* and *Newsweek*.

At only 26, he is also a Rhodes Scholar and an acclaimed historian. The historian Arthur Shlesinger, Jr., said of Shesol's new book, *Mutual Contempt*, an account of the relationship between Robert Kennedy and Lyndon Johnson, "This is the most gripping political book of recent years." President Clinton also read the book and was so impressed he invited Shesol to become a presidential speech writer. Asked what he thinks Generation X will add to politics, Shesol replied, "This generation brings a certain pragmatism to the political process. Those of us who have elected to be part of the system are not likely to be sweeping ideologues on either side. There is not an emphasis on creed, rather the premium is on results. The attitude is: Show us what you can do."

says Hans Riemer, the cofounder of the political action group 2030, is that "the act of voting is seen as buying in to what many believe is a corrupt and broken system"—one that Xers don't want to legitimize. Today's twenty-somethings grew up on the Iran-*contra* affair, Whitewater, the savings and loan debacle, the Clarence Thomas–Anita Hill confrontations, Filegate and Paula Jones. From our parents we learned about Watergate, the anger over Vietnam, the questions about the assassination of John Kennedy, Martin Luther King, and Robert Kennedy. The statistics show how far we have come from the trusting days of the 1950s. In 1965, according to a *Time* poll, 70 percent of the American public said they trusted their government officials. Today, less than 30 percent of Americans say this.

In the long run, the bottom line for attaining political power is voting. Generation Xers don't want to participate in a system they don't trust. Politicians listen to those who elect them. Many of the issues important to young adults get completely overlooked by Washington because we don't vote. That's why, year after year, Social Security reform is untouched; why the 1997 tax package included rebates for everyone but single working adults; why the environment always plays second fiddle to big business. As Riemer puts it, "I think the greatest weakness of the generation is its disengagement from politics at the national level. It's undermining everything we're trying to do at the local level." The importance of national politics seems to be one lesson Generation X has not yet learned.

A Lower Quality of Life?

We are told time and time again that our generation will be the first in American history to have less than our parents did. There is a good deal of support for this assertion. The incomes of households headed by people aged 15 to 24 fell substantially between 1980 and 1995. In 1980, households headed by 15-to-24-year-olds had a median annual income of about $23,500. By 1995 that group's median income was just under $21,000. Like their younger counterparts, households headed by people aged 25 to 34 also experienced a drop in incomes since 1980, but only by 3 percent. In contrast, in this period the incomes of people over the age of 65 skyrocketed 25 percent. Why such unequal statistics? Reasons include governmental redistribution of funds from young to old through programs like Social Security and Medicare, slower economic growth rates than previous generations experienced, stagnant wages, and perpetually low national savings rates that leave us with little money to invest in the future. Pages could be added to this list.

Despite this mountain of disheartening data, most young adults believe their standard of living is better than it would have been in years past and that it can get even better. Perhaps that is because we know that the future has not yet been determined. What happens in the American economy is largely up to us. True, we cannot return our country to the same set of economic factors that gave us the post–World War II boom. However, we can better the economy through our public and private decisions. As the saying goes, "We cannot control the direction of the wind, but we can adjust our sails."

Dead on Arrival

Is America in need of a resurrection? Despite our economic stability and our dominance in world affairs, many Americans have a negative outlook on our future. So far, those currently in power have set the limits for future generations. They have told us we will be the first generation of Americans who will have a lower quality of life than our parents. They say we are poorly educated and underemployed, that we have no capacity for concentration, no drive. The soothsayers tell us we will suffer high rates of income inequality and low standards of environmental health. As foreign competition gets tougher, America may lose its premier place in the world economy. It weighs on one's outlook when the polls tell us that Americans think our country's best days are behind us, and when our elders believe that our generation will make the world a worse place. It is unfair to blame us for the world we have inherited. It is unconscionable to tell us that we will not succeed. And yet our parents and grandparents have made that pronouncement: Dead on arrival.

Despite the predictions, this generation has a great deal of hope for the future. I have great optimism that we will resurrect the American spirit—in fact, we have already begun. Generation X is starting more businesses than any other generation in America today. By pushing the limits of technology, we are forcing the economy to follow us— surfing the Internet, exploring and creating cyberspace, traveling more, understanding more about our bodies and our universe, attending college in record numbers, and investing with greater understanding than any generation before. Everywhere, young people are challenging assumptions and forging their own futures by breaking new ground. We are building our own nest eggs, not asking for handouts, starting our own companies. We spend more time with our families and seem less obsessed with materialism than those who built their careers in the 1980s.

"Today's people will certainly improve society. . . . We are all stewards who have been trusted with the precious gifts of our own talents, earth's resources, and each other. We have the benefit of the experiences of those who came before us, and inherit the responsibility to leave behind an even better society for our children," says Bobby Jindal, who at twenty-six was appointed by President Clinton to lead the National Bipartisan Commission on Medicare. If any single characteristic defines us—one that surely grows from the decay from which we sprang—it is our unyielding, unconquerable, unrelenting spirit to marshal the exhausted energy of our predecessors and use it to fuel our quest for a totally new world.

Regardless of our style or the preconceptions others have of us, we will resurrect an America that, despite technology's triumphs, now is sabotaged by self-doubt and self-hate. Our fellow Americans need not worry, for we are far more confident, believing, powerful, and prepared for this massive construction job than anyone could have ever dreamed.

CHAPTER 2

The Next Moral Order

The Age of Economics

Caught in a relaxing interval between one moral code and the next, an unmoored generation surrenders itself to luxury, corruption, and a restless disorder of family and morals.
—Will and Ariel Durant

Every age has public ideas the expression of which is unique to its time and place. Religion dominated public thought in the Middle Ages. Art formed the discourse of the Renaissance. In the days of Bismarck, diplomats spoke of foreign policy and the delicate balance of power. World War II brought the fight against tyranny that spawned the world's greatest battle of ideology, the Cold War.

In 1991, when I was a college freshman, the Evil Empire whimpered its last breath. The world changed. Our ideological battle appeared to be won. Democracy and capitalism were conquering the globe, toppling ancient regimes, sweeping away the old world order. Historian Francis Fukuyama said we may have reached an "end of history." Arguably we had come up with history's best political arrangement: democracy. "Today virtually all advanced countries have adopted . . . liberal democratic political institutions . . . and moved in the direction of market-oriented economics. This movement constitutes an 'end of history' . . . as a broad evolution of human society advancing toward a final goal," Fukuyama said. Questions remain. What is our next big challenge?

Of course, the Soviet Union and the two-hemisphere world it helped create weren't the only institutions that were toppled in the eighties and nineties. Nearly every institution, from our churches, government, and families to our banks and corporations, was under siege. Callused by scandal after scandal, we lost faith in our government. The majority of families were transformed from the traditional structure of working father, homemaker, and children to every other conceivable combination. Divorce rates doubled. Single motherhood became a norm. In the global race for dollars, corporations downsized millions of people, which affected three fourths of American families, according to the Bureau of Labor Statistics.

This social turmoil left us confused about what we should expect from our government, employers, families, and selves. Gone is the old moral code of the postwar generation, based on nuclear families, corporate loyalty, government trust, revered religious leaders, and small, stable communities. It was dismantled in our parents' time, by Watergate, feminism, the sexual revolution, the civil rights movement, changing economies, and globalization. Some viewed saying good-bye to the old ways as a mistake, a "slouching toward Gomorrah," as Robert Bork put it. Others saw it as a needed revolution.

For our generation, the "why" or "how" matters much less than the "what"—what comes next? We're concerned about what moral structure, value system, code of conduct will rise from the ashes. "The biggest challenge for our generation will be cleaning up the messes left by the short-sighted, instant-gratification tendencies of the previous generation," says Jonathan Karl, a thirty-year-old CNN correspondent.

The Age of Economics

The economist John Kenneth Galbraith has written of our time, "This is not the age of doctrine; it is the age of practical judgment." Put another way, our society cares about outputs, results, deeds. We are after what produces the greatest good for the most people, not doctrine, rhetoric, dogma. We are not worried about staying within the guidelines of any particular system; rather, we seek the avenue that produces the greatest results. We adjust, maneuver, manipulate our choices around what seems to work in today's complex world. We are deductive thinkers rather than inductive. We experiment to find our answers. This experimentation is not rebellion, as it was for our parents. Rather, it is a way of life. It is the thing we do in the absence of any learned instruction or behavior.

In our trial and error we are constructing a new way of thinking, a new code of judgment. This code is based on the foundations of economic thought. I don't just mean what the average student takes in an introductory micro/macro economics course. The study of economics involves much more than supply-and-demand curves, equations, and inflation rates. It is a way of thinking, of approaching problems. Consider the inflammatory question of abortion. A philosopher might begin the debate with questions: When does life begin? Where does the duty of society lie, to the unborn or to the liberty of women to choose? A lawyer would turn to precedent, *Roe vs. Wade*. A politician polls his constituents for their opinions. An economist takes a different line of thought. She says: "If, whether you are pro-life or pro-choice, we can say that abortion is not the desired end of pregnancy, then the real question is, how do we reduce unwanted pregnancies?" We do it through sex education, teaching abstinence, or through the proliferation of contraception. The economist seeks what is common among differing factions and builds a solution.

Take a similar issue—the death penalty. The moralist asks whether it is ever right for society to take the life of another person. A politician wonders whether he will seem soft on crime if he opposes the death penalty. A lawyer might wonder whether the death penalty is constitutional. An economist might approach the problem in an entirely different way. In our society, it costs more to prosecute to get the death penalty, which has little value as a deterrent, than it does to keep an inmate in prison for life. For this reason, an economist may argue that the best alternative for people who commit heinous crimes, is life imprisonment.

Economic thinking provides the clearinghouse of our hopes and desires. That is because economics is a solution-seeking social science. It was devised to help us understand and therefore manipulate markets for best possible use. Economics is about the greatest benefit for the greatest number. The economist, unlike the lawyer, doesn't think in terms of legality or illegality, but rather in terms of incentives, education, and altering personal choices. The philosopher worries about the right questions; politicians, their constituencies. Economists worry about results, about finding the most suitable answer in a world that is rarely simple. This is the skill our society hungers for at our time in history.

How do we reconcile the claims of environmentalists and the business community? How do we distribute limited health-care resources among a very broad demand? How do we shore up Social Security and Medicare for the next generation of Americans? How do we promote racial and gender equality? How do we alleviate the poverty of single mothers? How should we encourage urban investment? These are questions for the economist. With many of our ideological questions settled, economics becomes the tool to implement our ideals.

To give us the answers, we have elevated a new breed of experts. Other ages had prophets, witch doctors, soothsayers, and voodoo gods. We have economists. Ask most insiders who is the most powerful man in Washington, and the answer will no doubt be someone involved in running our economy—maybe Alan Greenspan, who rules over the nation's Federal Reserve Bank. With a few words (like "irrational exuberance") he can shake the stock market and send the economy reeling. Or what about Clinton's secretary of the treasury, Robert Rubin, or the former secretary of labor, Robert Reich? Their world is one not of ideology but of interest rates, GDP growth, labor contracts, inflation, and trade. The army of economists who testify before Congress exceeds in number every other profession except, perhaps, lobbyists. As one Washington insider put it, "The President can't go to the bathroom unless he first asks an economist what effect it might have on the unemployment rate."

The Hobgoblin of Little Minds

This generation's desire for results molds our political outlook. We care less about who is a Democrat or a Republican, a conservative or a liberal. We don't care about titles; we care about deeds. We care about who can get the job done and what policy makes the most sense. According to a UCLA report, *The American Freshman: Twenty-five-Year Trends*, "Striking changes in political identification have occurred in the middle of the road category." The percentage of freshmen identifying themselves as moderates rose from a low of 49 percent in 1970 to 60 percent in 1983 and has stayed above 55 percent for every year thereafter. The study says that young adults reflect a fusion of political impulses, conservative in some areas, liberal in others, and all points in between and beyond. Add to that our support for independent candidates like Ross Perot, the can-do businessman from Texas, who won 23 percent of the youth vote in 1992, compared with 19 percent of the votes overall.

Heather Lamm, the chairman of the GenX political "action tank" Third Millennium, said, "The labels of conservative, liberal, Democrat, Republican hark back to another era. Young adults tend to think issue by issue, not along party lines." Young adults tend to be less

willing to toe the party line. This comes in part from a healthy cynicism toward Washington—a conviction that you just can't trust politicians, no matter what party they are with. The other element is the
strong independence of this generation—a desire to decide things
ourselves rather than be spoon-fed opinions. As Emerson said (and a
popular Reebok ad appealed to), "A foolish consistency is the hob-
goblin of little minds."

Perhaps that's why President Clinton has been such a successful
politician. He represents a fusion of our liberal and conservative traditions, taking from each camp what works. He borrowed from the
Republicans to form a "hands-off" economic policy. His deficit cutting, welfare reform, and overall downsizing of the federal government could be the envy of any conservative. From the Democrats he
took a commitment to civil rights and the environment, initiating reforms like the Family Leave Bill or the Everglades Restoration Act.
Where he needed to fill in the blanks of our political temperament, he
took a poll. Abracadabra—the unbeatable politician, a person of syn-
thesis, consensus building, workability.

Our desire for workability may be why Americans have refused to
be moved by allegations of wrongdoing by the White House. Clinton's ratings remained high through the many scandals that have
plagued his administration—Whitewater, Filegate, campaign finance
inquiries, Paula Jones, Monica Lewinsky. Why didn't Dole's points
about the erosion of American values carry over into the voting
booth? Simple. Our traditional moral codes have been replaced in the
public debate by the code of economics. The economy is good. Inflation is low. Growth is high. The deficit is down. It happened on Bill
Clinton's watch. We use our economic sensibilities to judge the political landscape, not our moral compass. As Bill Marr of the TV show
Politically Incorrect says, "The President is like the plumber who
comes into your home. You don't really care where he is spending his
nights as long as he gets the job done." That is the way most people
feel about politics.

Jennifer Klein, the former director of a GenX political action group, the National Association of Twenty-somethings, observed, "They're definitely thinking independently—they tend to side with the candidate that they like or agree with and don't necessarily vote the party line or vote a party down the ticket." This mixed bag of political preferences arises because we are not concerned with the lines drawn by the far right and left. We are not concerned with the philosophical questions of federalism versus nationalism, liberty versus equality, national security versus free speech. We want a government that W-O-R-K-S—that delivers the mail on time, protects the environment, fosters business, secures our future by deficit control, makes our streets safe, and stays out of our way as much as possible while doing it. We don't care whether the state or the federal government administers the welfare program, just so it works.

Politicians are getting the point. The buzzwords of politics show it: "reinventing government"; "It's the economy, stupid"; "The era of big government is over"; "15 percent tax cut—across the board"; "deficit reduction"; "making the thirteenth and fourteenth years of education as common as the first twelve"; "welfare to workfare"; and "plugging first-graders into the World Wide Web." Our political-speak is about action, restructuring, saving money. It is not about ideology. It is about practicality.

The Heart of It: Financial Concern

On a more basic level, generations worry about what they have to worry about. Having been reared on the statement that we would be the first generation of Americans to have less than our parents, it is no wonder that so many of us care about economics. We may live in our parents' basements. We make less money than our parents did at the same age. We have an average of $10,000 in college debt. We are faced with the constant possibility of corporate downsizing while we fill jobs for which we are too often overqualified. And economists tell us that after a long life of hard work and high taxes we will have a big IOU from the government on which to retire. We care about distribution because we are missing out in the soup line. So economics for us is as important as the battles over the union and taxation without representation were for our forebears.

This is the truth that unites America's next generation and separates us from those who have come before. Are we "slackers," "twenty-nothings," "MTV deadheads"? No. We are, to be coy, misunderstood. While our parents and grandparents may speak from the language of ideology, we speak the language of practicality. We are concerned with making it work. As popular young author Douglas Ruskoff points out, "Unlike the Boomers, who need to feel they are working to promote a positive system or to dismantle a negative one," we "fight social injustice head on . . . but these battles look different because we no longer fight for causes. We don't need causes to rally behind. The real issues, ones that agendas only mask, are quite plain to us already."

The issues are as visible as the cracked plaster and leaky faucets in our schools, a homeless teenager wandering the streets of the inner city, an overcrowded emergency room, a gray skyline. These are our problems to solve. And they cannot be solved by spouting political theory. They must be cured through an understanding of economics, of how to best deliver goods and services and how to teach people to care for themselves. A homeless person doesn't need dogma. He needs food, shelter, and access to people who care.

How do we solve these problems? Government? It has a poor track record in our time. So we, the next generation, must roll up our sleeves and do it ourselves. Mark Winston Griffith and Errol Louis provide the example. In 1993 they opened the Central Brooklyn Federal Credit Union in Brooklyn. Says Griffith of their financial center, also known as the "hip-hop bank," "We are going to have to find ways of innovatively leveraging the indigenous wealth of North America's largest black community and help reshape it in our own image, on our own terms."

Our obsession with economics is deeply reflected in our personal lives. According to a study conducted by UCLA and the American Council of Education, in 1967 more than 80 percent of entering college students said it was "essential" or "very important" to "develop a meaningful philosophy of life"; it was the top goal of college freshmen. Today that objective ranks sixth. The top goal, according to 64 percent of college freshmen, is being "very well off financially."

A New Code of Ethics

Some say that this is an indication that our concern for economics reflects a failure of our moral codes. Given the weaknesses of ethics, politics, and even the law to keep us in line, do we latch on to economics as a last-ditch effort to give structure to an amorphous world? Is money our lifeboat in a sea of failed families, lying politicians, jailed religious leaders, and walled communities? Lewis Lapham, the editor of *Harper's*, writes, "Unless we wish to say that what is moral is what an insurance company will pay for (which, in our present circumstances, comes fairly close to the truth), what other arrangement meets the presumption—accepted as revered truth on both the liberal and conservative sides of the bed—that ethics and politics constitute increasingly marginal subsections of economics?" Or, as high school teenager, Erin Ortiz, puts it, "As it seems that we cannot depend on love or acceptance, this generation has turned to the two things that we can depend on, material goods and ourselves."

Certainly the crumbling of institutions, from the family to our government to our corporations, has left us with a mammoth void. But in the void a new system is being created. A code of ethics is arising, one more responsive to our world's demands, being constructed largely by America's youth. That code is grounded in economics, and our study and preoccupation with economics can shed new light on morality. The modern philosopher John Rawls's theory of justice, for instance, depends on an understanding of the rules of distribution. Adding economics allows us to ask new philosophical questions: How much economic inequality is too much in society? Do current generations have an environmental and financial responsibility to future generations? With limited resources how do we distribute health care fairly?

The study of economics can cut through philosophical and political debates with numbers, and give new weight to old ideals. The Nobel laureate Amartya Sen calculated the economic costs of gender inequality in India to convince politicians they should protect women's rights. In one of his main texts, "The Missing Women," he discusses the difference between the number of women born and those who reach adulthood. In poorer countries women suffer from ill treatment, murder, discrimination and the inequality of health treatment and childhood opportunities. This discrimination means that little by little, as the age pyramid progresses, men begin to outnumber women. Sen argues that these societies waste their basic human potential. For Sen, economics has always been an answer to solving the most fundamental social problems: "I think if you are born in India and you watch a famine when you are nine and you believe that something can be done to change the world, it is not an unnatural thing to take an interest in economics."

Sen's philosophy applies well to our own society. What carries more weight with a corporate executive? Hire more women because it is the right thing to do, or hire more women because you are overlooking many intelligent people who could improve your productivity and increase profits? Twenty-six-year-old Gayle Turk was part of the top management of Catalyst, an organization to promote women in corporate America. Their message? Hiring women improves corporate profitability. According to Turk, "Advancing and promoting women is not just the right thing to do. It is also good business. If

Photo Courtesy of Jonathan Karl

JONATHAN KARL
Reporter, CNN

TV JOURNALIST, NEW DAD

When management told Jonathan Karl that he would be representing his generation for CNN, he wasn't afraid. He welcomed the challenge. Today, he can most often be seen covering the political scene and "keeping it real" so that the younger folks tune in. What tweaks the interest of younger viewers are "stories of individuality and self-reliance. This may be the most entrepreneurial generation in American history," says Karl. When he is not hunting down a story he spends time with his wife and new baby.

you are limiting yourself to only half the population, then you are not getting the best talent available." Catalyst studies show that retaining talented women increases corporate profitability. That's because most women who leave either start their own firms or work for competitors. Not only does that dispel the myth that women are leaving to take time off or to be with their families, it also shows that it is in a corporation's financial interest to hold on to its talent.

Especially in our own time, economics can help us to sort through the rubble and establish a framework for discussing issues of generational, race, and gender equality. For Heather Lamm of Third Millennium, our generation's most compelling political issue is the redirecting of our fiscal priorities. "I think that if we fail to invest more in the future in the form of training and savings we will not stay competitive. We spend far too much on today's political whims and not enough on tomorrow's realities."

Bobby Jindal, 26, was the Secretary of Louisiana's Department of Health and Human Services; his job was restructuring the Medicare and Medicaid systems for the millions of people in his state. "There is the growing political realization that limited resources will impact the structure and delivery of health-care services," he says.

Deroy Murdoch, a political consultant and marketer, has become the young guru of government retirement plans. He's worried about how the inequality of the races will rear its head when baby boom African-Americans and Hispanics who have been able to save little start retiring.

None of this is to say that economics alone will bring us to the promised land. Fukuyama says, "Although economic activity is inextricably linked with social and political life, there is a mistaken tendency, encouraged by contemporary economic discourse, to regard the economy as a facet of life with its own laws, separate from the rest of society." Of course, economics is not separate. Our system of economics exists within the context of our social and cultural norms. Economics cannot replace our moral compass, but it can enhance the instrument, if used properly.

Still, there are some historians who argue that our preoccupation with economics is a sign of America's eventual moral demise. They say that we have lost passionate causes to fight for. Our lack of crisis has made us fat, lazy, the perfect targets for the barbarians at the gate. Fukuyama echoes the French historian Alexander Kojeve, who wrote about the coming end of history: "[Men] would satisfy their needs through economic activity, but they would no longer have to risk their lives in battle. They would, in other words, become animals again. . . . A dog is content to sleep in the sun all day provided he is fed, because he is not dissatisfied with what he is. He does not worry that other dogs are doing better than him, or that his career as a dog has stagnated, or that dogs are being oppressed in a distant part of the world." Is Kojeve right? Do we need crusades to ennoble us?

The answer to this question is that of course we do. However, do we need events as all-consuming as war, depression, tyranny, or holocaust to awaken the human spirit? It seems a limited view of humans to assume we need always to have a prod at our backs to move forward. And yet so many have made that argument. Must great philosophy, great art, great men and women come only from turmoil? As Fukuyama puts it, "Human life, then, involves a paradox: it seems to require injustice, for the struggle against injustice is what calls forth what is highest in man." There are certainly times when crisis brings forth the best in us and creates heroes such as Winston Churchill, Franklin D. Roosevelt, and Abraham Lincoln. But there are also times when crisis brings only failure or despair—Vietnam, the bombing of Hiroshima, the Bay of Pigs. And there are times when virtually no specific occasion at all yields great deeds and heroes—the civil rights movement, the women's suffrage movement, Theodore Roosevelt's conservation initiatives. There have been great art and invention from war and crisis, but there has also been great art and invention in times of peace.

None of this is to say that we do not need challenges. We do. But our challenges need not involve marching off to war. Injustice is not dead in our time. Our society has the highest degree of economic inequality in the world. We are still battling prejudice, ignorance, and crime.

John Steinbeck said that the last frontier of man was "his unconquerable soul." Steinbeck said in his late writings, *America and Americans*, that America had fought England, settled the West, endured the Depression, and beaten tyranny back in the world wars. Writing in 1965, he too worried that America would rest on its laurels and slip from greatness. The answer, he told us, lies in seeking the challenges within: to battle prejudice, unkindness, apathy. To foster

Photo Courtesy of Steve Frank

STEVE FRANK
Journalist, **Wall Street Journal**

FINANCIAL GURU

At 25, Steve Frank is a staff reporter for the *Wall Street Journal.* He spends most of his day dealing with folks twice his age or more. "The people I cover assume I am a lot older. When they meet me in person they are stunned—but they get over it." Steve has always had a passion for journalism. He began his first newspaper back in second grade. It was called the *Brookside Times,* named after his school in New York. By third grade he had a staff of four and was charging ten cents an issue, which he donated to the Humane Society.

Steve has high hopes for the financial future of his generation. "We are the first generation to really plan for our futures though financial instruments like 401(k)s, IRAs, profit sharing, and mutual funds. We will be the first generation of Americans for whom liquid assets will be of greater value than our homes."

curiosity, understanding, tolerance. This is our challenge: to defend our nation when there is no clear and present danger, to find injustice without a headline, to battle tyranny where only its seedlings exist. In short, not to react, but to pro-act. The peace of our present gives us the time to secure our future. This generation of Americans must use the tools of logic, pragmatism, and economics with ethics to conquer this last frontier.

CHAPTER 3

Neither Elephant nor Donkey

A New Political Animal Emerges

Youthful passion, the most natural, universal thing in the world, a matter of great importance, used to be taken into consideration by statesmen. But this living, weighty matter is no longer accounted for by politicians, who consider it nonexistent.
—Giancomo Leopardi

Slow, corrupt, hot air, empty rhetoric, inaction, partisanship, hostage of special interests, easily bought, dishonest, criminal, and just plain unfair. These are the words and phrases GenXers use to describe our government.

It is easy to see why young Americans have an unfavorable view of Washington. We have seen one example of government corruption and ineptitude after another. Our birth years were marked by the assassination of President Kennedy and Watergate. Growing up, we watched the trial of Oliver North and the revelation of the Iran-*contra* connection. We saw the government take a bath in the savings and loan crisis and fail to catch on to Michael Milken and Ivan Boesky until they had illegally manipulated hundreds of millions of dollars in stocks and bonds.

We constantly hear about trillions of dollars in debt we'll be left to pay because of "voodoo" economics and a trickle-down effect of which we will never see a drop. We watch politicians, intimidated by the American Association of Retired Persons, defend mammoth social programs like Social Security and Medicare, which demographers tell us will crumble under the weight of an aging society. Watchdog groups continually dig up examples of government waste, from subsidizing Chicken McNugget campaigns in China to paying for the Internet access of legislative employees, who used it to surf "pornographic sites."

More recently we have been bombarded with more scandals than even a meticulous journalist can handle. From the Speaker of the House to the Democratic National Committee and Republican National Committee to the White House by way of China to the missing and the dead, every politico seems to have done something wrong. Pick a word, put "gate" on the end of it, and chances are you can link it to someone in Washington. Rob Nelson and Jon Cowan, the cofounders of Lead or Leave, the first political action think-tank for twenty-somethings, explained the political disillusionment of young people: "We're a generation that was raised on images of politics and government gone sour. While our elders may recall the glory days of John F. Kennedy or Franklin D. Roosevelt, we in this generation have no memory of a time when politics was considered a noble endeavor and the men and women who practiced it were revered as pure heroes."

In our own time, politicians are seen as the pawns of special interests. *Harper's* reports that only 5 percent of the public believe money *doesn't* buy influence in Washington. Political campaigns highlight scandal and corruption in our system. Why? Because political campaigns are about getting elected, and getting elected is about money.

To put things into perspective, 99.97 percent of Americans don't make political contributions of more than $200. In other words, .03 percent of the population has political influence and dominates the time of money-starved politicians. "American elections are paid for overwhelmingly by economically interested industries and a small handful of individuals," says Ellen Miller, the executive director of the Center for Responsive Politics. In our time, the amounts of money being raised are out of control. Miller estimates that the entire 1996 presidential race cost about $800 million—three times the 1992 campaign. It has been estimated that another $800 million was spent on the 1996 congressional races. So far, things do not seem to be changing. Campaign finance reform has stalled in Washington and fundraising rages on. According to the Congressional Research Service, the amount of soft money (money given to a party operation rather than a specific candidate) raised by political parties in 1997 for every campaign finance reform bill introduced (and defeated) was $404,000.

In light of these figures, it is no wonder that the pollster Louis Harris recently found that 78 percent of GenXers disagreed with the statement "Government can generally be trusted to look after our interests." In a 1960 *Newsweek* poll, a similar percentage of young people held the opposite view—they trusted government. The question for this generation is, where do we go from here? Will the trend toward corruption, distrust, and mismanagement continue, or will we make things better? What kind of politics will we practice—or have we become so apathetic that we won't practice politics at all?

"Who's the Enemy Here?"

Given our place in history, many say that it is not surprising that this generation of Americans is not engaged politically. To Curtis Gans, the director of the Center for the Study of the American Electorate, based in Washington, it's not surprising that young people aren't interested in politics: "It used to be that young people were the spear-carriers against the war in Vietnam, for civil rights, for the environment. But there doesn't seem to be an issue that captures the imagination of young people at this point." Every previous generation in this century has faced some specific challenge or enemy. From the world wars and Depression in the first half of the century to the Cold War and the civil rights movement of the second half, young Americans were able to imagine the better world for which they were

fighting. But Generation X grew up in an age with no readily identifi-
able enemy. "All the Big Causes seem to be settled. The nation beat
the Depression, defeated Hitler, stared down the Soviets and abol-
ished Jim Crow long before we were on the scene," John Meachum of
Newsweek reported.

In today's world, what is truly important? After all, there is no war
to be fought, no larger-than-life enemy to conquer, no obvious evil in-
carnate to stir the senses. We are all groping for meaning in a world
with fading black and whites, elusive summits. In this postindustrial,
post–Cold War, post-postmodern, neoclassicist, neocapitalist, stream-
lined, downsized, new ordered, reinvented World Wide Web of a
world, it is hard to know how to make a difference.

And yet, many problems exist in our time: economic inequities,
lingering racial discord, pollution, crime, deteriorating cities, and rising health-care costs and government debt. But these problems are
tougher to define or get hold of. It is often harder to cure a social condition than to fight a foreign dictator or protest a Klan rally. "Who's
the enemy here?" wonders Hans Riemer of the political action group
2030. This generation faces the confusing combination of general
contentment coupled with vague and gradually developing socioeconomic problems.

Civics Lessons Unlearned

"I've heard . . . about meetings behind closed doors . . . where
congressmen have basically just said, 'Oh we don't care about them
because they don't vote,' " Jennifer Klein says. This illustrates one of
our biggest problems: that Gen X doesn't vote. Despite efforts by national campaigns like MTV's Choose or Lose and Rock the Vote campaigns, or motor-voter registration, Generation X's voting remains
low. In the 1992 presidential election, only 38.5 percent of 18-to-20-
year-olds and 45.7 percent of 21-to-24-year-olds reported voting,
compared with over 60 percent for all other age groups. The youngest

Americans generally have the poorest rates of voting participation in any election. In the last twenty-five years voting rates in every age group except 65 plus have gone down. In the 1996 presidential election just 29 percent of us made it to the polls. The decline of voter participation has been faster for the youngest age brackets: In 1972, 18- and 20-year-olds were 20 percent less likely to vote than the general population. In 1992, they were more than 30 percent less likely to vote than the general population. In the 1994 congressional election 61 percent of voters aged 65 and older cast ballots, according to Census Bureau data, but only 17 percent of those 18 to 20 voted.

As a result of our low turnout, politicians have no incentive to heed our concerns because we are not the ones electing them. In turn, we become disheartened because no one seems to be listening. It is a vicious circle. The only way to break the circle is to pull the lever. It may seem simplistic—and so far it has been difficult to accomplish—but it is the only way to ensure our representation. Democracy requires participation. That civics lesson seems to have eluded us.

We need not only to vote but also to lobby for enlightened voter access and registration laws. For instance, why not vote on more than one day? That would give more people a chance to make it to the voting booth. Better yet, vote on the weekend. Living in a Dilbert World, it is actually hard to get off work. Let's face it, most bosses would rather have us faxing or photocopying than attending to your civic duty.

Add to the inconvenience of voting the problem of inconvenient voter registration. The motor-voter law, which registers people to vote when they apply for driver's licenses, was a needed improvement, but it wasn't the final answer. We need to make voter registration possible in every library, post office, and convenience store in our country. We could follow Oregon State's example; there, in 1997, citizens participated in a "mail-in" referendum. The referendum was mailed to every voter on record and gave people nearly two weeks to respond. The response, said officials, was much better than when people are asked to vote "on location." Best, we could be voting by e-mail or phone. A coded program can be written by our gifted computer whizkids to

HANS RIEMER
Cofounder, 2030

POLITICAL ACTIVIST, LIBERAL VOICE

In 1996 Hans Riemer and Chris Cuomo, Mario Cuomo's son, launched 2030. Their goal was for 2030 to be a "political action-tank" for Generation X. They are not membership-driven, like a lobby group. Instead, their mission is to make young Americans aware of political issues. "We have no choice but to make America a better place. If we don't, we'll have to get on the boat and move somewhere else. So much of what is going wrong today requires innovation and new thinking, and we can respond to these requirements at a more rapid pace than other generations could." So far Riemer and Cuomo have made quite a media splash, appearing on CNN and MSNBC, among other stations, as representatives of their generation.

protect privacy and assure honesty. A more embarrassing and shameful reason why some won't vote is, they feel, a practical concern: voting puts their existence on record, which means that they are fair game for jury duty—the last thing busy executives or overworked GenXers want to have disrupting business.

Perhaps we can take a lesson from Costa Rica, which consistently has the highest voter turnout in the Western world. They teach their children to vote early by having them participate in a mock vote along with the adults. Organizations in the United States like Third Millennium and Kids Voting are trying to duplicate the successful program here. Started in 1988, Kids Voting now operates in forty-one states. The result? According to Barbara Ganulin, an executive director of the program, where Kids Voting has been established, adult voter turnout has increased and students have developed voter habits that will stay with them into adulthood. Perhaps this model provides a good lesson in civic education.

Beware the Media's Role

In recent decades, the media have changed how news is presented. TV news has become an enormous industry, and in the race to capture the biggest audience share, the distinction between news and entertainment has blurred. The news media have become more sensationalized, constantly trying to shock an increasingly desensitized population. Perhaps this is a reaction to the current era of historical calm: "Without epic scope, every news story becomes a 'crisis,' and 'heroes' come cheap. The cumulative effect of such connected moments is to trivialize just about everything," John Meacham wrote in *Newsweek*.

When addressing themselves to national politics, the media have also shifted their focus away from the issues, dwelling instead on insider politics: Which politicians are more powerful? Where are the lines of allegiance drawn? This practice has decreased the relevance of news for the general public and made politicians seem ridiculous, like children fighting over insignificant matters. Furthermore, the growing overlap of individuals who become high-level politicians, journalists, and media personalities seems to create an incestuous core in the power structure. This trend is documented in the increasing number of politicians who slide into journalism (John

Sununu, Geraldine Ferraro, George Stephanopoulos, and Susan Molinari, to name a few).

One magazine that has taken advantage of the disappearing line
between politics and pop culture is *George*, the brainchild of John
Kennedy, Jr. Here politicians are spotted hobnobbing with entertain-
ers and other rich and famous. An average issue might chronicle Bill
Clinton socializing with Barbra Streisand, Dolly Parton with Henry
Kissinger, Alan Greenspan with the Spice Girls. Here is a magazine
that ranks both Anne Heche, "lesbian actress" and paramour of Ellen
DeGeneres, with our secretary of state, Madeleine Albright, as being among the "most influential women of our time."

If you have any doubt that the line between entertainment and
politics is becoming blurred, examine the parade of actors-turned-
politicians and politicians-turned-actors. Young adults are well ac-
quainted with the concept. After all we were told early to "win one
for the Gipper!" For most of us, the former actor Ronald Reagan was
the first president we remember. Other actors-turned-politicos are the
late Sonny Bono; Fred Grandy, who played Gopher on *The Love Boat*
and is a former representative from Iowa; and Clint Eastwood, the
onetime mayor of Carmel, California. Many are now touting Tom
Selleck as the next Ronald Reagan. On the other side, Senator Fred
Thompson of Tennessee who conducted the hearings on campaign finance reform in 1997, has dabbled in Hollywood, having a prominent
role in *The Hunt for Red October* among other movies. Bob Dole
now strikes a pose for Air France and Visa; President Clinton has
even done walk-ons for a TV drama, and he popped up once on the
silver screen albeit spliced in involuntarily, in the movie *Contact*.

In recent years, Hollywood's portrayals of Washington, specifically
the American presidency, have entered our public consciousness and
shaped our beliefs about government. From *Dave* and *An American
President* to *Air Force One* and *Primary Colors*, the motion picture
industry has explored everything from conspiracy theories to the
president's love life. *Wag the Dog*, in particular, had a powerful reso-
nance. It chronicled White House spin doctors' attempts to divert
public attention away from a presidential sex scandal by inventing a

Hollywood-produced and -directed war with Albania. The plot was surprisingly close to actual events—so much so that the media and the Iraqi ambassador to the United States questioned whether or not simultaneous United States threats against Iraq were just a "Wag-the-Dog Effect" to divert attention from the Monica Lewinsky story. Sadaam Hussein even ordered *Wag the Dog* to be played on Iraqi national television to show his people just what America was all about.

With entertainment this close to reality, it is hard to know the difference. Nowadays, the storytelling of Hollywood seems more real than the absurdity of Washington. David Samuels of *The Weekly Standard* put it best: "Perhaps the most outstanding feature of the moment is that the lines between fact and fiction, between personal experience and televised narratives and characters, have ceased, not to exist, of course, but to serve as a useful tool in interpreting everyday American reality."

Generation X's political education has come from this trivializing and insider-obsessed media. The entertainment focus not only has affected our political attitudes but has produced an acute distrust of the news media. Xers are more media-savvy than any previous generation. We're all too aware of the potential biases and predilections of media representatives who are often seen as interconnected with the newsmakers they "objectively" report on.

Rock the What?

What could be more American than Mom and apple pie? How about Madonna wrapped in an American flag? Or Al Gore doing the macarena? Or New York's mayor, Rudy Giuliani, as a drag queen in the Broadway hit *Victor/Victoria*? If you examine the political climate you will see ever more desperate attempts to win the attention of an uninterested electorate. Today we are selling politics like Coca-Cola—with fast music, sex, shock. Most of these attempts have been directed at young voters who, pollsters say, respond to this kind of entertainment-politics hybrid.

The trend gained speed with the 1992 elections. In the 1992 elections, candidate Clinton appeared on MTV and *The Arsenio Hall Show* to woo young voters. MTV and the corporate music industry joined forces with their Choose or Lose and Rock the Vote campaigns to rekindle the interest of young people in politics and to encourage them to register and to vote. Xers did respond to this new, direct attention. Many registered to vote at the Choose or Lose tents set up on college campuses or booths at Lollapalooza, and voting rates among 18-to-20-year-olds and 21-to-24-year-olds increased by 16 percent and 19 percent, respectively, from the 1988 election to the 1994 election compared to a 7 percent increase among the total population.

Despite the positive response, these initiatives have been criticized by young and old. Clinton's efforts were attacked for being empty gestures and making him look ridiculous to the rest of the nation. Choose or Lose and Rock the Vote were described as encouraging young people to participate in politics as if it were "just another facet of pop culture," says GenX historian Jeff Shesol. Shesol continues, "Who said politics was supposed to be fun, anyway?" Tabitha Soren and MTV News, of course, as well as John Kennedy, Jr.'s *George* magazine and any politician who makes wry reference to the macarena.

Each bows to the conventional wisdom that young people are not citizens but consumers, and that democracy darned well better be sexy, funny, and entertaining if it's going to survive the next millennium. Curtis Gans of the Committee for the Study of the American Electorate laments that "if we used that star quality to help kids figure out something they'd like to change in their community and showed them how to change it, then we'd have real politics."

Many members of GenX took a cynical stance, generally seeing Clinton as something of a phony politician who wore shades while playing a saxophone and answering questions about his underwear to get the GenX vote. One Xer lashed out at the Choose or Lose registration drive, asking, "Choose or lose what?" and handing out fliers that said, "Get it straight, MTV doesn't care about you making a po-

Photo Courtesy of Adam Werbach

ADAM WERBACH
President, Sierra Club

ENVIRONMENTALIST, CROONER

What does Adam Werbach have to sing about? A lot. As the youngest president of the 106-year-old Sierra Club, the largest grass-roots environmental organization in America, he has lunched with the president at the Grand Canyon; he manages more than 600,000 Sierra members, and, most important, he is doing what he loves—saving the environment. His goal is to make the environment America's number one issue. "People in my generation have a very different attitude about the environment. Environmental protection is a norm, not a fringe idea left to tree huggers. And young activists are out turning the tide. I'm sure that the next group that comes along will blow us out of the water, and it will be our job to step aside and let them have their chance, just as the Boomers had better do for us."

What is this generation's biggest challenge? "My generation has been charged with the daunting task of redefining the American Dream. This isn't the same country that our parents grew up in. Our society is changing rapidly, and we are charged with making sense out of these changes and making them work in an era of diminished expectations. It's a tall order, but I think we are up to the challenge." Aside from saving the environment, Adam has time for his second love, singing. He is lead vocalist of the Brown Derbies, a jazz band, and has recorded two CDs.

litical or cultural choice. Instead, you are a consumer to be sold to and made money from."

In 1996 Rock the Vote recruited 500,000 new young voters. Despite the high numbers of registrants, few young adults made it to the voting booth. "Do they go to the polls? No," complains Mark Strama, Rock the Vote's twenty-eight-year-old program director, feeling perhaps a bit betrayed by all those fresh-faced Lollapaloozers who pledged to do their civic duty. According to Gans, the youth vote reached a new low in 1996, hitting its lowest point (under 30 percent of eligible voters) since eighteen- to twenty-year-olds gained the franchise in 1971.

Some argue that GenXers are looking outside the system to make a difference in their world. Abrams and David Lipsky, the authors of *Late Bloomers*, point out, "The popular misconception [about GenXers] . . . is that declining interest in partisan politics and a lack of interest in inside-the-Beltway issues translates into political apathy." The fact is that most Xers are politically aware and active—just not in the traditional ways. Disillusioned with the national party system, Xers are less inclined to use its standard tools—sweeping reforms and policies rooted in ideology—for change. Instead, this generation has redefined politics for its own purposes, making it highly personal and individual, small-scale, local, accessible, and pragmatic.

An Independent Streak

A firm result of Xers' disillusionment with party politics is a movement among young people toward identifying themselves as independents. In 1994, 40 percent of 17-to-24-year-olds identified themselves as "Independent," "Independent Democrat," or "Independent Republican," the highest percentage of any age group. (Only 1 percent of the group identified themselves as "apolitical"—undermining the stereotype that Xers just don't care.) Young people are participating in politics at the national level, but they have rejected political parties as an avenue of participation. Even among those GenXers who still identify with one party, the affiliation is weak. Staffers on Capitol Hill used to socialize only along party lines; now "one good drink special can overcome party loyalty real quick," GenXer Bob Meagher, a former aide to U.S. Congressman William McCollum, a Florida Republican, told *Swing* magazine.

Earlier generations were raised with party loyalties and could choose party affiliation on the basis of real distinctions when it came to issues. But as Generation X grew up, the difference between Republicans and Democrats shrank. "There's not a strong party system at the grass-roots level these days. Often there's no moral difference between the parties—both are driven by special interests," says Kellyanne Fitzpatrick, a Republican political analyst. "The generation up to thirty-five rejects traditional politics. They don't trust government, don't like Washington, don't vote, don't read newspapers. They view themselves not as members of political parties but as a generational group."

So how *do* you describe the political temperament of this generation? Eric Miller, the author of *In the Shadow of the Boom*, says they are "liberal on some issues, conservative on others—neither Republicans nor Democrats, they are pragmatists." Farai Chideya, a twenty-six-year-old correspondent for ABC News, narrows it down; she says that young people tend to be liberal on social issues, conservative on the economy. And that view makes sense. While most of us grew up with the ideals of the 1960s, we also understand the financial realities of today.

Consider the popularity of the independent candidate Ross Perot in the 1992 presidential elections. Twenty-three percent of 18-to-24-year-olds voted for the Texas billionaire, who appealed to this generation with a no-nonsense, business approach to politics. His use of logic, numbers, and graphs coupled with his focus on "the issues of the future" won the hearts of many in Generation X. Above all, he is a political "outsider"—someone who was not corrupted by the system in Washington. As Scott Sanders of the College Reform party says, "Mr. Perot cares about our issues—like reforming Social Security and reducing the national debt. And he cares about restoring faith in government through real campaign finance reform. Those are issues Generation X can get behind."

The move away from traditional party politics is the reason so many politicians are jumping party lines. Indeed, the most successful politicians these days are the ones who do not toe the party line. On the Democratic side, Bill Clinton has abandoned the old line on welfare. On the Republican side, Christine Todd Whitman, the governor of New Jersey, and Bill Weld, the former governor of Massachusetts, split with their party on issues like abortion and gay rights. Representative Gary Condit, a Democrat from California, is the cochair of the Blue Dogs, a group of conservative Democrats who have become the glue of the increasingly powerful coalition of conservative Democrats and moderate Republicans. Mike Dayton, Condit's GenX aide who helps with the group, says, "We've been successful both at driving the Democrats to the center and at moderating the extremes. Both sides are fighting for the center because they realize the margins just aren't big enough."

As a result of these trends, both the Republican National Committee and the Democratic National Committee are having identity crises. The old-liners are having a hard time dealing with these renegades and are trying to rein them in. Who can forget Jesse Helms's fight against Bill Weld, Clinton's appointee as ambassador to Mexico? Helms thought he would teach the more liberal Weld a lesson by not even allowing him to have a hearing in the Senate. Even though Helms succeeded in winning the battle against Weld, the war between the hard liners and the new, more moderate politicians is far from over.

If the Democratic and Republican parties are to survive they have to adapt to the times. Political parties have to change to reflect the new controversial issues of this generation. Our parents were split on issues like the Great Society, the civil rights movement, and the women's movement; our generation has different issues. We are largely in agreement on the issues our parents warred about. We think

the Great Society failed. We're advocates of diversity. We're supporters of individual rights. And we want the government out of our lives
as much as possible.

The cofounders of Lead or Leave summarized just some of the differences between traditional political concepts and Generation X's
new watchwords:

The Old	The New
Left vs. right	Postpartisan
What I'm owed	What I can do
Mass rallies	Local guerrilla actions
Political parties matter	Solutions matter
Volunteering = a good cause	Volunteering = political statement
Special interests reign	Search for a common agenda
Reliance on government	Local and personal actions
Politics = Washington	Politics = life choices
Ideological	Pragmatic

Men from Mars, Women from Venus—
Politically, That Is

Despite our general independence, GenXers seem to reflect one
important voting trend—the gender gap. "The gender gap story has
always had two primary components. As women have been moving in
the Democratic direction, men have been looking more Republican,"
according to the Roper Center's *America at the Polls 1996*. What is
most surprising is that the gender gap is widest among young adults.
In the past two elections, 60 percent of young women voted Democratic, while 60 percent of young men voted Republican. Maybe men
really are from Mars and women from Venus.

Since 1992, when women made up 53.5 percent of the vote, it has been generally concluded that women have the potential to swing elections; in other words, if not for women's votes, we would be talking about Bob instead of Bill. The way the parties tried to woo women during their 1996 conventions reflected upon this nation's view of women's importance in the electorate. Because Republicans are for the most part seen as "antifeminist," they decided to showcase women during their 1996 convention. Their 1992 defeat, after Pat Buchanan had stepped up to the convention podium to attack the Clinton agenda as "radical feminism," was a lesson well learned. In 1996 they pushed Buchanan out to the wings and spotlighted Susan Molinari and Elizabeth Dole, political women who were politicians first and gave up nothing when they married.

As for the Democrats, this time they were more worried about potentially distancing themselves from the male vote. Democrats didn't put very many more women on the podium, and they spotlighted them in a family context. Most press releases, statements, or speeches aimed at women used the phrase "women and their families" or "women and children." The Democratic Congressional Campaign Committee created a "Families First Agenda," which brought "fair pay for women" and "affordable child care" into the mix of family programs. And Hillary Clinton, who was very outspoken in the 1992 election, was virtually silent in 1996.

Despite the two parties' efforts to moderate themselves in terms of the gender divide, more men still voted Republican and most women, Democrat. Maybe that had something to do with the issues each party stressed: the Democrats emphasized Medicare, Medicaid, education, and the environment, while Republicans pushed cutting taxes and balancing the budget. Whatever the reason, one thing is clear: the political gender divide is pronounced among Generation X's members.

Lending a Hand

The most visible result of the conflict between GenXers' distaste for national politics and their desire to solve the problems they see is the service movement. Xers are volunteering at astronomical rates. One study, done in 1996, found that 72 percent of college freshmen had volunteered in the past year—the highest percentage since the study began in the 1960s. "We're pretty skeptical about how government is handled," says Shareka Nelson, a student at Georgia's Albany State University. "We see it more as our responsibility to solve problems. That's why young adults choose hands-on volunteerism—delivering food to cancer patients instead of demonstrating in front of the White House."

According to another study, by Independent Sector, which monitors the nonprofit sector, the most active volunteers are young adults, with 55 percent of that population volunteering at least once in the past year compared to 48 percent for the general public. A survey of the nation's undergraduates found even higher percentages: a quarter of us volunteer five hours a week for a community service organization. "Service" can mean anything from mentoring to working on a suicide hotline to building homes for poor families. Volunteerism appeals to this generation because we can see the difference we are making. Dana Deaton, 20, of Nashville, Tennessee, said, "I can help this little girl read, but when you take it to a broader level—abortion or affirmative action—I think our generation is a little overwhelmed."

One of the most successful volunteer organizations has been City Cares of America. The organization has 13,000 volunteers and membership of more than 75,000. Their secret? Flexible and varied volunteering for busy young professionals. The movement began in 1986, when six young friends decided they were frustrated with their options for volunteering in New York City. It was difficult for them to find flexible volunteer work given their long work weeks. Since then the program has grown to twenty-six cities throughout the nation, from Los Angeles Cares to Chicago Cares. Now, in New York City alone, the organization has 2,500 volunteers and participates in

200 projects annually. They do everything from mentoring under-privileged kids to building houses and planting trees.

The program includes people like Kevin Arsnol, a New York City investment banker who spends an average of eighty hours a week at work and a lot of time traveling. It is hard to imagine someone like Kevin having time to volunteer. But New York Cares makes it easy by allowing Kevin to stop by a Harlem middle school in the morning to teach a sixth-grade history class. "Volunteering puts me back in touch with reality. With what is really going on out there. It is easy to lose touch when you're working in glass offices. And it reminds me of how fortunate I am." Kevin is a far cry from the old image of *Wall Street*'s Gordon "Greed Is Good" Gekko.

Another volunteer organization is Do Something, founded in 1993 by a group of young adults that included Andrew Shue, the costar of *Melrose Place*. Although it is a national organization, its focus is local. Anna Marie Nieves-Bryant, the executive director of the New York office, explains that Do Something is about teaching young people "to build safe and happy communities." Do Something supports local action by giving grants and awards to entrepreneurial young adults who start up community service projects—anything from a drug rehab center to a legal services office for recent immigrants. Do Something spreads the "good news" by publishing a bimonthly magazine on young adults who are taking action in their communities. Nieves-Bryant uses her political and business savvy to win support for the organization. "The greatest strength is my ability to be real and to be political—to be bilingual. By that I mean being able to talk to young people hanging out on the corner about what they're doing and then going into the boardroom and speaking to investors about why they should fund what I am doing, and to be respected by both groups fully." So far their sponsors include MTV, Blockbuster, Applied Materials, and *Mademoiselle* magazine.

Jumpstart is another volunteer organization with a local focus. In 1993 Jumpstart was founded by two Yale students who believed that university and college campuses provide a natural resource to communities in need of additional support for their young children. The first Jumpstart Corps members worked one-on-one with their assigned children to teach and reinforce the basic academic and social skills. Today, Jumpstart exists at eleven universities and has just formed a partnership with President Clinton's Americorps. In 1996 Jumpstart volunteers gave eighty thousand hours of their time to helping some of America's most disadvantaged youths.

The push for volunteerism is being fostered by our national government. In his first term, President Clinton created Americorps to encourage volunteerism among members of our generation. Volunteers spend at least a half an hour with a child every day and visit the child's home weekly to involve parents as well. The president's plea for young Americans to get involved stems from shifts in ideology about the role that the federal government should play in people's lives: big government is out and personal responsibility is in.

This shift is also illustrated by our new welfare policy, which has relegated most of the financial responsibility for welfare to the states and has mandated strict work requirements. As a result of the federal government's shrinking welfare role, corporations have now been asked to share the burden by encouraging volunteerism among their ranks. The 1997 Summit for America's Future, inspired by General Colin Powell, brought President Clinton, political leaders, and top CEOs together to discuss prospects for such a venture. The conference asked participants to commit their employees and resources for volunteer work with at-risk youth. Many companies jumped on the bandwagon; Timberland pledged its employees for a week of paid-time volunteer work every year, and Coca-Cola doubled the $50 million it was already giving in aid to education. Whether these companies will stick to their commitments remains to be seen, but if CEOs listen to public opinion polls, they know that the majority of Americans think it's important that the companies they buy from or invest in have a major volunteer program to help the community.

Lobbying like the Pros

GenXers have been quick to learn about getting the establishment's attention. It's as if we're finishing up Lobbying 101 and have enrolled for Advanced Lobbying 901. GenXers learn from their elders. If special interests work in Washington, then let's have our own political action group.

Third Millennium is on the front lines as a growing national advocacy and educational organization for young people. It defines itself as standing outside standard structures: "Third Millennium isn't liberal, moderate, or conservative, but postpartisan. We look beyond the ideologies of both parties to focus on pragmatic solutions," says Richard Thau, the executive director. Its focus is national, "to build consensus around solutions to America's national debt, Social Security, health-care, environmental, racial, and educational crises."

Although it fizzled out in 1997, the National Association of Twenty-somethings (NAT), attempted to create an advocacy organization based in Washington. NAT took as its model the American Association of Retired Persons (AARP), offering benefits as well as information on pertinent political issues affecting members. NAT's benefits included a Web site offering help with résumés and some insurance reductions. However, NAT was never able to reach the "critical mass" that was needed to make the organization viable.

The name of the "action-tank" 2030, launched by Chris Cuomo, the son of the former New York governor Mario Cuomo, and Hans Riemer, is appropriate to this generation: 2030 is the year Social Security is projected to be bankrupt. Leaders of 2030 call themselves a political action group geared toward revitalizing politics for Generation X. Though they are small and have few members, they hope to rev up operations in the years to come. Some of their goals are cutting the costs of education and health care, increasing young workers' wages, and changing the priorities of government subsidies. "We're subsidizing the industries of fifty years ago . . . not the industries of the next generation," Riemer told *Swing* magazine. While the group may be on target with most GenX issues, they get a particular amount of attention for the one issue on which they seem to side with the older generation. They generally oppose the privatization of Social Security, saying that Social Security is too important a program to be left to the whims of the stock market or individual investors.

Xers are also starting to work through establishment lobbying groups. A growing number are taking part in lobbying via America's traditional political action committees, or PACs. In 1996, at just twenty-three years old, Adam Werbach was elected as the youngest president of the Sierra Club, an environmental and lobbying organization with traditional appeal to older people. Werbach came up from the grass roots, founding the Sierra Student Coalition, which is a college-based volunteer and lobby group. It currently boasts more than 30,000 members. Now he has more to deal with—the Sierra Club's 600,000 members and a budget of $40 million. He has set the 106-year-old organization on its head by lobbying politicians and educating voters in the 1996 election with over $7 million, producing rock-and-roll CDs on the environment, and launching a college campus–based "Bash Newt" campaign (participants got to take a swing at a piñata caricature of House Speaker Newt Gingrich). Werbach says, "The environment is the primary issue that prompts this generation, my generation, to take social and political action. Our job is to get the word out to them and to give them a place to act on their anxieties and convictions."

Of course, something can be said for starting early. Werbach began his environmental crusade at the tender age of eight, when he circulated petitions demanding the ouster of the then secretary of the interior, James Watt. For Werbach, college remains a prime place for youth political movements. According to him, one out of every hundred calls coming in to officials on legislative issues is from a college campus. "Anytime you're told you're too young to do anything, that's a time that you could sign a petition or write a letter."

What is special about the GenX lobbying groups is that they are remarkably ethical (and therefore poor). Riemer says that 2030 takes no money from labor organizations or AARP, despite the fact that the three groups are frequently aligned on political issues. Their funding comes from corporations and private individuals. Thau says Third Millennium takes money from a wide variety of interests— businesses and private individuals, liberal and conservative—but is careful not to accept too much money from any one source, to avoid becoming the pawn of any one interest. As a result, such groups can maintain their independence, even if on a small budget. These young people want to battle what they see in Washington so they are careful to keep their consciences clear and their accounting open and clean.

GenXers really shine in the important area of media savvy. Though Third Millennium has under 5,000 members, the group has testified before Congress sixteen times, has been written up on more than one occasion by the *Washington Post*, the *Wall Street Journal*, *Newsweek*, *Time*, and numerous other publications. Third Millennium originated one of this decade's most often cited statistics in American media. In a poll they conducted and released on September 26, 1994, Third Millennium found that more GenXers believe in UFOs than in the future of Social Security. The poll was the subject of a cover story for *Time* and was the most-quoted statistic of that year. Today, when *The McLaughlin Group*, CNN, MSNBC, or just about any political talk show or network wants the opinion of GenX, someone at Third Millennium is called.

2030 also gets excellent media coverage. With no members and Riemer as its only full-time employee, this action-tank has already been mentioned on CNN and MSNBC and in *New York* magazine, *Parade*, the *New York Observer*, the *Washington Post*, and dozens of other media. Whatever else can be said of GenX, we know our media. We understand what sells and we can be responsive. That turns a small or no-member organization (paling by comparison to the AARP's 30 million plus) into a formidable political force.

Retooling the News

Young people are attacked for their low rates of news media consumption. According to one study, in 1990 only one person in three under the age of 35 read a newspaper daily, compared to nearly seven out of ten in 1965. But in rejecting mainstream news, Xers have turned to alternative political media over which they have more control and in which they have more faith. From rock to rap and computer to cable, Xers are clawing and scratching to establish a strong media presence. Political shows on alternative radio and cable-access TV plus political articles and chat groups on the Internet are ways in which Xers trade political information.

A number of Xers are also getting a foot in the door of the mainstream media. The attention that Generation X has been getting in recent years makes the Xers' viewpoint a valuable one for the modern news media. Stations like CNN and MSNBC have hired young people to provide the GenX perspective and commentary. Kellyanne Fitzpatrick and Farai Chideya were both hired by CNN as young political commentators during the 1996 election. Appearing throughout the day as two faces of Generation X, they provided "from the left" and "from the right" viewpoints. On MSNBC are MSNBC's friends, a young, diverse group of budding pundits asked to participate in a kind of on-camera coffee klatsch after the anchors have delivered the news. Even Barbara Walters has launched a new show, the View, with a GenX representative, Debbie Matenopoulos. Collectively, we are making inroads into the national media. The fact that television is taking a chance on us allows Xers access to the national political discourse our predecessors never had.

Xers are also following their parents in using music as a political medium. Politics is sometimes expressed in song lyrics and in political agendas advanced and promoted by certain musicians. But the politics in today's music is not necessarily as overt as in the past. A member of the band Jawbox said, "We are [a politically oriented band] by the virtue [of the fact] that we want to be responsible for

what we do. . . . All good music and all good art are inherently political because they are about understanding the world and getting dia-
logues going among people."

The increasingly popular political movement focusing on the
plight of Tibet has become an important issue among young people
because of the attention music makers like the Beastie Boys have
drawn to the cause. Their "free Tibet" organization, Milarepa, raises
money for the cause through concerts. "In the three years that Milarepa has been around, the influx of young people to the Tibetan
movement has been incredible. Looking at history, it's young people
that have always made the difference in a social movement, whether
its antiapartheid or civil rights or antiwar," says Erin Potts, the organization's director. The Beastie Boys' last concert brought in over a million dollars for the cause.

The Lead or Leave Example

The national group Lead or Leave, founded by Rob Nelson and
Jon Cowan, was created in 1992 around the idea that young people
can be rallied for national change and that the most pressing issue for
young people is the national debt. Nelson and Cowan picked the
name "Lead or Leave" to combat the slacker myth and to demand that
politicians either lead America to fiscal responsibility or relinquish
their positions. The group asked members of Congress to pledge to
halve the debt in four years. Lead or Leave earned plenty of media attention and appeared to be succeeding in politicizing the "slacker"
crowd. They staged a rally on the doorstep of the headquarters of the
AARP and declared the issue of entitlement reform "our generation's
Vietnam." At the height of their media attention, they claimed one
million members (a number later discredited). Despite an initial
strong showing, the group disappeared a few years later because of a
loss of members and bad management, which led to the alienation of
financial backers.

The story of Lead or Leave is sometimes cited as a case study for what is wrong with much of young people's involvement in national politics: the catchy gimmicks and exciting, fun methods needed to get Xers involved will eventually wear off as their "short attention spans" drift elsewhere. Steve Johnson, founder and director of Democrats with an Attitude, a group organized to get young people into the "fun" aspect of the Democratic party, subscribes to the view that "precinct caucuses, conventions, issues meetings—young people don't like them much. . . . [They do like] fun events, fun logos, fun things. Politics needs to be made fun for them. First, you get them active and then you feed them the issues." Lead or Leave's methods were fun, but the group didn't fare so well with the issues. The Lead or Leave pledge did not specify how the debt should be shrunk. Tax hikes? Military cuts? Social Security cuts? The message was: Just do it. This was politics without politics. No hard choices. A gimmick. Without a concrete agenda, the group couldn't hold together.

One critic of the Lead or Leave approach cautions, "Who said politics is supposed to be fun, anyway? . . . The conventional wisdom [is] that young people are not citizens but consumers, and that democracy darned well better be sexy, funny, and entertaining if it's going to survive the next millennium. . . . Fun, quite simply, is not enough to build a political cadre." Many of the national groups now do not follow the sequence of fun first, issues later. However, they are also not capturing the attention of Xers as effectively as Lead or Leave did.

Taking the Plunge

"It is the death of politics if you start calling vegetarians who recycle politically active. The young are not as cynical and selfish as they have been depicted, but it's wrong to say that invisibly they are as politically active as ever," warns Helen Wilkinson of the think-tank Demos. While being on the fringe and being a "rebel with a cause" are attractive to those of us who are wary of mainstream politics, we must also realize that to complete the job we have to reach critical mass. We must get involved. On a very basic level, we must vote. Alexander Jutkowitz, twenty-nine, who works for Global Strategy Group, a firm that conducts polling and market research of young adults, says, "It is disappointing, but the political reality is that if you usually don't vote in great numbers, or don't lobby with any force, no one has any reason to pay attention to you."

Time and time again young adults get overlooked. This is seen in both the political neglect of Social Security and Medicare and the fact that we do not get the tax breaks other groups do. We must realize that politicians ignore us because there is no negative consequence to doing so. We do not vote. We do not give money. We are virtually invisible on the political landscape. Rob Nelson, in his book, *Revolution X*, reported Senator Phil Gramm (R-Texas) as saying, "Do you know why we continue to borrow from your future, racking up huge debts? Because you don't get involved and you don't vote." One congressional intern said his boss once bluntly told him off the record, "Generation X should burn this place down for the way they're getting screwed." In order for us to start making big differences, that must change. Richard Thau, of Third Millennium, said that former Senator Alan Simpson (R-Wyoming) once candidly told him that any lobby group needs at least 10 million members to be taken seriously on Capitol Hill. That is the political reality of our system.

Furthermore, we must educate ourselves about the issues. An ongoing study of generations born from 1940 on found that the differing interest in and knowledge of politics between generations were generally marginal, or that those who at that time were under thirty knew *more* about the issues than older people. But today, the trend has reversed and young adults are drastically less aware than their elders; a full 20 percent are less likely than middle-aged and older Americans to know even basic facts about current events. If we followed politics, we would understand that we do have causes as real and important to the future of our nation as Vietnam, the civil rights movement, and the Cold War were to our parents. Generally, they are economic issues—the debt, bankrupting Social Security, funding education, balancing business interests, and environmental protection.

We should take a lesson from nineteen-year-old Danny Seo, who believes that this generation has what it takes to lobby and change government. The founder and president of the 25,000-member activist group Earth 2000, Seo is an animal rights activist whose massive letter-writing campaign inspired new statewide laws on animal rights in his home state of Pennsylvania. In a similar campaign against Eddie Bauer's and Lerner's use of animal fur in clothing, Seo convinced thousands of young people to send letters of protest along with their parents' cut-up credit cards. Sure enough, animal fur disappeared from store racks. Yet even with all his drive Seo identifies with the situation faced by young adults. "Our generation faces problems that didn't exist when our parents were our age. It is not surprising that young adults feel hopeless about the future."

It is true that our issues are sometimes harder to get excited about or even to understand. Who has time to grapple with problems of the Social Security system or figure out the national debt? These are not issues that can be summed up in one-liners like "Make love, not war." The AARP and others who lobby opposite Generation X in Washington know that. They use our lack of understanding to one-up us on political issues. As Evelyn Morton, an AARP lobbyist, says, "The Social Security issues that are being raised are not ones that the [younger] generation is ready to focus on yet. So I think there's a built-in limit to what they can do."

We must prove these lobbyists wrong—that we indeed are focused on the future. We have been told, and we believe, that we have been born into an age that has no causes, no crusades, no battles. Some of the greatest injustices in America today are waged against future generations: the debt we will face; the taxes we have to pay; the promises our politicians cannot keep. If any group should be politically active, we should. Our economic well-being, the core of any political system, is at stake. Meanwhile, our generation, lulled into a fundamental distrust of government and political parties, is headed into the prophetic doom that has been forecast for us—one in which we will experience an era of less.

Our generation does have a crisis—we are just failing to face it. Our generation is charged with overcoming the accumulating debt caused by the gigantic pyramid scheme of entitlements we face. It is frightening to think that we will be responsible for trillions of dollars in debt of our elders, who will be long buried when their bills come due. We won't have any money for ourselves, let alone future entitlements. Is it any wonder we put more faith in UFOs than Social Security? If we fail to marshal our generation on this political issue, fail to vote, fail to run for office, and, yes, fail to lobby and fail to reduce our most powerful enemy, our national debt, then we will fail as a generation and most tragically as a democracy.

CHAPTER 4

A Whimper, Not a Bang

Shouldering the Great Society

Children should not have to save up for their parents, but parents for their children. —2 Corinthians 12:14

Imagine that it is the year 2015. Over 70 million members of the baby boom generation have started to reach retirement age. Generation X—a more ethnically diverse and poorer generation— becomes the prime mover in the workforce. Amid higher taxes, a depleted government treasury, and less job opportunity, Generation X is asked to pay for the retirement of its parents. What happens?

Today we are told by economists that the government is transferring huge quantities of wealth from future generations to current generations by fostering unsustainable retirement plans like Social Security and by running up debt that future generations will have to pay. We are told that Generation X will be the first generation of Americans who will be poorer than their parents were. Our public education system is in a shambles with many of our young people lacking the skills to compete with the rest of the world. Many of us grow up in crime-infested cities and attend schools that are literally falling apart. Thirty percent of us were abandoned by our fathers.

Should GenX support expensive government programs for those of an older generation who are better educated and richer; had better employment opportunities and lower taxes; discriminated against ethnic minorities; allowed our child poverty rate and violent crime rate to be the highest in the industrialized world; and whose lack of planning for our future created trillions of dollars of debt and a damaged environment? Ask Generation X to support that system and what will be the answer?

By 2030, the U.S. Census Bureau projects, nearly 40 percent of the population will be Hispanic, African-American, and Asian. Imagine what happens when a predominantly white elderly population demands that its benefits be paid by young working minorities. Will members of these minority groups remember growing up in greater poverty than their white counterparts, going to less well endowed schools, battling over affirmative action, facing corporate discrimination?

Today, for every dollar we spend on our youth we spend five on our elderly. If this kind of inequality existed between the races or the sexes we would hear a great public outcry. We would see protests, riots, marches on Washington. But this subtle discrimination gets only a footnote in the political debate. Our concerns are overshadowed by those of the more powerful, the older, the more entrenched.

Given our economic condition, our voices should be the loudest in Washington. Entitlement reform and debt reduction are issues of great significance. They do not hold the drama of the issues of the 1960s or the 1940s. There is no larger-than-life enemy like Hitler or Mussolini. There are no assassinations, riots, or Woodstocks. Yet our problems are as serious and have consequences as dire as any faced by America's previous generations. History shows us that societies and cultures do not end with the crescendo of a great musical work or the climax of an action-packed motion picture. Great powers tend to wither; they do not combust. It was true of the Roman Empire, of British imperialism, of the Ottomans. Many historians argue that America could be headed down the same path of demise. We are faced with supporting a system of social guarantees that the majority of our economists and historians say are financially unsustainable. Perhaps boring issues and yet they have profound consequences for America's future. T. S. Eliot wrote, "This is the way the world ends / Not with a bang but with a whimper." If we do nothing, the whimperings of this generation could, indeed, be the end of American hegemony.

Accounting Teaches a Costly Lesson

The economic field of generational accounting became popular in the late 1980s when economists realized that many industrialized countries were systematically making their future generations poorer by spending too much on people alive today. Simply put, generational accounting is a way of measuring the impact of government programs on the economic equality between generations. Generally, economists have found that industrialized countries transfer wealth to current generations by overspending current funds, causing a buildup of debt for future generations and establishing pension funds and retirement plans that overpromise benefits to retirees.

The economist Allen Auberach, at the University of California at Berkeley, calculated that in 1990, a seventy-year-old man would receive net benefits from the government over his lifetime of $46,000. In contrast, a twenty-five-year-old man in 1990 could expect to make net payments over his lifetime of $226,000 dollars. That's because the older man can expect to receive full Social Security benefits, Medicare, and the like. The young man will likely face the scaled-down version of these programs—if they exist at all—and will of course pay higher taxes.

To pay for the spending on older generations, Generation X will face huge tax burdens. The combined cost to the federal budget of Social Security and Medicare, expressed as a share of workers' taxable payroll, is projected to rise from the already burdensome 17 percent in 1995 to between 35 percent and 55 percent in 2040. This doesn't include the many other costs, from nursing homes to civil service and military pensions, that are destined to grow. The Congressional Budget Office projects that by 2040 our overall tax burden will amount to 82 percent of taxable income if we do nothing to curb our spending. Our children might get to keep $18 of every $100 they earn. And those numbers don't change very much even with the balanced budget agreement. That's because the agreement doesn't even begin to reform our entitlement programs like Social Security and Medicare.

We already see the effects of this generational transfer of wealth. The child poverty rate in America is twice that of the elderly poverty rate. Since 1973, the year I was born, families with household heads 18 to 34 years old have lost an average 10 percent of real income. Families with household heads over 65 years old have experienced income growth of nearly 30 percent. With a national debt of more than $5 trillion and growing, it's no wonder Generation X is told we will be the first generation to have less than our parents. As the author Alex Abrams writes, "When it comes to the tax-versus-entitlements game, Generation X is on the verge of becoming the first group of Americans to get slammed at every stage of their lives—to experience tax hikes during their prime working years only to see their benefits cut upon retirement."

The United States is not the only nation transferring debt to future generations. Germany, Italy, and Sweden are among other nations creating large future obligations. Even Japan, with its graying population and large state pension liabilities, will face crises. Estimates indicate Japan's net debt as a percentage of GDP (gross domestic product) will jump from an estimated 13 percent this year to more than 300 percent in 2030, mainly owing to the huge pensions the nation has promised its retirees.

Why are advanced nations building up so much debt for future generations to pay? Let's take a look at how the United States has gotten into the business of transferring funds—by running huge deficits and constructing unsustainable social programs.

Photo Courtesy of Heather Lamm

HEATHER LAMM
Chairman, Third Millennium

ENTITLEMENT CRUSADER, BUSINESSWOMAN

Working on her master's degree in business administration at Kellogg doesn't stop Heather Lamm from taking part in national politics. Maybe she gets it from her dad, the former governor of Colorado, Richard Lamm. But she certainly has her own passion—entitlement reform. Sound boring? Not if you have your eye on the future. Lamm is worried about the huge tax bill we will be paying for Social Security. "If we fail to invest in the future in the form of education, training, and savings, we will not stay competitive in the next century. We spend far too much on middle- and upper-income individuals and not enough on children."

As chairman of Third Millennium, a twenty-something political think-tank, Heather is trying to change that. She says the biggest challenge for this generation is "learning to care about our communities and our nation. We are currently so cynical and so detached from politics that I worry how we will survive the next century as a nation. I worry that as we assume leadership positions, we will have no vision or loyalty for our country or its citizens."

Our Inheritance: A Big IOU

In New York City's Times Square, a "national debt clock" records the level of America's debt. In January 1997 the federal debt was $5.2 trillion, or 72 percent of our entire gross domestic product—about $20,000 worth of debt for every man, woman, and child living in America. The debt can be defined as the accumulation of all of our deficits. It is the amount that we have continually borrowed and owe to our citizens and foreign lenders in the forms of U.S. bonds and notes.

Steven Moore, the author of *Government: America's #1 Growth Industry*, provides examples to illustrate the enormity of our debt. He states, "If Congress paid down the debt a dollar every second, it would take 130,000 years, or roughly the amount of time that has passed since the Ice Age, to pay down the present debt." Or "If you laid the debt out in dollars from end-to-end, it would reach out into space four times the distance between the earth and the sun."

Most of our current debt was accumulated in the 1980s. The deficits that began to be so high throughout the 1980s and into the 1990s resulted in part from a dramatic rise in our federal government spending. Since 1960, the government has grown faster than any other segment of the American economy. The government now consumes about 25 percent of the U.S. gross domestic product. It is estimated that by the year 2010, that will shoot above 30 percent.

The largest share of government spending—67 percent—is mandatory spending. That's the money the federal government spends automatically—unless the president and Congress change the laws that govern it. As a share of the budget, mandatory spending has soared in recent decades owing to the rise in entitlement spending and in net interest on the national debt. It includes entitlement programs such as Social Security, which accounts for 23 percent of all federal spending, and Medicare, which accounts for 12 percent. It also includes interest on the national debt, which since the 1970s has doubled, as a percentage of the budget, to 15 percent today.

Meanwhile, discretionary spending, the money the president and

Congress must decide to spend each year, has shrunk to just 30 percent of the budget. National defense discretionary spending totaled an estimated $259 billion in 1998, 15 percent of the budget. Nondefense discretionary spending—a wide array of programs that include education, training, science, technology, housing, transportation, and foreign aid—has shrunk as a share of the budget from 34 percent in 1966 to an estimated 15 percent in 1998.

Future increases in government spending will come from hikes in mandatory spending, with Social Security, Medicare, and interest on the debt leading the way. According to the Social Security Administration, Social Security will run a projected $766 billion deficit and Medicare will run a $934 billion deficit by 2030. Despite a narrowing deficit, in the next few years we can expect catastrophic increases. These exploding deficits will continue to expand our debt, making it a projected $17 trillion in 2030.

And we have to pay more and more interest on the debt we create. The third-largest expense for government is interest on the debt. When the government borrows money it has to pay the money back with interest, just as an individual or corporation does. In 1998, that interest is projected at $250 billion, or more than four times what the federal government spends on education. The amount we spend on interest uses up money we could be putting toward valuable government programs or money we could return to citizens as lower taxes.

A Poorer Generation X

Facing these huge obligations of debt, is it any wonder economists say Generation X will be the first generation to have less then their parents? If the debt isn't enough to make us worry, there's also concern that the way the government spends our money is making us poorer.

Many argue that debt isn't a problem. After all, nearly every corporation in America borrows money. Corporations borrow to invest in new ventures and grow. Some have argued this is what America does—borrow to grow and provide needed services. However, there is a large body of evidence that government expenditures largely promote consumption rather than savings and investment. For instance, the federal government spends less than 1 percent of the budget on education, technology, and research. We spend the majority on Social Security and Medicare (income mostly consumed, not saved by recipients) and on debt interest. The point is, our government does not "spend to grow."

And we have a tax system that also encourages consumption over savings. The current system taxes interest savings and capital gains at the corporate and individual levels, creating double taxation. So the tax system creates a bias against investment favoring current consumption while discouraging savings. Not surprisingly, America has one of the lowest savings rates of any industrialized nation. Total net savings, including public and private sectors, is less than 5 percent of our nation's output, down from an average of 11 percent in the 1960s.

This low savings rate translates into fewer funds available for domestic investment, which in turn translates into lower growth rates for our economy as a whole. For the past two decades, our growth rate has hovered around 2.5 percent, a sharp decline from the 3.5 to 4 percent rate that we averaged in the post–World War II era. If the economy had grown over the past twenty years at the pace it did after the war, the average American household today would have an income at least $12,000 higher than it does.

If the United States continues on its course of the past two decades, with a growth rate of about 2.5 percent, we can expect our per capita personal income to be about $40,000 in 2020 and $65,000 in 2040. Compare that with what we would have with a 4 percent growth rate (the rate at the end of World War II): $60,000 in 2020 and $130,000 in 2040. A couple of points in growth rate can make a huge difference in the long run.

What Rose Garden?

Why have we allowed our spending to rise so quickly? The culprits are entitlement programs like Social Security and Medicare. What went wrong with these programs, which were intended to provide for some of the neediest citizens—the elderly? Simply, politicians promised us a "rose garden" that, given current demographics, we can never hope to deliver to future generations.

Evidence suggests that Medicare and Social Security were pretty good deals for the generations that have enjoyed their use. According to Urban Institute economist C. Eugene Steurele, the author of *Retooling Social Security for the 21st Century*, a current retiree couple will receive $308,000 more in Social Security and Medicare benefits over the course of their retirement than they paid into the system. That's largely due to longer life spans and favorable tax laws. The Congressional Budget Office calculates that benefits from entitlement programs have grown more than three times as fast as inflation since 1965.

That's certainly not a bad investment for those involved. Unfortunately, our entitlement programs are financed by a huge pyramid scheme. Their success is predicted on the existence of a growing number of young workers to provide for the retirement of the elderly. With the aging of our society, the scenario is very different.

America is in the midst of a process of graying. Between 1960 and 1994 the percentage of the population age 65 and older doubled, compared to a 45 percent increase for the overall population. At the same time, the percentage of Americans age 18 years of age or younger declined from 36 percent to 26 percent. Over the next forty-five years, the number of people 65 and older will increase by roughly 40 million, a rate of increase five to eight times greater than the number of people between 20 and 64. In the worst case scenario, in 2040, one in four Americans may be over 65.

Our aging phenomenon results from two trends. First, life expectancy is up. In 1935 the average number of years spent in retirement was 12.6; now it is 17.2. By 2040 it will be at least 30 years.

The most rapidly growing group of Americans is made up of those 85 and older—up a tremendous 232 percent from 1964. Second, the birthrate is down. We are barely replacing our population. Immigration accounts for 30 percent of our small population growth.

This aging of our nation puts pressure on the resource most demanded by the elderly—health care. Our growing elderly population demands more health care of all kinds, especially Medicare, which services those over 65. Furthermore, as our medical technology has become more complex and varied, overall costs have increased. The government adds to the problem by inflating health-care demand through tax subsidies and breaks for health insurance and services. As a result, household health-care costs have soared in recent years. Between 1987 and 1993, health insurance costs increased 105 percent overall. The amount each household spent on health care rose 56 percent. By comparison, household income rose only by 28 percent between 1987 and 1993. One in every five dollars spent in America today goes for health care.

Our aging population and soaring health-care costs mean that paying for Social Security and Medicare as they now exist will become a nightmare for Generation X.

I Believe in UFOs

Social Security has the very real potential to cause a generational conflict because benefits depend on the taxes of young workers who don't believe they themselves will ever receive benefits. Generation X has good reason to be skeptical.

Social Security was signed into law by Franklin Roosevelt in 1935. The program was created to ensure the economic stability of the elderly. Since then the program's benefits have mushroomed and now it is our most expensive social program, costing 23 cents of every dollar of tax revenue ($384 billion in 1998).

The Social Security system is a pay-as-you-go program. The elderly are supported not by the payments they made during their working lives but by young workers' current taxes. Workers and employers each contribute an equal amount to the Social Security program to pay for retirement, disability, and Medicare benefits. Current FICA (Federal Insurance Contributions Act, the law that authorized the Social Security payroll tax) deductions are about 7.65 percent of earnings from workers and 7.65 percent of gross salary that is paid by employers.

In 1998, almost 50 million people received some sort of Social Security benefits. In addition, Social Security accounts for 40 percent of the total income of those over 65, keeping 38 percent of this group out of poverty. The average monthly benefit for a male retired worker is about $760 ($550 for a woman). The retirement age is 65. It will increase to 67 starting in the year 2000.

Social Security's problem is that we have a growing number of elderly and a shrinking number of younger workers to pay for benefits. When the program first began, there were 15 workers to support each retiree. Today, there are 3.3, and by 2040 there will be no more than 2. As the Baby Boomers (born between 1946 and 1965) reach old age in the next few decades, the Social Security system faces serious problems. The Social Security Administration is projecting that it will begin to suffer huge cash deficits by about 2015, and the entire system will go bankrupt by 2029. Professor Martin Feldstein of Harvard University reports that the present actuarial value of the system's expected tax revenues is about $11 trillion short of its promised future benefits. That is more than 1.5 times our annual gross domestic product.

What, then, is the future of Social Security? Has the government foreseen these problems? In 1983 the Greenspan Commission, a bipartisan congressional panel, created a Social Security savings account to cover the future claims of Baby Boomers. This was accomplished by bringing in more tax revenues than benefits paid out. It created a surplus that was invested in government bonds and could be drawn down when Boomers reached retirement. Originally, the commission thought the reform would keep Social Security solvent for seventy-five years, or until 2058. However, their predictions were overly optimistic. Now, economists are predicting the erosion of the Social Security Trust Fund and the bankruptcy of Social Security by 2029.

Social Security has a racial element to it. According to the Rand Corporation, Social Security accounts for 44 percent of the wealth of Hispanic Americans and 40 percent of the wealth of African-Americans but only 25 percent of the wealth of white Americans. That's because statistically white households have better retirement plans and have had higher wages. Any weakness in Social Security will affect minorities more than whites. There are other demographic factors to consider. In thirty years a majority of the working population will be nonwhite, meaning that ethnically diverse young adults will be paying for a richer, white population—and that spells racial conflict. Richard Thau, the director of Third Millennium, says, "If blacks and Hispanics will be the largest segment of the working population in thirty years, and mostly white Boomers are the retirees, aren't we sowing the seeds for not only a generational but a racial battle?"

CPI—Not User-Friendly for GenX

In March 1997 I testified before the Senate Finance Committee as a representative of Third Millennium. I was there to speak up for young people's interests in regard to the Consumer Price Index (CPI). This index, which is the most commonly used measure of inflation, had become a major sticking point in the political debate over entitlements and taxes. The reason? The CPI is used to index Social Security benefits as well as taxes. In fact, 30 percent of all government spending is linked to the CPI.

The CPI may well be the most used and most important statistic Washington produces, but its accuracy has been questioned vigorously. In 1995 the President appointed the Boskin Commission, headed by Michael Boskin, Stanford University economist, to judge the accuracy of the CPI in gauging inflation. The Boskin Commission reported that the CPI overstated inflation by 1.1 percent.

Now, you may ask, what is a percentage point here or there, and why should we care? The commission estimated that the current bias would contribute about $148 billion to the deficit before the start of the next millennium. That would make the bias in the CPI our fourth-largest federal program, after Social Security, health care, and defense. By 2008, the bias would contribute more than $1 trillion to the national debt.

Unfortunately, this problem isn't new. The commission said that CPI has almost always overestimated inflation because it isn't "a cost of living index." Rather, it measures the changes in cost of a fixed market basket of goods. But everyone knows when you live in a dynamic economy like ours no one buys a fixed market basket of goods for long. Even my freshman college economics textbook said that the CPI overestimated inflation. According to that book and the Boskin Commission, in 1982 the CPI overestimated inflation by 6.5 percent, and in 1984 the bias was 4.7 percent. The CPI overstatement has already cost us billions. This problem is older than most people in this generation. So why has it taken this long—more than three decades— to seriously address the issue?

Also testifying on the CPI were members of the AARP and AFL-CIO. Simply, they didn't want their constituents' programs, primarily Social Security, reduced. Politicians were reluctant to do anything. Despite the best advice of our nation's best economists—including the Federal Reserve chairman, Alan Greenspan, who said the CPI with "one hundred percent certainty" overstated inflation—Congress chose not to act. Not because it was right or sensible, but because of sheer lobbying power. Our political system is filled with missed opportunities like this because our generation doesn't get involved; we don't have lobbying muscle; and because we don't follow the issues. Undoubtedly, when we are older we will regret that we didn't speak up. We'll regret it where it hurts the most—in our pocketbooks.

Looking to Other Nations

Perhaps we should investigate the policies of other nations for hints on how to solve our elder support dilemma. America isn't the only country experiencing problems associated with an aging society. Many European countries and Japan are quickly approaching the same fate. The unfunded liabilities of retirement programs in most European countries are significantly greater as a proportion of GDP than ours. A 1996 World Bank study, *Global Capital Supply and Demand: Is There Enough to Go Around?*, reports that the present value of unfunded pension liabilities in major European countries ranges from 150 to 250 percent of GDP: "This means that the implicit social security debt is a multiple of an already large explicit public debt, which . . . averages more than 70% of GDP in industrial countries, up from 40% just fifteen years ago."

In Japan, the age wave will hit much sooner than anywhere else because of Japan's huge elderly population. The good news for Japan is that their savings rates are higher than ours, allowing them to absorb some of the shock. Furthermore, the Japanese seem more willing than Americans to sacrifice for the future. In 1986, when Japan enacted a major reduction in pension benefits, the Ministry of Health and Welfare issued a concise justification that cited "equity between the generations." Few if any objections were heard in a society where most of the elderly at all income levels live with their extended families. The day he assumed office, Prime Minister Ryutaro Hashimoto referred to the "imminent arrival of our aging society" and said it was a priority "to overhaul those social arrangements premised upon a life span of two score and ten to suit our new expected life span of four score."

Developing countries are following Japan's model. In South Korea, where the household savings rate runs at about 35 percent, companies routinely fly banners on the shop floor with messages like *Working to Make a Better Life for the Next Generation*. In Singapore, workers' account balances in the mandatory pension savings system equal nearly three quarters of the GDP. In Chile, the average worker has an account of $21,000 in the fifteen-year-old national funded retirement system—a sum about four times the average annual Chilean income. Argentina, Peru, and Columbia are following Chile's lead in setting up funded systems.

Australia has made employer-sponsored pensions mandatory, boosting coverage from under 40 percent to nearly 90 percent of the workforce. These pensions, invested by the private sector, earn higher rates of return than our Social Security system. Iceland has means-tested its social insurance system. Germany has enacted retirement age increases, and France, Sweden, Italy, and the United Kingdom are debating making such a move.

Most other industrialized nations are able to budget their public spending on health care and have much greater control over this potentially explosive aspect of aging. Unlike the United States, most countries tax public benefits and health-care benefits as they do any other income. Most have fairly healthy household savings rates (generally well over 10 percent of disposable incomes, versus about 5 percent here) and can absorb public-sector deficits much better than we can.

Medicare's in Critical Care

According to a Third Millennium poll, young adults believe that the television soap opera *General Hospital* will outlast our Medicare program—both of which started in the 1960s. Fifty-three percent chose *General Hospital*, while 34 percent rooted for Medicare. Unless Medicare is fixed, the majority of young adults want out. We will pay our own medical bills when we retire. Why do we feel this way? Just look at the system and you'll see.

As the rising number of elderly stretches resources, and health-care costs increase, the nation faces the impending bankruptcy of

BOBBY JINDAL
Secretary of Health and Human Services, State of Louisiana

HEALTH-CARE GURU, *BRADY BUNCH* FAN

At just twenty-five Jindal has one the most important jobs in the nation. He is the director of a national bipartisan commission which will recommend ways to rescue the nation's 230 billion dollar Medicare program which serves 38 million citizens. Jindal was hand-picked from his position of Secretary of Louisiana's Department of Health and Human Services where he turned $400 million in deficits into a surplus of $170 million. Louisiana governor Mike Foster's gamble on the young Rhodes scholar and former McKinsey consultant paid off. Jindal is now spreading the word in Washington. Not bad for a guy who is a first-generation American. Incidentally, he gave himself the name Bobby, his American name, after Bobby Brady. Did we mention, he has been accepted to Yale Law School and Harvard Medical School?

Medicare. That's frightening when you consider that Medicare provides health-care coverage for over 38 million elderly Americans. The program has three parts: Part A, hospital insurance; Part B, insurance for doctors and other services; and the recently added Part C that provides a limited menu of new choices like HMO-care and medical savings accounts for Medicare recipients. Since its inception in 1965, Medicare has accounted for an increasing share of federal spending—now more than 12 percent. Under current conditions, Medicare spending is projected to double every five to seven years.

Medicare takes care of the medical expenses of the elderly and disabled. Those eligible for these funds are over 65 or disabled and qualified to receive Social Security, or over 65 and paying a monthly premium ($43.80 in 1997). Medicare provides such help as in-patient hospital care, short-term skilled nursing facility care, home health care, doctors' services, diagnostic and lab tests, outpatient hospital services, home dialysis, and ambulance services.

In fiscal 1997, Medicare's Hospital Insurance Trust Fund, which pays hospital bills (Part A), spent $9.9 billion more than it received in taxes. In fiscal 1995 the fund had begun losing money (nearly $36 million) for the first time since 1972. Democrats and Republicans both admit that the data showed a need to shore up Medicare. Even more dire, the fund was expected to be wiped out entirely by 2001 and start piling up deficits.

In 1997, Congress passed into law Medicare Part C. Among the changes designed to save the government money, lawmakers agreed to incentives that encourage more beneficiaries to join HMOs and other managed-care organizations. Under congressional plans, for example, new types of managed-care plans giving beneficiaries greater freedom in choosing their doctors were approved. And hospital and physician networks—known as provider-sponsored organizations—also were given the go-ahead to offer Medicare plans. To help beneficiaries choose from the expanded menu of managed-care options, all health plans faced new requirements on disclosing information on how their programs work.

Congress also decided to give beneficiaries a third option: medical savings accounts. Beneficiaries would be given government payments to set up tax-free medical savings accounts to cover routine expenses, such as doctors' visits, and to buy high-deductible insurance policies for illnesses that are expensive to treat. This third option, beyond the traditional fee-for-service program and managed-care program, was criticized by some consumer advocates who argued that beneficiaries using medical savings accounts would have to foot more of their medical bills. But supporters contended the accounts give beneficiaries greater freedom of choice about their medical decisions.

Other Medicare changes that gained congressional approval included money set aside to help low-income beneficiaries pay the premiums for doctors' services.

Meanwhile, other changes proved too controversial and failed to get a green light from both houses of Congress. The Senate voted to gradually raise the eligibility age to 67 from 65 with the change phased in by 2006. The Senate also voted to charge higher premiums for the most affluent beneficiaries. These proposals, which met stiff resistance from senior citizens' groups such as the politically powerful American Association of Retired Persons, failed in the House of Representatives. Even with this new legislation, economists warn Medicare still has not been preserved for our Baby Boomer parents who start to reach the age of 65 in 2011, much less us.

Taking Our Chances on Health

The United States spends far more per capita in health care than any other nation on earth. One of every seven dollars spent by the government goes toward health care. Public and private health-care spending represents 20 percent of our gross domestic product. Increased technology and lengthening life spans make health care more expensive. Costs are also driven up by fraud and the lack of incentives in our system to use health-care services wisely. Despite all our spending, statistics show that our overall health-care quality has not been keeping pace with the rate of our economic growth. The Index of Social Health produced by the Fordham Institute in Social Policy reported that "the overall picture of the 1990s is not very encouraging. Of the eight worst years, in terms of health care coverage, since 1970, six have been in this decade. The social health of the nation has not kept up with the recovery of the economy."

Part of the problem could be that many are uninsured. The number of uninsured Americans has risen 41 percent since 1976. My generation, and our young children, make up the majority of the 41 million Americans who are presently uninsured, a number that is increasing by about 1 million per year, according to the Washington-based People-to-People Health Foundation. Of the uninsured, 53 percent reported problems obtaining or paying for health care in the previous year. The American Health Association estimates that health insurance problems had a negative impact on the physical or mental health of 17 million people in 1996. Similarly, a study by the Harvard School of Public Health reported that at some time during the past year, 37 percent of Americans had difficulty obtaining or paying for medical care. Those individuals receive insufficient preventive care and often end up flooding emergency rooms, usually the most expensive type of health care.

The principal reason for not being insured is cost. Insurance premiums have increased by 90 percent from 1970, four times the increase in wages. Many businesses have been able to control health-care costs through employees' use of health maintenance organizations (HMOs) and other less expensive forms of managed care. Other businesses continue to provide health insurance but are reducing or eliminating their coverage of employees' family members in order to reduce labor overhead. Employee health-care coverage is one of those expenses that is falling by the wayside in the overall scheme of business planning and profit seeking. About 70 percent of uninsured say they are employed either full-time or part-time but do not have health coverage through their jobs.

According to a 1996 poll done by Third Millennium, private corporations' commitments to financing the health-care coverage of their workers is eroding, with 40 percent of companies surveyed saying they would prefer to contribute only 50 percent or less of a worker's premium. While 27 percent said they now paid the full premium, only 9 percent believed they should continue that practice. Half of the companies surveyed believed they should contribute less toward the health coverage of employees' spouses and children, a growing sentiment among corporations that some researchers believe has added to the ranks of the uninsured.

Almost 2 million welfare families may face eventual loss of government-sponsored insurance coverage through the 1996 Welfare Reform Bill as they are forced to go to work, many in low-wage, part-time, or temporary jobs that do not provide benefits. Among those making less than $7 an hour, the percentage who buy insurance decreased from 80 to 63 percent between 1987 and 1996. (The percentage for those earning more than $15 an hour dropped from 91 to 86 percent.) Although the new welfare law extends some transitional coverage to people moving into jobs, the lack of skills, education, and work experience among many welfare recipients may make it hard for this group to land jobs that provide health-care benefits.

Why should young adults care about these facts and trends? After all, we are young and in a stage of our lives when people pay less attention to health-care issues. We should care because a majority of people without insurance are young adults with their children. We should care because our generation will be paying for the health insurance of our elders when they retire, through Medicare, Medicaid, and other government programs, while we ourselves have none. Whether we like it or not, a chunk of our paycheck every week goes to Medicare programs. We should care because health-care costs have soared during our lifetime, sucking up more and more of America's GDP. As we age and our life spans lengthen and more expensive technology is developed, costs will continue to rise. Even at this early age we have to be prepared for big future health-care bills for ourselves, our children, and our parents.

For our generation, health insurance stops when we graduate from high school or college. Yes, some of us can stay on our parents' plans until we reach a certain age. But this is an ever-increasing problem, as our parents are dropped from health insurance coverage programs in their companies, or, having been downsized or fired from the corporation, are out on their own.

Most of us who work are insured through employers, and that generally means we are part of an HMO. Membership in HMOs grew tremendously in the first part of the nineties. The percentage of American workers belonging to managed-care plans has grown to 74 percent, up from 55 percent in 1992, when Clinton began his campaign for health-care reform. A study of employers of all sizes found that those offering HMOs as a health-care alternative have reduced the number of alternative health plans available to their workers during the last year. Among midsize employers, 52 percent now offer only one plan.

Simply put, health maintenance organizations underwritten by insurance companies or other groups were designed to reduce overall health-care costs. HMOs traditionally limit members to a specific group of doctors in their area and encourage people to see primary-care physicians before seeking more expensive advice from specialists. The advantages of belonging to an HMO include reduced paperwork in filing claims and significantly reduced cost, but there are drawbacks to HMOs. Doctors throughout the country say HMOs have limited their ability to talk to patients about costly treatment options or care. Sixteen states adopted laws in 1997 to curb the use of these gag clauses, and Congress is considering legislation to eliminate them altogether. Some HMOs have revised portions of their contracts, but doctors report that gag clauses are still a serious problem. Furthermore, hospital stays were so strictly limited by some insurers that Congress recently stepped in and required that new mothers and babies remain in the hospital for at least forty-eight hours.

HMOs contend that they cannot legally be held accountable for the quality of care, because they don't make medical decisions. HMOs argue they are protected against malpractice claims and lawsuits by a 1974 federal law, administered by the Labor Department, that regulates employee benefits. The former Secretary of Labor Robert Reich says that not being able to sue HMOs would compromise the right of many consumers to be compensated for injuries resulting from negligence.

In addition, HMOs have strict rules about what they will and won't cover. More nontraditional forms of healing such as chiropractic, homeopathy, acupuncture, and psychotherapy are not necessarily covered by HMOs. Often, neither are medical emergencies. Some plans won't pick up bills if you don't notify the HMO within twenty-four to forty-eight hours of being admitted to a hospital. And if you get sick while traveling, your HMO may not cover you outside your area. Many HMOs won't cover sports-related injuries, because they've decided it's beyond basic care. HMOs can severely limit your hospital stays.

Regardless of the drawbacks, the majority of GenXers who have health care are enrolled in HMOs, because in the companies we work for, HMOs are often the only alternative. For those of us who get a choice from employers, most choose the cheaper HMO option. This is in stark contrast to the majority of elderly in America. Those over 65 generally receive traditional health care paid for by Medicare. One of the most popular plans for reducing Medicare costs is to move our elderly population from traditional plans to HMOs, which are generally cheaper.

Despite the growth of HMOs, a good many GenXers are simply forgoing expensive health insurance altogether. They are just winging it, paying for doctor's visits out of their own pockets and hoping that nothing more serious happens. Sarah Snyder, an analyst at the Employee Benefit Institute in Washington, D.C., says, "Younger people in general are in a transition period. They are leaving their parents' homes, going to college, leaving college, and their incomes are not very high. They feel that they're healthy and the risk doesn't seem great."

This is especially true for GenXers who have chosen the entrepreneurial route or freelance work—representing millions of people. "I am running my business out of my studio apartment. I can't even afford paper clips, much less health insurance," entrepreneur Jeff Branson said. Caroline Brandner, a hopeful model freelancing in New

York said, "I'll just have to take my chances. Paying for health care is the last thing I can afford right now."

Despite some risk taking, Generation X's attitude toward health insurance is certainly not cavalier. Elgin Summerfelt, associate director for Career Services at Bentley College, said, "I'm hearing twenty-one- and twenty-two-year-old graduating students tell me that the benefit program on health coverage is the significant factor that they are using in making career decisions. I'm hearing students choose lower salaries in somewhat less desirable positions because of health coverage."

Insurance companies haven't stepped forward in any way that our research shows to meet the needs of young people who do not have health-care coverage. That's ironic, because Xers' statistical risk of being hospitalized or facing serious major illnesses is lower than other groups', so the cost to insure us would be minimal as a pool group for insurance companies. It is remarkable that insurance companies are not offering reasonable policies that our generation can afford.

But the news isn't all bad. Washington has been taking baby steps to improve health-care availability in America. That is largely because of the political failure of Clinton's 1994 health-care package, which promised a complete overhaul of the health-care system and offered complete health-care coverage for all Americans. One of the more notable "baby-step" bills was the Kassebaum-Kennedy bill, passed in 1996, which allows workers to maintain health insurance coverage if they change or lose their jobs and bars insurance companies from denying coverage to people who have preexisting medical conditions. The law also makes it easier for self-employed workers to afford their own insurance by increasing the portion of the cost that they can deduct from their income taxes from 30 to 80 percent. And it toughens penalties for Medicare and Medicaid fraud, reduces paperwork, and offers tax breaks for those receiving long-term care.

Voters Get the Spoils

This financial crisis precipitated by the demise of our social programs may make us America's first generation to have less than our parents. Early indications of this trend are evident. Since 1973, families whose head of household is 15 to 34 have suffered decreases in income, while families whose household heads are over 65 have enjoyed an income increase of over 25 percent. Not surprisingly, the poverty rate for children is 22 percent—twice that for those over 65. Finally, a majority of the poor are under 35 years of age, and 52 percent of all households in poverty are headed by young single mothers.

The lack of economic power in our youth is reflected by our lack of political pull in Washington. The sheer number of the elderly combined with their economic power has resulted in the growth of groups like AARP, which have been tremendously successful in bringing the concerns of the elderly to the forefront of political debate. The power of these elderly coalitions has avalanched over the concerns of poorer and younger Americans. Most important, younger Americans haven't developed the ability to organize themselves into a strong lobbying force. And they simply don't vote.

It's no surprise that issues such as welfare and education that concern the young get put on the back burner. In 1996 the federal welfare system was completely overhauled, allowing government savings of $55 billion over the next seven years. Meanwhile, Medicare reform was stalled—even though we are told the system will go bankrupt by 2001. The reason? Older people vote. Young single mothers and children don't.

If you have any doubt about the political power of the elderly just look at the hold of the elderly in Florida. For a week every year, the Silver-Haired Legislature, whose 300 members include former judges, teachers, doctors, business owners, and even former legislators, takes over the state's senate and house chambers to consider dozens of issues of concern to the state's elderly. They pick five top-priority issues and take these to churches, civic clubs, condominium boards, and mobile-home park associations to enlist support; then they go and promote them among real lawmakers. Now in its twentieth year, the Silver-Haired Legislature is a working example of grass-roots politics and demonstrates why older adults are a powerful lobby in this nation. During a recent annual session, they were courted by the Democratic governor, Lawton Chiles, at the executive mansion for two hours, by the attorney general, and by the secretary of state, among others.

About half of the states now have similar bodies, but Florida, a state where 3.5 million of 14 million residents are sixty or older, has one of the most active and politically influential senior legislatures. Its members estimate that more than one hundred of the issues they have debated have gone on to become state law. Their greatest achievement: the creation in 1988 of a State Department of Elder Affairs. With this kind of resolve and entrenchment, it is easy to see why the weaker voices of young adults are shut out. As Kellyanne Fitzpatrick of The Polling Company notes, "The real challenge: getting engaged in the political process to protect our own interests. This generation has to be appealed to as selfish stake holders to get them involved." If we do nothing, things will only get worse. You know what the demographers say: Florida is the future.

CHAPTER 5

The Education Economy

Our Standards of Wealth

*Human History becomes more and more a race between educa-
tion and catastrophe.* —H. G. Wells

What is the most important determinant of a nation's wealth? For the Mongol leader Genghis Khan it was land. He and his armies extended the Mongolian empire from the Pacific Ocean to the Black Sea, spanning most of Asia. He became the greatest conqueror the world has ever known. Other great civilizations have sprung from favorable natural conditions and remarkable resources. The earliest documented human civilization arose in Mesopotamia in the "Fertile Crescent" between the Tigris and the Euphrates rivers. For the Greek city-state of Sparta, power resided in superb military strength. Great Britain built its imperial power on industry, shipbuilding, and big-scale production.

In today's world, what is the basis of wealth? It's not land. Japan, just three fourths the size of Texas, moves the world's financial markets and, with no military to speak of, has become a powerful political player. Nor is influence derived from the conquest of other civilizations. Indeed, in 1997 the British bid good-bye to the lingering vestiges of their empire as the last British boat sailed from Hong

Kong's harbor. And countries need not depend on their own natural resources. The rise of the free market and the quick movement of goods and services has brought oil to Japan, missiles to Pakistan, Bibles to China, wheat to the Congo, mangoes to Siberia.

What, then, is today's source of power? Which nations are destined for hegemony and which for decline, and to which category does America belong?

Every great civilization has put a high premium on the education of its members. Whether the greatest value was attached to education as a soldier, a farmer, or a politician, human history has shown that acquisition of the appropriate skills are vital to the continuance of a nation-state. As the adage goes, "Knowledge is power." Or, more recently, as Education Secretary Richard W. Riley put it, "Education is the engine that drives our economy." But it is not enough to say that our populace must be "educated." That is as true and established in our society as it was in Plato's. The more important question is, *how* should we be educated? Indeed, living at the end of the second millennium of the Common Era, what does it mean to be an educated person? And how does that definition formulate America's future?

As every futurist, as every social commentator, as every pundit and politician has observed, we are living in the "Age of Technology," but however often that statement is uttered, it does not fully account for the profound ways in which technology has changed and is changing our world. Technology has made our lives faster, more complex, and more demanding. The skills required of our time are those of quick thinking and communications, creativity, adaptable reasoning. The nations of great success in the future will be those that best train their citizens to meet the challenges technology presents. What the spear was for the Spartans, the hoe was for the people of Mesopotamia, the factory was for the Englishman, the computer, the Internet, and telecommunications are for us.

Many would argue that technology has dumbed us down and made us into television-mesmerized, video game–playing Bart Simpsons who barely have the intelligence to operate a cash register. But technology should not be thought of as diminishing the importance of traditional education. Consider the other images that technology conjures up: the MIT student creating microbiotic robots to hunt down the body's infirmities, the eager investment banker who churns out dynamic merger models at the flick of a button; or the young law associate who can search the vast databases of our legal history finding precedents to prove her case.

Technology gives us immediate access to endless stores of knowledge. It allows us to sort through information, to categorize, to find that which is relevant to us. In exchange, technology requires much of us. It exponentially increases the speed at which we are required to make decisions. Our family doctor is beamed into the ER, where he deals with dozens of patients hour after hour. The banker who once tediously recorded trades by hand in a ledger plugs in to worldwide networks of buyers and sellers trading billions of dollars in seconds. Our international policy once carried by envoys is now broadcast in real time over CNN.

Technology has called us to make decisions concerning life and death, fortune or bankruptcy, war or peace with mind-reeling speed. Many say technology has made us inhuman, cold, out of touch. In fact, it has expanded our humanity and put us in greater control of our destiny. Technology has empowered the individual with so great a task that we are stunned and just trying to catch up emotionally and intellectually with our newfound responsibility. That is where the importance of education comes in.

Today education must give us the tools necessary intellectually and emotionally to deal with the world technology is creating. How do we train people today for a job that might not exist tomorrow? How do we teach concentration when we are surrounded by split-second video imagery? Is there time to learn history when today's news takes up twenty-four hours? Is there a point to teaching spelling, simple math, and grammar when computers can take care of it? Put these questions in the backdrop of growing ethnic diversity, tight budgets, and fading familial support and you get . . . well, you get our troubled school system.

Why have Americans become so dissatisfied with our school system? Is it really as bad as we think and where did we go wrong? If our kids aren't as well educated as the children of other nations, what does that mean for the future of America? Where do we go from here?

It's a Jungle in Here

Reverse the tape to the 1950s. There's Sidney Poitier fighting to teach in the ghetto of *Blackboard Jungle*. This film, along with *Up the Down Staircase*, shocked everybody beyond New York City—how could schools deteriorate this way?

Now, fast-forward through the seventies, eighties, and into the nineties. The *Blackboard Jungle* of my generation is the "representative" public high school. Many Generation Xers and those that follow us have come to accept rat-infested, dilapidated buildings, standing-room-only classes, terrified teachers, drug pushers lurking at lockers, and stabbings in the hallways. According to a report published by Public Agenda, half of parents think that public schools fail to give kids a good education and 70 percent say drugs and violence are a problem in their public schools. At my public high school in Florida, it was a rare day when there wasn't a fight in the courtyard, a drug deal during lunch, or blood splattered in our hallways. I witnessed my principal getting knifed; watched a kid on acid run screaming from my first-year Spanish class; saw policemen remove guns from people's lockers; stood on our school lawn for hours because of a bomb scare; and watched one classmate go into labor during graduation ceremonies. I have seen teachers threatened with their life if they didn't pass someone. To say that our schools have reverted to a state of nature is kind.

For the teens of the 1950s, often called the Silent Generation, the rather mild "wildness" included sock hops, a rare out-of-wedlock pregnancy (prompting marriage), Elvis, James Dean, and drive-in movies/making out. America rode a crest of good economic conditions. *Life* in 1954 called the Depression babies "the luckiest generation in American history." The birthrate in the mid-1930s had dropped to an all-time low, assuring those babies a bigger piece of a larger economic pie than any other generation in history. College, new cars, swimming pools, unshackled optimism made up what Secretary of State under President Eisenhower, John Foster Dulles, called "a paradise."

Two phenomena were about to transform it into a paradise lost. First, America was on the eve of bursting with the largest baby cohort in history (79 million born between 1946 and 1964), and explosive social upheavals were on the horizon—the New Frontier; the assassinations of John F. Kennedy, Martin Luther King, Jr., and Robert Kennedy; public school integration; the civil rights movement; the Great Society; the Vietnam War; and the women's movement. These factors became turning points in our history, writing enormous changes into our educational system that will be felt well into the new century.

Through all of this, we have isolated school problems from the rest of society. Yet schools mirror our families or lack of them, our sense of responsibility or lack of it, and our ethical standards or lack of them. Schools show our political dishonesty, the low priority given to caring for our young, and lack of belief in and trust of the future. More important, schools showcase our future potential on the world stage.

And the statistics do not bode well for our future. We are told time and time again by one study after the next that we are failing our children. A good portion of us can't read or find Canada on a map, much less write a coherent paragraph or solve an algebra problem. In the most recent International Mathematics and Science Study (a comprehensive study of science and math achievements by students in forty-one countries) U.S. students ranked twenty-eighth in math, behind Singapore, Germany, England, and Japan. We ranked seventeenth in science, behind Bulgaria, South Korea, and the Czech Republic. That makes us below average in math and just slightly above average in science. Any way you slice it, we are far from achieving President Clinton's aim of ranking first in the international education competition by the year 2000. A study by the Department of Education and the National Assessment Governing Board reported similar findings: high school–age students have made some gains in math and science but have made no improvement in reading and writing since the early 1970s, when the group first started testing.

In *The Devaluing of America*, the Secretary of Education under Reagan, William Bennett, wrote that from 1950 to 1989, "We probably experienced the worst educational decline in our history. Between 1963 and 1980, for example, combined average Scholastic Aptitude Test (SAT) scores fell 90 points, from 980 to 890." Since then, combined SAT scores have grown by only 1 percent. Paul Copperman's *A Nation at Risk* spelled out an ominous future for our generation. The government-commissioned education study claimed that for the first time in our nation's history, the educational attainments of one generation will not surpass, equal, or even approach those of their parents.

Of course there are arguments that the statistics don't tell the whole picture. The problem with comparative education analysis among nations lies in the unquantified differences in their schools and testing systems. Many countries weed out low-ability students early through stiff exams, admitting to higher education only those who attend specialized college-preparatory high schools. It may be that comparative data from those countries are collected only from such high-ability schools. A quality-control observer for the International Association for the Evaluation of Educational Achievement describes highly divergent testing conditions in South Korea: "The math teacher calls the names of the thirteen-year-olds in the room who have been selected as part of the sample. As each name is called, the student stands at attention at his or her desk until the list is complete. Then, to the supportive and encouraging applause of their colleagues, the chosen ones leave to [take the achievement test]." Only the cream of the crop are tested. That does not happen in America.

School systems testing better than America's also differed from ours in a number of other ways. Top-scoring Koreans and Hungarians, for example, attend ethnically homogeneous schools. The Taiwanese spend 1,777 hours in school per year, while we instruct our kids for only 1,003. Students in the former Soviet Union spend at least two hours more on their homework each night than American children.

In *The Manufactured Crisis: Myths, Fraud, and the Attack on America's Public Schools* (1995), Davis C. Berliner and Bruce J. Biddle account for the plunge in SAT scores in terms of participant increase. Since the test's inception in 1941, the percent of students taking it has risen, and the ethnic diversity of this larger group has dramatically increased, all due to the rise in the number of college-bound students. Today more minority students, more students from lower-income families, and more students from lower academic class ranks take the SAT.

In this case, the problem often is not the student's inherent ability. Average SAT scores decrease by 15 points for every $10,000 decrease in family income, and this leads some to believe that because poor families can provide their children with less educational support (like private schools, tutors, and special preparatory courses), their kids score worse. Furthermore, going to college now is less "selective" than it was in the past, so more students are going to college, and thus more students are taking the SAT. We should not be surprised to find lower overall average scores. The College Entrance Examination Board also adds a warning against using aggregate SAT scores to compare the educational quality of states, schools, and teachers: because the test is voluntary, the results don't include all students.

Finally, Berliner and Biddle point out that the SAT was designed in

Photo Courtesy of Anna Marie Nieves-Bryant

ANNA MARIE NIEVES-BRYANT
Executive Director, New York City's Do Something

COMMUNITY ACTIVIST, NEW YORKER

Anna Marie Nieves-Byrant became the executive director of the grass-roots organization Do Something in 1995. The organization focuses on rebuilding individual communities by making grants to over thirty young adults working in local charities and by providing forums where young people can share strategies.

According to Anna Marie the first step in building communities is to gain the trust of the people in those communities. "Motivating and inspiring people seem to be the first steps in achieving change. From what I have learned, we must first build relationships and gain the respect and trust of the people in communities and organizations and only from there can you truly effect change."

For Anna Marie, her job has a personal element to it: "My success is measured by the impact that I have had on the community around me. I came from a background where there were problems and I was able to escape them. And now I can go back and address them without being afraid. My goal is to make New York City a wonderful place to live for everybody. That probably won't happen in my lifetime, but I still have my eye on the prize."

1941 to predict students' college achievement when the college-bound were primarily white, Anglo-Saxon, and middle- or upper-middle-class. "We should not be surprised, therefore, to learn that minority and immigrant students tend to have lower scores than the group that first took the SAT fifty years ago." Because minorities have often had less educational opportunity, they do worse on standardized tests. The good news is that minority students have been steadily gaining on whites' scores since 1976. Berliner and Biddle suggest that this should be cause for joy, not lament. Myron Lieberman, the author of *Public Education: An Autopsy*, takes another view. He cites a top-down chain of causation as the reason for falling SAT scores: when more states required public universities to accept high school graduates regardless of classes taken or performance level, high school students didn't study as diligently. Twenty states have this open-enrollment policy.

Though some say that America's test results are not disastrous, Secretary of Education Richard Riley points out, "You can put the results together and say our results compared to the rest of the world are average, but . . . in this education era, average is far too low." In any event, rationalizing poor test scores does not explain away America's dissatisfaction with our education system. According to the Center for Education Reform, 93 percent of parents surveyed thought their local schools needed improvement. Forty-three percent thought a great deal of improvement was necessary. This dissatisfaction is fueling a rising political debate at both the national and the local level.

After decades of deteriorating education, we may finally be realizing that if we can't train our children to sustain American productivity, leadership, and competitiveness, then we'll slip back, as have other world powers throughout history. As the National Commission on Excellence in Education put it, "If an unfriendly foreign power had attempted to impose on America the mediocre educational performance that exists today, we might well have viewed it as an act of war. As it stands, we have, in effect, been committing an act of unthinking, unilateral, education disarmament." Our fate will be a poorer quality of life with less ability to purchase conveniences and staples, a vulnerability to the political power of other nations, and loss of American-style democracy.

On the Eve of a Revolution

However troubled our education system is, it must continue to function for the short term. Nearly 52 million children are crammed into our elementary, middle, and high schools, causing a burst of construction and a strain on our resources. A surge in enrollment will continue until 2006, says the U.S. Department of Education. We are still educating the children of some 73 million Baby Boomers. High birthrates among minorities, lower dropout rates, plus immigration to cities such as Los Angeles, Miami, and New York put a heavy strain on the system. In a recent *New York Times Magazine* interview, Rudy Crew, the chancellor of New York City's one million–student system, said of our predicament, "We don't have a lot of time, which is why I feel this incredible urgency. I think we have ten years to turn the system around before the public gets fed up and begins to replace it with something else." Crew's assessment can be applied to many of America's public school systems. So what are our alternatives?

One option that has been gaining political steam is school choice through vouchers or autonomously operated charter schools. Successful voucher programs have been launched in Detroit, Chicago, Cleveland, and Milwaukee. In Ohio the program has scored significant educational achievements. In just one year, voucher students increased their math scores by fifteen percentage points and their reading scores by five points. And parents are happy with the program. According to a Harvard University study, two thirds of parents using the voucher system are very satisfied with the program—twice as many as families sending their kids to public schools. Republicans have been strong to support these local efforts. In fact, many want to transfer our federal dollars from Washington to Hometown, U.S.A., in the form of vouchers, and dismantle the Department of Education. They argue that the Department of Education is a haven for bureaucratic waste held hostage by the National Education Association, and that the voucher system will spur competition among schools and increase the quality of teaching.

Crew cautions that none of these "choice" systems have achieved critical mass. The charter school movement, although almost a decade old, accounts for only 200 public schools out of the 85,000. Since 1992, the Edison Project, a for-profit group, has raised $100 million to set up just 25 schools and has yet to turn a profit. In Milwaukee, a voucher system pilot program handles just 1.5 percent of the overall student population. "Those who would welcome the abolition of the current system," Crew says, "have never demonstrated an ability to bring in its place a system that works on the massive scale." There are also legal issues. Because vouchers are often used to pay for tuition in religious (mostly Catholic) schools, opponents say vouchers violate the separation of church and state. Court battles are raging in nearly every district where vouchers exist and will likely make their way up to the Supreme Court.

Even so, popular support is leaning toward a system of choice, as Americans become increasingly dissatisfied with the status quo. In fact, according to polls done by Gallup and the Joint Center for Political and Economic Studies (JCPES), a Washington research group, a slight majority of Americans may actually favor school choice. In addition, the polls found an overwhelming majority of black and hispanic respondents favor vouchers 72 percent (Gallup) and 65 percent (JCPES), respectively. As Mary Jenkins, whose son participates in the Chicago voucher system, said, "This is the best alternative I've seen for my son. And he is happier. And he is doing better than he ever has." Another parent, Karl Teeter, says, "The public schools in our district aren't much more than day care—and dangerous. Vouchers give my family the same opportunity as the rich people get—instead of letting us waste away in a failed system. I think that's a pretty good deal." In 1996 even Bill Clinton said in the second televised presidential debate with Bob Dole that he would support a voucher system at the state level and supports magnet and charter schools which use nontraditional and experimental methods of teaching.

Still, most Democrats oppose these proposals. They contend that vouchers would offer only a minority of students greater opportunities, leaving the majority behind in an underfunded public school system. Under the voucher program the private schools can pick and choose their students, leaving tougher-to-educate children behind. Others say the program favors families whose children already attend private schools and tend to be the least needy. And the Democrats tend to oppose further decentralizing educational decision making, because, according to IEAP, the countries that perform best in international comparisons tend to be the ones where national standards are set and implemented, unlike the United States, which has largely decentralized standards. Secretary Riley echoes that view. "I'm a former governor, and we have complete respect for the state and local role in education. But this is the education era, and the future of the country is dependent on the ability of children to master the basics and get a good education." For him, as education becomes increasingly critical to the nation's economic future, improving student achievement must be seen as a state responsibility, a local function, *and* a federal priority.

The Political $olution$

If education is a national asset, then the government has a stake in fostering good learning. The federal government advanced a new role for itself with the Education Department's landmark 1983 report, *A*

Photo Courtesy of Andrea Batista Schlesinger

ANDREA BATISTA SCHLESINGER
Program Director, Social Security Challenge

EDUCATION ACTIVIST

During her senior year in high school she was the voice of New York City public school students. As the sole student representative to the New York Board of Education, Andrea liked to "shake up the system." She felt the Board ought to listen to the students first. They are the ones that really know what's going on.

Today she is continuing that work as the Program Director for the Social Security Challenge, a program sponsored by the Pew Charitable Trust. The Challenge is designed to get students involved in America's Social Security debate. As program director, Andrea is "teaching young people how to get their point across, how to access the media and how to gain legitimacy." Andrea says Generation X will put a different face on leadership: "Our generation will breed a new profile of what a leader is—a more colorful face, a woman's face, I hope."

Nation at Risk, which said the nation's economic future was imperiled by a declining school system. David Tyack, an education professor at Stanford University, reports that in some ways the intense global competition for educational achievements created pressure for a concerted response from Washington. There's intense pressure to think internationally, to compare ourselves to other nations, to look at a much smaller, more interdependent world. That demands a national response.

In spite of these new realities, the United States still has one of the most decentralized education systems in the world. Overwhelmingly, the money and power still reside in state governments and local school districts. Only 6 percent of the nation's education spending comes from the federal government. This is not to say that Washington has not been involved in education issues. The federal government has dabbled in education, from the G.I. Bill after World War II to the Great Society programs to development of special education and college financing for low-income students in the 1970s. In Generation X's lifetime, there has always been a national debate over education. Comparing generations, education historians say that earlier periods didn't have the sustained national attention on education that the current education-reform movement has garnered for more than a decade.

If we examine the Clinton administration's spending on education, we see that big government isn't ending, it's just beginning. In Clinton's second term, federal spending on education may reach levels not seen since Lyndon Johnson was in the White House. At $6,000 per student per year, America spends more on education than any country on earth. Five million teachers, administrators, and support staff are employed by our nation's schools. Federal, state, and local governments spend nearly $400 billion annually to run our public education system, accounting for nearly 8 percent of our gross domestic product. State and local governments each individually spend about 47 percent of the total. The federal government picks up the rest.

Despite this financial momentum, America lags behind most other industrialized countries in the results of elementary and high school education. We spend more than any other industrialized country on education and yet get some of the worst results. Since 1970, funds for public schools have increased by 80 percent, yet my generation has seen little improvement in school conditions or in measures of educational achievement.

Many say that the problem is not how much we spend but *what* we spend our money on. According to the Organization for Economic Cooperation and Development, America has by far the world's most bureaucratic educational system. Nearly 60 percent of America's educational workers don't teach. We are spending less now on student classroom instruction than at any other time in recent history. Between 1960 and 1984, a time span affecting Generation X, school spending on administration and other noninstructional functions grew by 107 percent (adjusted for inflation), whereas money spent on teachers' salaries dropped by 56 percent.

The one thing we've learned is that money isn't everything. Indeed, the one-room schoolhouse in the North Carolina mountains where my grandmother taught produced better-educated students than most of the high-tech, cyber-linked, hundred-room schools of today. Of course, we have more problems now—language barriers, less parental support, more students to educate, urban decay, drug use. However, there's still a lesson to be learned from our past. No amount of money will replace dedicated, well-intentioned and well-trained teachers and caring parents.

Yes, we need to replaster our schools, improve the plumbing, build new classrooms, and link up to the Internet. But we also need to be smart about how we teach kids. As the political analyst Kellyanne Fitzpatrick says, "What young people mean when they say education, if you get beneath the data and probe intensely and get the qualitative anecdotes, is not necessarily spending more money per pupil. Ironically, they actually want to make sure the basics are being taught in our curriculum, and want parents to be more involved."

Photo Courtesy of Rachel Bell

RACHEL BELL
Founder, co-CEO, JobDirect

RISK TAKER, WORKAHOLIC

When she dropped out of college, most of her friends told her she was crazy. But Bill Gates did it, right? And he did okay. She and her childhood friend, Sara Sutton, founded JobDirect, now the largest on-line student résumé database in the country. JobDirect matches up employers with new graduates. In just two short years they have more than 100,000 résumés and over 250 student interns spreading the word on over 175 campuses nationwide. Just some of the companies participating are IBM, Intel, Random House, and Price Waterhouse. What does Rachel do with her free time? "What free time?" she says. "We work twelve-hour days—sometimes more. Being an entrepreneur is tough business."

Taking risks. That is what Rachel Bell says makes our generation different. "Our parents would not accept the kinds of risks we do. When I dropped out of school right before my senior year to follow through on my ideas with JobDirect, my parents were really upset. But to me, success is following through on your ideas, making things happen. You've got to take the chance when it comes."

High Tech—A Magic Wand?

Some politicians, like President Clinton, have seized on high tech as the new magic wand. Clinton promised a computer in every classroom by the year 2000. More than half of America's public schools already have access to the Internet and the percentage is growing.

Emphasis on computer education, starting with elementary students, must delight business leaders of the Department of Information Technology's *Technology Task Force*, the group that helped pique Clinton's interest in electronic classrooms. Keep in mind that two thirds of that group work in the high-tech and entertainment industries. The task force's report, *Connecting K–12 Schools to the Information Superhighway,* cited numerous studies which found that computers improved student attendance and performance in many subject areas, including math, science, and language arts. Others complain that these studies are largely anecdotal and inconclusive. Edward Miller, the former editor of the *Harvard Education Letter,* wrote, "Most knowledgeable people agree that most of the research isn't valid. It's so flawed it shouldn't be called research."

The most obvious end result of computer education is to increase a student's competitive edge in a high-tech world. According to the Department of Labor by the year 2000, more than half of U.S. jobs will require computer skills and will pay roughly 10 to 15 percent more than jobs requiring no computer skills.

The argument for high tech in the classroom is valid if in fact teachers are integrating lessons with hands-on experience and becoming more creative in their teaching styles—and students are actually using the computer to learn. Unfortunately, this is not always the case. "When they do work," writes Todd Oppenheimer in "The Computer Delusion," which appeared in *The Atlantic Monthly* in July 1997, "their seductive images often distract students from the lessons at hand—which many teachers say makes it difficult to build meaningful rapport with their students." And all too often, teachers aren't equipped to fix computers, which frequently develop glitches.

Cyber-proficiency also comes at the expense of traditional disciplines. Oppenheimer reported that a 1996 poll discovered that a majority of U.S. teachers found computer education instruction more important than teaching European history, biology, chemistry, and physics or literary standards like Steinbeck, Hemingway, Plato, or Shakespeare.

Adapting to a global, computerized economy has sent educators, politicians, and business executives scrambling for ways to improve students' preparation for functioning in the computerized workforce of the future. But the gargantuan effort to make sure every child can log on to the Internet by age 12 seems somewhat misguided in view of the biggest challenges: teaching children reading, writing, and basic arithmetic.

The Graduate, Revisited

Because the new job market demands at least a bachelor's degree for a competitive salary, more and more people are entering or returning to college. They do it for the practical reason of getting a better job rather than for purely scholarly pursuits. Today, 60 percent of 18-to-19-year-olds and 45 percent of 20-to-21-year-olds are in school. A fourth of 22-to-24-year-olds are enrolled in college and a quarter of 25-to-34-year-olds have at least a bachelor's degree. Many students are older than you think—virtually half of today's undergraduates are 22 and older. About 40 percent attend school part time. Just over a third finish college in four years. That is more than any other generation in American history.

A major question is posed to each generation: Should all of our tens of millions of students be encouraged to go to college? Does everyone need a college education? Who will pay for it? Part of the answer to that question lies in the answer to another question: How does our nation benefit from a degree-carrying workforce? While a college degree may hold more financial cachet than a high school diploma, economists, educators, and experts continually dispute the connection between a healthy economy and the educational attainment of its workers. In "College Is for Suckers," Ted Rall, a writer for *Might*, a magazine geared toward life in your 20s, insists that politicians like former Labor Secretary Robert Reich and Federal Reserve Chairman Alan Greenspan are lying when they claim that downsizing, the trade deficit, and the widening gap between haves and have-nots can be blamed "on the need for more education." He says it has to do with other issues like the lowering of trade barriers and government policy.

Mike Ross, an education professor at the University of California–Los Angeles, says, "If you look at a hundred years of industrial history, there's nothing close to the one-to-one link between education and the economy that we assume today." Larry Cuban, an education professor at Stanford University, says there's "a false kind of connection about how lower productivity in the economy, particularly in the late seventies and eighties, was somehow related to lower productivity in the schools."

However, what seems to be true in the conflict of views is that, at the very least, the education-economy connection can be proved on a person-by-person basis. We can definitely point to higher education—its high costs and relatively high financial returns—as a factor in further separating the rich from the poor. The gap between the earning potential of workers with and without college degrees has increased by almost 100 percent since the early 1980s: then workers with college degrees made nearly 40 percent more than those with a high school diploma; today the figure is 73 percent. And ethnicity compounds the lean job prospects for those without a college degree. A 1996 Bureau of Labor Statistics Survey showed that African-American and Latino high school graduates were three times more likely to be unemployed than whites. In addition, education has become a factor in determining future levels of income. Those without a high school degree are six times more likely to end up below the poverty line. Those with a college degree are more likely to end up in the middle class or in the upper levels of income distribution. As *BusinessWeek* observed in 1995, "The well-paying blue collar jobs that gave U.S. workers rising living standards for most of this century are vanishing. Today, you can all but forget about joining the middle class unless you go to college."

Job security used to be one reward of a college education. Today that idea has become antiquated. It's well noted in the workplace that a college degree is essentially what the high school diploma used to be—a ticket to work, but not to especially demanding or well-paying work. We suffer, ultimately, because we have no choice but to get the credentials to compete for jobs that, in reality, do not require specific skills related to our degrees. There's a glut in the market and now too many degree-carrying members face "education inflation" in the number of credentials it takes to secure a job.

The Problem of Cost

Of course getting this ticket to a "brighter future" is not cheap. Indeed, a lot has changed since the last generation went to college. College costs have soared. Today, paying back college loans can be a decade-long event. Parents put a second mortgage on their home; students either plead for financial aid or incur what can add up to tens of thousands of dollars of debt.

The College Board found that the increases in average yearly tuition for four-year colleges in 1996–97 were greater than the rate of inflation. Private colleges now cost an average of $12,823 annually (a 200 percent increase since 1980), and four-year public colleges cost approximately $6,000 per year for state residents and $11,000 for nonresidents (a 214 percent increase since 1980). Two-year public colleges cost about $2,000 a year for state residents and $4,000 for nonresidents. However, the College Board reported that more than half of all full-time undergraduates paid an annual tuition of less than $4,000, while three quarters paid less than $8,000. To keep up with costs, many students work full- or part-time jobs in addition to school. Between 30 and 40 percent of students aged 20 to 24 work. "Many of them are going to school and working a couple of jobs and paying to go to school," says Jennifer Klein.

As colleges have begun to give a greater share of financial aid in the form of loans, many students cannot avoid going into debt. The Department of Education states that student borrowing has almost doubled since 1993, from $18 billion to $33 billion in 1996. Most of these loans are awarded under the most popular federal education aid plan, the Stafford Program, under which student loans from private institutions are guaranteed and subsidized by the government. This year, the average Stafford loan balance for students leaving four-year colleges jumped 15 percent, to $10,146, according to U.S. Group Loan Services, an organization that administers a $10 billion educational portfolio. Frederic Gilbert, the group's president, said, "Student debt has grown because of the rising cost of attending college, higher loan limits, expanded eligibility, and the growing proportion of federal student aid offered in the form of loans rather than in grants."

This financial quandary has led to a trend among private colleges who have abandoned their once need-blind admissions policy. In fact, some colleges have adopted a policy known as geo-demographics. In reaction to the dwindling number of students who can foot most of the tuition bill, schools will garner information from census reports, mailing lists, even product warranties to find students in middle-to-upper-class neighborhoods to recruit.

Some argue that college is still a bargain. The average daily cost amounts to about $90 a day for private colleges and $35 for public institutions. In exchange, students generally receive instruction, room and board, three meals a day, free counseling services, and job placement services. In the end the most enticing part of the deal is that a college education generates future rewards in the form of higher salaries.

Financing Higher Education

In 1997 President Clinton launched two programs to make higher education more affordable. The Pell grants program is a system of federal aid geared to low income students seeking higher education. Since the program began more than twenty-five years ago, it has given over $100 billion to 30 million students. Where President Reagan allowed the value of Pell grants to erode with inflation, Clinton has increased their maximum amount from $2,700 to $3,000. In general, however, the government grants "free money" less and less. In the 1970s, 75 percent of federal student aid came from Pell grants. By 1988, they made up only 30 percent of federal student aid.

Clinton also proposed a $10,000 tax deduction for college, graduate school, and technical school fees and tuition; this proposal made it into the 1997 Balanced Budget Act as a $5,000 tax credit for any but the first two years of education. The full value of the deduction won't be available until 1999. Middle-class families will be the primary users of this aid since most kids who go to college are from middle-class or upper-middle-class homes. For lower-income families, Clinton has proposed a $1,500 tax credit for the first two years of higher education. One catch: Those using the tax credit will have to maintain a B− average and must not have a prior felony conviction for drugs. The only rule for middle-class families who take the tax deduction is that their income must not exceed $100,000. The Institute for Higher Education Policy and the Boston-based Education Resources Group came to similar conclusions about the president's plan: they said the program would benefit the middle and upper classes who already attend college in large numbers but would do little to encourage the poorest Americans to attend.

Larry Smith is a community college professor at Texas College of the Mainland. Most of his students work part time and receive Pell grants or some other form of aid. Smith notes that many of his students won't benefit from the tax credit, because they don't earn high enough grades to qualify. He laments the possible effect of the B− rule on students whose families have no history of higher education. Many of his students are adults who have been out of school for years, "nontraditional students" who, he says, "don't really have the basic skills and background they need to do well in college." They develop these skills in college, but need more than a year, he maintains. Usually a C is considered a quality grade for them in the first year. Many of them go on to successfully earn a degree.

According to the Commission of National Investment in Higher Education, a panel of academic and business leaders, even with new loan availability, college costs are expected to soar to such heights that nearly 7 million students will be shut out of the system by the beginning of the next millennium. The group also found that since 1976, college costs have risen because public support per student has crept along with the rate of inflation, while real costs per student jumped roughly 40 percent owing in part to a greater demand for college education. If current enrollment, spending, and financing trends continue, higher education will fall $38 billion short of what it needs to serve the projected student population in 2015. Tuition would double by then. Imagine paying $10,000 tuition yearly for state universities and $40,000 for many of America's private colleges.

Bigger Bang for the Buck—Right at Home

At roughly $1,000 per year, community colleges may offer the most accessible ramp to the higher-education highway. They may not be the prestigious colleges, but they are among the most affordable. As a result, more than half the freshmen in higher education study at one of the 1,500 community colleges nationwide. These schools enroll 44 percent of all undergraduates, 45 percent of all black students, and 52 percent of all Hispanic students.

Community colleges illustrate the problem of cachet. Cynthia Inda is a Harvard undergraduate who transferred from a community college. Inda explains the difference in people's reaction when she informs them she's a student at Harvard. "Now people ask me what I'm doing when I graduate. Now they ask me what my major is. Now they take more of an interest in me. Yet I'm the same person, with the same work ethic, the same intelligence, and the same aspirations." The prevailing myth is that the type of college a person attends signifies his or her level of intelligence—as in Ivy League equals brilliant; community college or state school equals ignoramus. The equation simply doesn't hold, because multiple factors determine who can and who cannot attend the elite schools. Both state schools and community colleges offer quality education at an affordable price. To dismiss a person who doesn't hold a degree from the nation's top ten schools is to hold a person accountable for more than sheer brainpower.

In Columbia University's history department, teaching assistants teach a fourth of all history classes offered in any given semester. Though there is discussion time during the lecture, it is limited. What ensues is more of a question-and-answer scenario between one student and the professor. A friend of mine, now enrolled in Columbia, was excited by the prospect of taking a final oral examination for her Asian humanities class, taught by the East Asian scholar William Theodore de Barry, the editor and coauthor of many volumes on the Indian, Chinese, and Japanese traditions. "I was disappointed when I went to the classroom and found de Barry's two teaching assistants waiting for me. Of course, I was also relieved because I no longer had to endure questions from a renowned scholar, I just had to answer to a couple of grad students."

In *Everybody Else's Education*, Louis Menand, a professor of English at City University of New York, discusses the distorted view Americans have of a college education. Most imagine ivy inching up brick facades, rampant elitism, and a sprawling manicured lawn. Not true. Menand insists that less than 1 percent of all students pay more than $20,000 a year for a college degree, and the overwhelming majority—nearly 80 percent—attend public, not private universities.

Given these statistics, we need to reevaluate our assumptions and conclusions concerning college education. In many cases, students attending big-name schools and state schools are receiving a comparable education and yet we give the elite institutions a better rap. We should keep in mind that some schools are largely selective for the ability to pay.

Degrees of Separation

As knowledge becomes increasingly valuable in this information age, access to its sources depends all the more on economic standing. The imperative of having a healthy bank account to attend college is likened by some to voting laws during the Reconstruction era, which required that voters own real property in order to vote. That effectively disenfranchised blacks and women. Inflationary costs for higher education may create a similar trend. Both freedom to vote for one's representatives and ability to increase job options have a direct bearing upon one's economic and political resources. Just consider: Fewer than 60 percent of the poorest Americans attend college, while almost 90 percent of the wealthiest do. That's a 30 percent difference. Whereas the barriers in the post–Civil War era were mandated by law, today the discrimination has become more subtle, dictated instead by resources.

Possession of a college degree makes possible just about the same average annual income formerly acquired with a high school diploma. In 1970, males with a high school diploma earned a median income of about $32,000. By 1993 they made not quite $21,000. Meanwhile, those with a college degree earned about $32,700 in 1993. As long as college graduates can expect to earn what a high school education used to bring, college should be as accessible as public high school.

Still, students' ability to complete degree programs is increasingly dependent upon their ability to finance college. In 1995, the General Accounting Office said high debt increases student drop-out rates. Among 25-to-29-year-olds today, more have completed only some college as opposed to four years or more, a reversal of the trend twenty-five years ago. Our student loan system may be more efficient and user-friendly than the antiquated options previous students faced, but the astronomical sums we borrow for higher education also take more from our limited available cash. It keeps that golden ring farther from our reach.

The Future of Affirmative Action

Generation X can bring the compelling purpose to questions about affirmative action, a social experiment that has come in for critical review in recent years. Many high schools in America are dominated by one or two ethnic groupings, white, black, or Hispanic. Unlike elementary and secondary education, college has become for many a bastion of diversity, at least in its intentions. Higher education enables students of different races to study under the same institutional roof.

Louis Menand writes, "Between 1984 and 1994, the total enrollment in higher education increased by about two million, or 16 percent. Not one of the students contributing to this rise was a white American male. . . . The number of 'white men' actually declined. People classified as 'minority' and 'foreign' now account for 27.8 percent of all students in higher education." Menand praises the "democratization of higher education," citing the public universities that have accommodated the influx of minority and foreign students. There are 6.3 million more students enrolled in public institutions than thirty years ago, compared to 1 million more in private ones.

Two of our largest, most ethnically diverse states, Texas and California, employed affirmative action in their admissions decisions to foster diversity in their state university systems. Until recently, that is. The *Hopwood vs. Texas* suit, filed in 1992 by four whites who were denied admission, ended in 1996 with the ruling to ban race-based admissions. California's Proposition 209, which bars state and local governments from using race- or gender-based preferences in education, contracting, or hiring, went into effect this year. Minority applicants are already down nearly 8 percent for African-Americans and almost 6 percent for Latin Americans. In Texas, the University of Texas Law School shows the staggering difference anti-affirmative action decisions made. In 1966 sixty-five black students and seventy Hispanic-Americans were admitted; last year, only six black and eighteen Hispanic-Americans were admitted.

The consequences of California's Proposition 209 can be seen in the University of California–Berkeley's law school admissions for the 1997–98 academic year. Of the 792 accepted, only 14 were black, and not one of these enrolled. A leading opponent of affirmative action and regent at the University of California, Ward Connerly, suggests that while the numbers are not entirely good, they do have their merits: "No one talks about the good news, that fourteen black students were admissible, and if they had chosen to attend, no one would have

questioned their right to be there." Connerly argues that racial preferences make the public question a person's inherent abilities, and create a feeling of inferiority among minorities. "Black kids don't go
into an athletic competition thinking they're going to lose," he said in
the *New York Times*. "They save those feelings of inferiority for the
classroom. And do you know what reinforces the idea that they're in-
ferior? Being told they need a preference to succeed."

When the Supreme Court rejected an appeal of Proposition 209 in
November 1997, some say it marked the beginning of the dismantling
of affirmative action. Moves were and are being made on federal and
state levels to end preferences. "It is time for those who have resisted
Proposition 209 to acknowledge that equal rights under law, not special preferences, is the law of the land," Governor Pete Wilson of
California told the *Los Angeles Times* concerning the Supreme
Court's decision. Others are worried that we are retreating from the
promise of equal opportunity; they say that minorities, because they
have been afforded less opportunities as youngsters, deserve special
consideration in admissions. A great many of America's liberal arts
schools have protested the decisions in Texas, saying that it not only
hurts minorities but it also infringes on the rights of the public university to choose its student body. One thing is for sure, affirmative action is an issue young adults will grapple with into the next
century.

Seeing the Big Picture

Some argue that one of the major problems of our system is that
our leaders do not see the big picture. We see college, high school,
and elementary school as separate entities, each with its own unique
problems. However, if we are truly to solve the problems of America's
educational system, we have to look at how all the parts fit together.

One of President Clinton's solutions is to extend education by two years. GenXers, especially, should be asking, "Will two more years accomplish what the system fails to do in twelve years?" The enormous expense of cranking up and subsidizing two more years would come out of the taxpayers' pockets. In addition, taxpaying parents would be responsible for the brand-new expense of two more years' worth of room, board, meals, hospitalization, and other out-of-pocket costs. And what of the students who after twelve years of public education graduate without good reading or math skills, then spend two years in remedial courses in college? Why not catch the deficiencies in the four years of high school? Better yet, why not get the whole thing right the first time, and pour our money—wisely—into strong elementary and middle schools? Chester Finn, a former assistant secretary of education, writes in *The Weekly Standard* in June of 1997, "Assuring everyone a free ride through grades 13 and 14 is like paying for high school twice. It signals the futility of reforming grades 1 through 12." Colleges must already backpedal to bring students up to speed to cope with their curriculums.

The City University of New York (CUNY) system is trying desperately to put an end to this "backpedaling." CUNY would restrict remedial courses to first-year students and would deny entrance to students they believed would take longer than one year to complete remediation. In 1994, 15,000 of the four-year schools' 143,000 students were enrolled in remedial classes, which represented roughly 10 percent of the classes those schools offered. CUNY schools estimate a savings of $2 million if their proposal gets approved by the state. Concurrently, CUNY has been trying to implement basic course requirements for high school students to gain admittance to colleges in the system, in hopes that the need for remedial courses will decrease. Under CUNY's twenty-seven-year-old open-enrollment policy, the university accepts any New York City high school graduate, though not necessarily in the college of his or her choice. By the year 2000, though, students will be admitted only if they have completed four units of math, three of social studies, two each of a laboratory science and foreign language, and one of fine arts.

College time spent doing remedial makeup work may only take pressure off high schools to demand higher standards for graduates. "Our government's best inclination today is the movement toward investing in education, though I feel that investing in K–12 education is at least as important as offering tax breaks to college-bound students," says Beth Kobliner, a GenXer who wrote *Get a Financial Life: Personal Finance in Your Twenties and Thirties.* We are so intent upon making higher education more affordable that we push productivity in the primary and secondary schools to the back burner. "We already have more college than high-school students and the world's loftiest matriculation rates: two thirds of all high-school graduates go straight to college and more follow later," writes Finn. "The great problem is that so many of those who enter aren't prepared for college-level work because they learned so little beforehand."

There are some encouraging signs. *USA Today* reported in October 1997 that school systems throughout America are tightening up standards in response to criticism. Denver sent about 2,360 students to mandatory summer school because their test scores were too low. Florida schools are raising standards by requiring a C average for a high school diploma. In Cincinnati eighth-graders who get low grades in their classes now must repeat the school year, rather than proceed to high school unprepared.

A Global Vision with a Local Commitment

America needs a combination of local care, high national standards, and a global focus. We know that the problems facing New York City are different from those in Gerring, Nebraska. To a large extent education has to be locally directed, but all decisions cannot be made locally. We as a nation must communicate to every corner of our country what is expected of our schools. We can learn from nations like Singapore, Japan, and most of Western Europe that setting high national standards works to give people goals. At the very least, such standards should ensure that every student who graduates from high school can read, understand basic algebra, use good grammar, and recall basic historical facts. Such requirements would force us all to work to fulfill the same expectations, which would make our students and teachers reach rather than coast.

Despite an endless cornucopia of ideas, education falters when dealing with cultural factors that complicate our schools' task as in few other nations. Language, racial, and ethnic differences must be considered in any reform. Today they are viewed primarily in simple political terms. But we must get beyond school images of the 1950s, where homogeneity ruled. We are diverse, and we will be for centuries. We must solve our language differences through the educational process. This is not a political question. It is a matter of economic and social necessity. No nation has ever survived without one central language. At the same time we must take advantage of our ethnic diversity to gain a global vision. Generation X has the opportunity to turn these roadblocks into America's superhighway to trade, commerce, and the arts as the world becomes less bound by geographical divisions. GenXers must act on our best instincts of cultural cohesiveness, turning a deaf ear to the voices of divisiveness and hatred.

My generation is the result of a broken system and we haven't emerged unscathed. We have much to say and do to heal and rebuild our schools. We are and will be paying for them and dealing with the resulting products in the professions, industry, science, technology, government, and politics. Educational reform is one of our great priorities. As a reminder, we of Generation X retain the painful memories of schools that failed us in so many ways. Our financial future is at stake. We don't need to add the costs of educational waste to the Social Security and medical bills we've inherited, but we must not pass on to the next generation the waste in human potential caused by today's bankrupt education system.

We must commit personal emphasis, time, energy, and care into solving the problem. That means getting involved in the politics at every level, working with educators, and doing what we do ever so well: go on TV and talk radio, write, and commit to changing attitudes. We each have our own areas in which to commit. Here are just a few things we can do.

- Work to take the bureaucratic overhead out of education. Reduce administrative costs from 60 percent to under 10 percent. Put much of the savings into training and hiring quality teachers to reduce the teacher-to-student ratio in classrooms. Put the rest of the savings into direct material support to students.

- Return to tried-and-true basics from K through grade 12.

- Place the emphasis on high tech where it belongs—as a tool, not an end unto itself.

- Take the best from foreign education and adapt it to our needs.

- Learn from and use the best of pilot programs and successful systems. Study big-city programs such as those in New York City and Chicago. Study the myriad of pilot and proven programs in states, counties, villages, and townships throughout America.

- While speaking the language of economics, we should maintain perspective. Improving education should not be implemented solely to produce efficient or necessary workers. If business interests influence too strongly the content of education, it could limit a person's ability to choose the way he or she uses education. As University of Pennsylvania's Richard Gibboney, an education professor, explains, "Education does many things, from teaching kids how to read to teaching ethics and responsibility. If you focus too much on the economy, you squeeze out some of those other values. When businessmen get into the educational business, and they are focusing on the kind of work-ers they need, the curriculum becomes narrow, technical, de-liberal."

- Above all, do it with our known Generation X traits: analytical probing, open minds, and individuality.

CHAPTER 6

All the Ships at Sea

Maneuvering Through
Financial Tides

Let us be very clear on this matter: if we condemn people to in-equality in our society we also condemn them to inequality in our economy.   —Lyndon B. Johnson (1908–1973)

The 1940s radio news host Walter Winchell began his nationwide telecast with the words "Good evening, Mr. and Mrs. America and all the ships at sea." In the 1940s there was a "Mr. and Mrs. America," prototypes of average citizens. And the news for this couple and all their little Americans was news for everyone. What concerned the economic well-being of one American family was important for other American families. "All the ships at sea" rose and fell on the same tides.

During the last fifty years new tides have lapped at the shores of America, bringing historic demographic and social changes. The sweeping tides of globalization, rapid technological change, free-flowing labor and capital markets, and increased competition from abroad have left Americans in unknown waters.

In the 1970s and 1980s we began to doubt our economic dominance. National growth rates stagnated compared to those of previous decades. The national debt swelled. The difference between what we bought and sold forced us to mortgage off symbols of American corporate grandeur: the Japanese bought Rockefeller Center and Columbia Pictures. The globalization that allowed the purchase of American assets drove huge, persisting trade deficits with Japan, Mexico, and China. Foreign cars, electronic equipment, and textiles hammered American products. We could no longer be sure America made the best products, had the greatest quality of life, or offered its citizens the highest-paying jobs. Meanwhile our own historians and soothsayers, like the Yale historian Paul Kennedy, author of *The Rise and Fall of the Great Powers*, told us that America was going the way of the Roman and the British empires.

Perhaps the most profound change in our economy, a constant source of political battle and social turmoil, is that as a people we no longer face a common economic destiny. While globalization has brought us closer to the rest of the world's citizens, it may have driven us apart as Americans. Consider a few examples:

- NAFTA (North American Free Trade Agreement) set American tomato farmers against American wheat growers. The former feared losing market share to their lower-cost counterparts in Mexico. The latter wanted to sell to Mexico.

- Our trade relations with China pit investment bankers seeking opportunity in Chinese capital markets against producers of media and entertainment who want assurances their products won't be illegally copied and against laborers in America who fear losing their jobs to workers who work for much lower wages.

- The threat of Soviet aggression, which drove the Cold War missile race and high defense spending may have done much to open doors to engineers in Southern California, but did little to improve the standing of public school teachers who saw federal spending on education stagnate.

- The soaring stock market of the 1990s provided nearly a billion dollars in Wall Street bonuses in 1997 alone. Meanwhile, most blue-collar workers in 1997 made little more than they did in 1970.

Why the disparity? On a basic level, increased free trade brings a better allocation of resources in the sense that business goes to the least-cost producer regardless of country. National borders once insulated our workers from foreigners who may have been more skilled or cheaper. As trade liberalization and technology eat through our national borders, more of us are exposed to fierce competition from abroad. Let's face it, money follows the action of the free market.

Our growing need to create technology also drives a wedge between the destinies of our citizens. The growth technology puts a greater premium on education than ever before. Skilled workers get rewarded in the marketplace. Meanwhile, unskilled workers face falling wages because their jobs are moving abroad or disappearing altogether.

Increasingly, our fates are linked to our own individual abilities rather than to the country in which we live—or even the company for which we work. Ask any employee who was downsized in the 1990s. When AT&T announced layoffs of more than 40,000 workers in January 1996, its stock price soared. The CEO earned millions of dollars in increased stock value and was pretty well assured of a golden parachute into retirement, while middle managers got their walking papers and limited severance pay. The same was true for companies like General Motors, Chemical/Chase Manhattan, and Bell Atlantic/NYNEX. They won hefty rewards in the stock market after they eliminated tens of thousands of workers.

The lesson learned is one we young adults have heard before: be prepared to fend for yourself. "Your security is in your skills," advises Xer John Lampe, a software industry entrepreneur. The way to survive economically is to make yourself the most attractive product by acquiring a wide and deep skill set—and always remember, you are on your own. As former Secretary of Labor Robert Reich wrote in *The Work of Nations*, "No longer are Americans rising or falling together, as if in one large national boat. We are, increasingly, in different, smaller boats."

How does the next generation in those smaller, individual boats maneuver through the waters of globalization, technology, and the often unpredictable motion of people, products, and capital? Will this generation be America's first to be poorer than our parents, as the soothsayers tell us? In order for us to prove the prediction wrong, we have to understand the macroeconomic winds that have led us to this point in history and learn how we can trim our sails to make the most of their force.

Does Reality Bite?

Who can forget Winona Ryder's character in *Reality Bites* who goes bust and tries to buy groceries on her father's gas card? Or the characters in the Broadway musical *Rent*, whose theme song is "How We Gonna Pay Last Month's Rent"? Most of us are getting married and having children later in life (a full two years later than our parents did) simply because we can't afford a family. We're called boomerang children because many GenXers end up back at home living in mom's and dad's basement (30 percent of us). And our home ownership is down.

So what happened? Why has it become harder for this generation of Americans? When *Newsweek*, *Time*, or CNN tells us that we are going to have a lower quality of life, they're relying on statistics generated by economists and statisticians. They are looking at three intertwining measures of our economic well-being: (1) America's growth rate as indicated by the changes in gross domestic product (GDP), (2) the change in our personal income levels over time, and (3) our net worth individually and as a nation.

In looking at these three measures, you'd be inclined to agree with the doomsayers: it seems like Generation X has and will have a lower quality of life than our parents. However, that isn't the whole story. Let's look at the issues to understand the story behind the statistics and what weight we should give them. Then we'll see that Generation X can act, putting a positive slant on the story. You can be sure of this: we're going to take Paul Kennedy's place and write our own "rest of the story."

Crowded Out

One reason people say we'll have a lower quality of life is because the United States has been experiencing lower growth rates than previously. For the past two decades our growth rate has hovered around 2.5 percent, a significant decline from the 3.35–4.0 percent average in the post–World War II era. The growth rate is generally measured by the change in GDP, which is the sum total in dollars of all of the products that are created in America in a given year. If the economy had grown over the past twenty years at the same pace it did after World War II, the average American household today would have an income at least $12,000 higher than it does today.

There are many theories as to why our growth rate has dipped. Some argue it would be impossible ever to recreate the post–World War II boom. Then, so much of Europe and Asia had been destroyed that American manufacturers and business could grow to fill the void. Many say that America has become such a mature economy that it can't sustain the high growth rates of the past.

However, many economists believe we could do better. They say our low growth rate reflects the fact that we save very little. Our national savings rate, including public and private sectors, is less than 5 percent of the nation's output, down from 11 percent during the 1960s. Japan and Germany have 13 percent and 11 percent savings rates, respectively. Compounding the situation, our consumption rate for goods and services is first among industrialized nations. Americans consume 80 percent of our net national product. By contrast, the Japanese consume under 70 percent leaving more money for savings and investment. By not saving we rob future generations of keeping pace with other nations such as Japan or Germany. Over the last decade, both have average growth rates higher than ours. This means the people of other nations are becoming richer at a faster pace than Americans are.

Why do savings matter and why is our savings rate so low? Savings matter because these monies provide a nation with investment funds. Without savings, there would be no money for investments in new ventures such as house building, new businesses, and education. The presence of foreign investment has helped to mitigate our lack of savings somewhat, but foreign investment has its drawbacks. Foreign investment means foreign ownership. That can be dangerous for our national interest. For instance, if we are heavily reliant on Japanese investment, then the Japanese have greater bargaining power in issues of international relations. In addition, when foreign investors own our assets they have the potential to earn the profit they spin off—not Americans. That profit often leaves the country. Finally, economists warn us that foreign investment does not fully replace domestic savings. Regardless of global capital markets, the majority of funds available for domestic investment still come from domestic savings. The bottom line is that if a country doesn't save, it can't invest in its future.

America fails to save and invest on both the public and private levels. Despite the growth of tax-deferred savings plans, our personal savings rate has fallen from 8 percent of disposable income two decades ago to about 4 percent today. Some argue it's because our wages have stagnated and more disposable income is used simply to survive. Others claim our tax system encourages consumption because it taxes investment earnings like capital gains at corporate and personal levels, robbing us of money for savings. Still others say our consumption is cultural. They blame credit card companies, Madison Avenue marketers, and retailers who feed off and nurture consumption.

Private citizens aren't the only poor monetary stewards. Government spends a majority of our tax dollars on consumption-based activities. It buys products like missiles, redirects money through Social Security and welfare, buys services through Medicare, and pays administrative salaries. While these activities improve the national welfare, they aren't, in the strict sense, investments. More important, our nation has been overspending and running consistent deficits for decades. In order to finance the deficit, the government must entice people to buy its bonds with higher interest rates. According to Harvard economist Benjamin Friedman, this financing draws money away from private to public sector. It means less money for private investment. Or, as Friedman says, government debt "crowds out" investment.

Some argue that because we save less, the cost of capital (the interest rate we pay to borrow money) is much higher than it was in the 1960s. Then, the top-rated corporations could issue long-term bonds at 5 percent or real rate of 2.5 percent and still outpace the inflation rate. In the 1990s overall inflation has averaged 3.3 percent, but corporate inflation rates have averaged 8.2 percent, a real rate of almost 5 percent. That's double what it was in the 1960s.

Uncle Sam Shrank My Paycheck

And guess what? This all affects GenXers—now. Our lower growth rates are reflected in our paychecks. The Census Bureau's latest data show real median household income at just over $32,000. That's .3 percent less after adjusting for inflation than it was in 1992 and 5.2 percent below the 1989 peak. Median family income grew only slightly during the 1980s and fell every year between 1989 and 1993. Moreover, real per capita personal income grew just 2 percent per year from 1993 to 1995, with the 1995 per capita income at $22,790.

Young workers were especially hurt between 1980 and 1995. In 1980, households headed by people aged 15 to 24 had a median annual income of $23,540. By 1995, it was only $20,980. Like the younger group, people aged 25 to 34 have experienced a drop in their incomes since 1980, albeit by a smaller percentage.

Why are GenXers experiencing low wages? Yes, America isn't

growing as fast as it was when our parents were our age. But there's another reason. It's government redistribution. Through programs like Social Security and Medicare, the government has become a kind of intergenerational Robin Hood—taking money from the young and giving it to the old.

According to the Census Bureau 1973 to 1990 the change in real median incomes of families with household heads aged 15 to 24 has decreased 15.3 percent; aged 25 to 34, 9.7 percent; aged 35 to 44, 2.3 percent. For households with heads aged 45 to 54 it has increased by 7.7 percent; aged 55 to 64, by 6.1 percent; and 65 and up, by a whopping 28.4 percent.

Here's another indicator. In families with children under age 30, incomes have decreased 28.6 percent. Income in families with all members over age 30 increased 4.1 percent. Not surprisingly, the poverty rate is 22 percent for those under 17 and 11 percent for those over 65. The rate is lower for older Americans because of benefits like Social Security and Medicare. And it isn't just in income that older people have a marked advantage. The average household net worth in 1998 for those under 35 was $29,450 and for those over 65 was $133,760. For those under 25, home ownership is down 32 percent in the past eighteen years. For those over 65 it has grown 8 percent. Older people are also more likely to be medically insured. Nearly all people over 65 are insured, whereas 73 percent of those 18 to 24 and 80 percent of those 25 to 34 are insured.

But there's more. Younger people pay more in taxes despite earning less and having more responsibilities (like raising children). A working-age couple with $30,000 in wage income pays eight times more in taxes than an elderly couple does with $30,000 in retirement income. A lot of the difference comes from what young workers pay in FICA taxes, which go to Social Security and Medicare. The elderly no longer pay those taxes, but receive benefits from the programs.

Po' Folks

Most people think of Generation X as college grads who wear flannel and watch too much television in their parents' basements. But there is another population of GenXers who are not portrayed in the movies, on television, or in magazines. They are the young and the very poor.

The U.S. Census Bureau estimates that the majority of the poor are Generation X households. Adults aged 18 to 24 are much more likely to be poor than the average American. Fourteen percent of Americans live in poverty, but the rate is 18 percent among the 18-to-24 age group. While most of America experienced low unemployment rates (5 percent range) in 1996 and 1997, it was another story for those under age 30. A staggering 11 percent were unemployed, up sharply from 8 percent in early 1996. Young women especially face poverty and unemployment. Twenty-two percent of women aged 18 to 24 are poor; 36 percent of these are black and 35 percent, Hispanic. People aged 18 to 34 account for 45 percent of all poor adults, of whom 47 percent are black and 54 percent Hispanic. Poverty rates are highest among children under the age of eighteen.

On August 22, 1996, President Clinton signed a Republican-sponsored bill that ended the 60-year-old New Deal system of welfare and sent the problem of welfare back to the states. The bill dismantles the entire federal welfare system and replaces it with dozens of block grants to states, which will craft their own policies. Of course, there are controls on how the money can be used, like putting time limits on how long states have to get people off the welfare rolls and into jobs. Many see the bill as a tremendous step forward that breaks the "cycle of dependence" and encourages a smaller federal government. Others say it is doomed to fail—it doesn't solve any problems, just moves them around. Still others see it as a continuation of the war against young adults and their children.

It's too early to draw any firm conclusions. Our strong economy has generated enough jobs to make the transition from welfare to workfare a real possibility, but questions remain: What happens in a down economy? Are the people being moved off welfare getting sustainable jobs that have a future or are they stuck in a low-paying service sector economy? Should we be educating low-skilled people rather than forcing them to work? Is safe and affordable child care available for them? What about health care? Is there equity among states? These are questions this generation should care about since it is our age group that is being affected.

No Net Worth

It's a "worthless" world they're passing on to Generation X. The federal government's net worth is calculated by the Treasury Department each year by calculating assets and subtracting liabilities. In 1995 it was a negative $4.5 trillion. Wow. In the simplest terms, that means that if the government sold all its assets and paid all its liabilities, America would be $4.5 trillion in the hole. That translates into $17,000 for every man, woman, and child in America.

That $4.5 trillion doesn't begin to include future net costs of paying Social Security, Medicare, Medicaid, or veterans' benefits. Add those to the equation and you have national obligations of more than $20 trillion or $80,000 for every man, woman, and child in America.

What happened? Our politicians built up debt by overspending and mismanaging and by creating unsustainable social programs like Social Security and Medicare. Financial writer Beth Kobliner observes: "The government's worst inclination is its continued avoidance of long-term, systemic problem spots like the budget deficit, Medicare and Social Security. This lack of political courage will have serious economic repercussions."

Adding salt to these wounds, our national private net worth is being depleted because of the large trade deficits we have run for more than two decades. The trade deficit is the difference between what America buys as imports and sells as exports. To buy more than you produce, you (person or country) must go into debt or sell off assets to finance the buying. For instance, if I want a new stereo system but have no money, I either open a charge account and pay later or mortgage my house to get cash. As a nation, we finance our buying sprees of Yamaha wave runners, Chinese textiles, and French wine by going deeper into debt and selling off our American assets like real estate, stocks, and U.S. bonds.

In 1995 America had a trade deficit of $159 billion. Simultaneously America was the single largest destination of foreign direct investment, attracting a total of $41 billion. That's money foreigners invested in the United States either by moving their corporations here or by buying our real estate and other permanent resources. In other words, they own a big "piece of the rock."

Creating Two Nations

One of the toughest macroeconomic problems we face is growing income inequality. The United States has the highest level of income inequality in the industrialized world. Today we are experiencing the widest gap between rich and poor since the Census Bureau began tracking such statistics in 1947.

Economists measure income differentials by dividing the population into five income groups with an equal number of people in each group. By comparing the percentage of total income earned by each group economists keep track of wages and income disparities. The latest statistics show that the top quintile brings home 44.6 percent of our total income, compared to 4.4 percent for the bottom quintile. From 1979 to 1994 the incomes of the top 5 percent of American earners grew by 45 percent, compared to the lowest quintile of earners, whose incomes dropped by 13.5 percent in real terms. What about the squeeze on the middle class? Those in the middle of income distribution received proportionally less of the nation's income. In

1968 the middle 60 percent of households received only 53 percent of aggregate household income, but that figure had declined to 48 percent by 1994.

The strong economic growth of the mid-to-late 1990s has somewhat reversed this trend. A soaring stock market fueled by higher corporate profits and historically low unemployment caused wages at the low end of the scale to edge upward. A 1996 increase in the minimum wage (the first since 1991) raised wages of low-paid workers. However, it's uncertain whether these gains will do anything to decrease the income gap. They could be washed away with the next wave of economic stress.

What's causing this increase in inequality? Some economists think it is caused partially by the growing premium on education. Currently there is less demand for blue-collar workers than in the past. Cheaper labor abroad has lured many blue-collar jobs out of the country. Technology has eliminated the need for others. The well-paying blue-collar jobs that gave workers rising living standards during the post–World War II era are vanishing.

Today, you can forget about being in the middle class unless you go to college. Households in which both husband and wife have some post–high school education were the highest wage earners. In fact, 44 percent of such households were among the top fifth in income. In 1979 workers with college degrees earned nearly 50 percent more than those who had only finished high school. By 1993 the differential was 89 percent. Of men who turned age 21 after 1980, only 32 percent with a high school diploma or less earned the median income by age 30. Almost half of those who turned 21 before 1980 achieved that standard.

Because more women have joined the workforce, there are now more double-income households, which adds to rising income inequality. These households are more likely than ever to enter the upper middle class than single-worker (often single-parent) households. The average earnings for a two-income household increased 44 percent between 1969 and 1994 to $42,000 as a result of higher wages and women joining the labor force. The Labor Department reports that in 1993, 30 percent of all double-income households were in the top quintile, compared with 14 percent of single-income households.

While two-income households continue to outperform the rest of American families, the rise in female-headed households continues to bring down the average household income. According to the Census Bureau, 13 percent of households were headed by unmarried females in 1993, compared with 11 percent in 1980. Many of these women were jobless, forcing the family to live on welfare. Households headed by unemployed women had the steepest drop in average 1996 income, as earnings fell 11 percent, to under $10,000.

Another persistent reason for income inequality is gender and minority status. While income equality between men and women and between the races is increasing, we are certainly still far from parity. Since 1961, women have progressed from earning 59 cents for every dollar earned by a male to 74 cents. One of the biggest problems remaining for women is not workforce participation but type of work and position. Women are still far from equality in male-dominated businesses like manufacturing and are underrepresented among America's top executives.

Inroads into corporate America have been made, but many women have gotten only as far as the entrance ramp or have remained stuck in the slow lane. Of the women who hold the title of vice president in their companies, less than a third "are in roles today that traditionally lead to the senior-most positions," according to Catalyst, a nonprofit organization that promotes the business interests of women. Catalyst reported in 1996 that roughly 80 percent of Fortune 500 companies have at least one female corporate officer and 49 percent had two or more, but these women are not necessarily in top positions. Only 57 women, compared to 2,373 men, hold positions in the highest ranks of the corporation. That comes to just 2.4 percent of those positions. Twenty-five Fortune 500 companies do have women filling a quarter or more of their corporate officer positions, but overall, women account for just 10 percent of America's corporate officers. And of the

2,500 highest income earners in America's corporations, only 47, less than 2 percent, are women.

Of the twenty-five Fortune 500 companies mentioned above, all except one are in service and retail, and their female managers are primarily in entry to midlevel management. These women are in the pipeline for advancement within their companies. In manufacturing companies, where few women are in the management "pipeline," the chances of finding women among corporate officers decreases. Industries that have a low representation of women among their corporate officers include brokerage, industrial and farm equipment, aerospace, electronics and electrical equipment, motor vehicles and parts, engineering and construction, chemicals, and forest and paper products—industries we have been socially conditioned to consider "unfeminine."

Inequality of pay occurs not only between men and women. There are inequities in job opportunity and compensation among groups of women, too: African-American, Latin American, Native American, Asian American, and white, non-Hispanic women all experience discrimination differently. Women of color have the added burden of facing damaging racial and ethnic stereotypes on top of gender biases.

Black families earn just 58 cents for every dollar a white family earns. This is partially because many black families are headed by a single female, and the lower income of single female–headed households brings down the average. Black married couples where both spouses work are the closest to income equality with similar white families, earning 87 cents to the white dollar.

The proportions of black Americans in service jobs compared to those in professional positions still causes worry. In March 1996, white males were two times as likely to hold managerial and professional positions as black males, while blacks filled more than twice the number of service-industry jobs as whites. Among operators, fabricators, and laborers, 31 percent were blacks and about 18 percent were whites. Ten percent more white women held professional positions than black women. A majority of blacks find themselves in unskilled, low-paying jobs, while whites are more often in specialized administrative, professional, or managerial work, where they earn higher salaries. Even among blacks with a college degree, the shortfall in earnings is drastic: on average, blacks with bachelor's degrees or more earn $6,452 less than non-Hispanic whites. Whites are 12 percent more likely to obtain a bachelor's degree than blacks.

Despite these numbers, we do seem to be making progress. The good news is that in 1996, for the first time since the Census Bureau began recording statistics in 1959, the percentage of African-Americans living in poverty is below 30 percent and the median income for black families has risen by 3.6 percent—more than that for white families (2.2 percent). In addition, the proportion of young black adults who have completed high school has now caught up with that of young white adults. By the year 2005, the Labor Department estimates, half of all the labor force entrants will be women. More than one third of the workforce will be Hispanics, African-Americans, and Asian Americans. *BusinessWeek* reported in a 1997 cover story entitled "White, Male, and Worried" that we have seen a significant decline in the past ten years in the percentage of white male managers and professionals in the workforce.

Some people argue that a better measure of equality than annual income is income mobility, the ability to move up the income ladder. Economists at the University of California–Santa Cruz claim that within five years almost half of the population aged 25 to 55 will have moved up or down by at least one income group. Mobility seems highest among middle-income Americans, but the poor frequently jump groups, too. The Census Bureau says that less than half the people who were below the poverty line in the 1980s remained there for more than a year. Nearly all of the poor who were employed full time managed to rise above the poverty level. However, there's evidence that income mobility may be slowing down. A University of Michigan study found that before 1980, more than a third of low-income families moved up to the middle class over a five-year period. After 1980, only a fourth did.

So should we be concerned? After all, America promises equal opportunity, not equal outcome. Still, there are fears that our high level of inequality is dangerous for our nation. Historians tell us that a strong middle class is needed to support a democracy. If the gap between our haves and have-nots continues to widen, our economic system, which is anchored by our middle class, may well collapse, putting our democracy in peril. Furthermore, there is some evidence that high levels of inequality can actually retard economic growth rates. That's because businesses need skilled laborers. When a large portion of the society is poorly educated and lacks skills the economy is limited. We see elements of that problem in our American economy in the late 1990s. Our fastest-growing industry branch, high tech, is frantically looking for skilled workers that just don't seem to exist. That hampers economic growth.

We could regress; we could easily develop into a country of rich and poor, like so many Third World countries. Ridiculous, you say? Tell that to the average American who works extra hours—sometimes two jobs—just to make the rent or mortgage or car payments. No matter how prosperous our country appears, look much closer and you will see a nation maxed out on credit cards and terrified of the financial demands of tomorrow.

How can we change the trend? Should we? America has never embraced the ideals of equal outcome the way European democracies have. The large role redistributive social programs play in Switzerland or Scandinavia will probably never be replicated on our soil. But perhaps we can do more to ensure greater equality of opportunity. Two ways to do this, according to Isabel V. Sawhill and Daniel P. McMurrer of the Urban Institute, are to (1) "creat[e] a level playing field, on which all individuals have equal opportunity to seek the rewards of the market economy, regardless of race, sex, nationality, or religion," and (2) "[equip] individuals with the necessary tools for success on that playing field by broadening access to education." If education is really the best way out of poverty then we have to make the opportunity for education affordable for everyone. With the limited success of our public schools and skyrocketing prices of college, it is getting harder and harder for poorer Americans to pull themselves up.

Building a New Economy

What should GenXers do to make it in this new economy? What should we do to make this economy stable and enduring for our children? From the long-term economic perspective, we must work on three essentials: education, savings, and rebuilding our communities.

It all starts and ends with education. It's the most important determinant of how a person fares economically during a lifetime. Put simply, just possessing a college degree (quite apart from the intrinsic value of the knowledge you acquired) will greatly increase your marketability. Of course, there are exceptions, like the genius Bill Gates who dropped out of Harvard University, then made a fortune estimated at nearly $40 billion. But the vast majority must face reality. You're dead in the water without an education. That's why President Clinton said he wanted to make the thirteenth and fourteenth years of education as common as the first twelve. Here, Clinton is "politically" correct: he knows that an American high school diploma means little to an employer. In order to be an attractive candidate for a job you have to have something more—a college education, an advanced degree, or specialized technical training.

Second is a four-letter word, S-A-V-E, and it's something America doesn't do. According to Federal Reserve Board researchers, only about half of Baby Boomers have retirement accounts, including 401(k)s, individual retirement accounts (IRAs), and Keogh plans. The median value was $15,600 in 1995. Even while the stock market boomed between 1992 and 1995, the Fed research showed that the value of assets in retirement accounts grew significantly for only one group, families with incomes of $100,000 or more. The median value of their accounts climbed from $55,600 to $85,000, while that of all other income groups remained flat.

Photo Courtesy of Kurt Von Emster

KURT VON EMSTER
Portfolio manager, Franklin Templeton Group

STOCKS AND BONDS, RHYTHM AND BLUES

He is one of the youngest and one of the most experienced mutual fund managers in the country. At just twenty-nine, Kurt Von Emster oversees $180 million of assets for the Franklin Global Health Care Fund. Under his management the fund has risen at an annual rate of 24 percent over the last three years. "I am motivated by my successes and my failures. And this is very different from the stereotype that defines my generation."

Kurt does not see his life as "all work." He plays the bass guitar as well as he plays the stock market—in a rhythm and blues band called The Flyers. And he has plans for the future. "Ten years from now I hope to be a doting father. Work will be a secondary priority."

You might think we young adults are doing better than our parents, given our exceptional incentive to save for retirement. Don't forget that more of us believe in UFOs than in Social Security. Regardless of the future role of programs like Social Security and Medicare, we know that they won't be so generous for us as they were for our grandparents or parents. We know from the political climate that the social safety nets won't exist in the way that they have. And Generation X, with our highly entrepreneurial, libertarian mentality, will not likely restore the Great Society.

There are some encouraging signs. According to pollsters at Yankelovich Partners, Inc. more of us (69 percent) think about retirement than our parents did at our age (51 percent). And according to a 1997 survey conducted by Employee Benefit Research Institute almost 20 percent have more than $50,000 stashed away for retirement. Only 18 percent of the Boomers have this much, and they are older. However, the prognosis is not entirely rosy. The majority of GenXers couldn't get by for more than three months if they lost their jobs, according to the Yankelovich Partners poll. In a nationwide survey, 54 percent of people in their twenties and thirties admit that if they lost their jobs tomorrow, their savings would last three months or less. One quarter of young Americans (26 percent) say they couldn't get by for longer than a month.

Forty-three percent of people in their twenties and thirties say the overall economic outlook for their generation is getting worse, compared to only 19 percent who think it's getting better. Fifty-five percent of those polled don't believe Social Security will be there when they retire—yet 55 percent haven't contributed to an IRA or 401(k) in the past year; 35 percent have no idea what a 401(k) plan is; 57 percent in their twenties and thirties save less than 5 percent of their incomes regularly—possibly nothing at all; 68 percent say they often feel as though their paychecks disappear from month to month. Despite the national obsession with weight loss, 67 percent of young Americans would rather get rid of $1,000 in debt than lose ten pounds.

This is the bad news. Despite our large college and credit card debts, we seem to keep buying. Economists say that we are purchasing on the basis of an idea of our future incomes. If that's true, we had better take decisive action to make sure our optimistic ideas of our future come to fruition. We know from history that all economic dreams don't materialize. So our best route to success is to take decisive action through saving and investing. If we are to have a better quality of life than our parents and grandparents, our only option is to save. And we must save more than they did. In the absence of government planning, it's up to our generation to save and invest for our own futures, to think long term. We can bypass short-term pleasures like a second VCR, the Dolby surround sound system, the new pair of jeans, in favor of saving for a rainy day, paying back college loans, and putting money away for our children's expensive education.

Third, we have to build strong communities and families. It takes a village, right? In the 15-to-34 age group, married households have the highest median income while households headed by females have the lowest. This is not a "family values" advertisement. For many single parents, it does not make sense to marry. Perhaps their potential spouses are abusive or irresponsible or just incompatible. But the statistics do seem to say that two people working in tandem makes for a richer household. Whether you are living with your parents, a spouse, or a friend, "togetherness" seems to make economic sense.

As young adults we have to make sure we understand all the economic forces at work on us individually and as a nation—to understand the mechanisms of interest rates, trade deficits, inflation, inequality. These are some of the most important issues facing us. They are not what MTV wants to tackle, but they are crucial to our well-being in the real world.

CHAPTER 7

Keeping Our Hats On

Reshaping the Workforce

Boomers had a paradigm of models. They started breaking down structures; they paved the way for Generation Xers, who are building from the ground up. Xers will have to make it up as they go along.
    —Leslie Evan, vice president of the human resources consulting
                                  firm Goodrich & Sherwood Associates

A strange relationship exists between Generation X and corporate America. We don't trust them and the corporations don't know what to make of us. One thing is clear from the outset, though. With our tremendous high-tech abilities and a reinvigorated entrepreneurial outlook, we will play a major role in corporate America before all is said and done. What kind of workforce will we be? How will we change corporate America? What kind of corporations will we create? That depends largely on what we as children, teenagers, and now young adults have seen of corporate life—our parents' experiences and our own early ones.

When our parents and grandparents entered the job market they felt they could hang their hat at one company and stay until they got the gold watch and a reasonable pension. The late eighties and nineties taught us different. The downsizing of giant corporations like General Motors, IBM, and AT&T obliterated our generation's confidence in the job security a corporation life once promised.

GenXers were hit hard by the 1990–91 recession. While 400,000 Americans over age thirty lost their jobs, one million under age thirty lost theirs. In previous recessions, recent college graduates got a majority of entry-level jobs. This time, 55 percent of job openings were filled by older workers. The job-loss rate hit a peak of 3.4 million in 1992 and has remained nearly that high ever since, despite a growing economy and booming stock market. The Bureau of Labor Statistics shows that during most of the 1980s one in twenty-five workers lost a job in any two-year period. In the 1990s it has risen to one in twenty. A *New York Times* poll reports nearly 75 percent of all households experienced a close encounter with layoffs since 1980 and a third of households contained someone who lost their job. Job dislocation spread to include every sector of the economy. Blue-collar workers still make up the majority of layoffs, but in the 1990s layoffs have increasingly hit white-collar workers, professionals, and administrators.

As a result, the overwhelming majority of graduates see their career at graduation not as a straight line of advancement in one company but as a zigzag path from company to company, job to job, skill to skill. GenXers were at least teenagers when most of the downsizing happened. We saw the layoffs of parents, friends, and relatives. We understand that there's no such thing as lifetime employment. Career decisions are our responsibility. Laura Hanigan, in the career services department of Columbia University, said, "You ask [students] how many know someone who is laid off and every hand in the room goes up. They believe it is part of life, like getting a cold, so they know job tenure is a short-term thing, not a long-term commitment. It's an economic transaction that lasts only so long as it works for both sides."

The statistics reflect the apprehension. Nearly half (46 percent) of workers say they are frequently concerned about losing their job in 1996, up from 31 percent in 1992, according to the International Survey Research Corporation. And few stay at their job very long. According to a 1995 study by Ohio State University, three out of five workers aged 27 to 30 stay at their job more than four years. So despite a robust economy and a good job market for the latter part of the 1990s, GenXers are hedging their bets. Recent graduate John

Warneke, 23, who went to work for Icon Office Solutions at a starting salary of $30,000, was able to choose from among four offers. But he recalls his father being laid off as a plant manager when Warneke was a high school junior. Warneke relates, "Fear drives you. I am motivated by the idea that nothing is secure, that you had better produce or you could be gone. In fact, when I was talking with companies, I was always keeping in mind where they might be five or ten years down the line. I think you have got to keep that fear because it's when you get in a comfort zone that you lose your competitive advantage."

Marilyn Moats Kennedy, who runs CareerStrategies, an employee-employer consulting group, puts it this way: "If Boomers were spoiled, Generation X was left to rot. . . . Generation X is influencing the workplace more than the three generations before it. How? GenXers state their boundaries and have no company loyalty. . . . They saw how attached Dad was to his big company. One day, he was eliminated, thrown away like a used Kleenex. They saw his pain." Generation X doesn't want the boardroom. They want a laptop and freedom. "For people over fifty, there was nothing wrong with having an 'executive dining room.' Those under thirty wouldn't be caught dead there. They invest minimal time until they can pass out their own business cards. Their notion of a leader is Bill Gates, not John F. Kennedy."

McTruth About McJobs

Almost as many Americans—one in seven—have worked for McDonald's at some point in their lives as GenXers currently working in "professional" positions. It is no wonder they call us a generation of McJobbers.

Since President Clinton took office in 1993 the economy has created more than 10 million new jobs, at a rate of 245,000 per month. However, two thirds have been service and retail positions that tend to be lower-paying jobs. And guess who is filling those positions?

Over half of all young adults work in the service sector and retail sales, making up the majority of workers in this sector. The 16-to-19 age group alone accounts for 10 percent of all sales workers and 13 percent of service employees. People in their early twenties (20 to 24) are also concentrated in sales and service. Only a fifth of young adults are in manufacturing.

To escape this service sector economy, more and more young people are attending college and technical and professional schools. More than a quarter of us over twenty-four have at least a B.A.— more than any other generation in American history. Is that good news? Not entirely. Many of us with the degrees are finding that it doesn't get us any further than a high school diploma did our parents. As we have seen, many jobs that previously required a high school diploma now require a college degree. That's underemployment— college graduates holding low-paying, low-responsibility positions. Through most of the nineties, the percentage of college graduates in noncollege jobs has been remarkably high: at least one in five employed college grad was in a noncollege job, according to a 1994 Bureau of Labor Statistics survey, and the bureau predicts that this phenomenon is likely to continue into the year 2005.

Examples of what the Bureau of Labor Statistics defines as a college job are manager of a chain video store, legal secretary, and police officer. In many occupations, "college job" is when the boss prefers to hire someone with a college degree and someone with a B.A. takes the job. A MacArthur Foundation study found that 9.2 percent of the working poor in Chicago have B.A.'s. While holding noncollege jobs is temporary for some, the Bureau of Labor Statistics found that the percentage of B.A.'s in noncollege jobs is high in all age groups.

Members of the class of 1994 at the University of Illinois–Urbana/Champaign were asked a year after graduating if their college training is being put to good use. Almost 40 percent consider themselves underemployed, nearly double the percentage of recent years. Unable to find appropriate full-time employment, many young adults are turning to part-time work. According to Manpower, one of the world's largest temporary employment services, among young adults, part-time work is common (23 percent aged 16 to 34 are part-timers), and this age group makes up half of the part-time workforce. Nearly half (48 percent) of temporary workers are under age 34. People aged 16 to 24 make up nearly a fifth of the temporary workforce. Nearly three in ten temporary workers are aged 16 to 24. New Yorker Kevin Smith registered with a temp agency five months after graduating from college. "It pays the bills. It will have to do until I can find something I'm really interested in, and it gives me time to look for other jobs."

This is not a problem limited to America. According to the March 1997 monthly U.S. Labor Department report, nearly all the OECD (Organization for Economic Cooperation and Development) nations now suffer from reduced job prospects for young adults. The department said, "Lack of occupational prospects, together with low pay, contributed to the uncertain labor force status of many young adults. Young workers experienced declines in earning relative to older workers in most OECD countries. Moreover, the expansion of 'youth-incentive' industries—hotels, restaurants, retail trade—has perhaps not always offered desirable occupational prospects." What is most revealing about the OECD report is that it attributes a good part of the problem to the rise in "noncomponents" of labor cost, the "extras" employers have to pay when they hire a worker, like FICA taxes (Social Security and Medicare), health insurance, and pensions. Since such costs are often higher in other countries (40 percent of GDP) than in America (30 percent of GDP), most other nations seem to be in worse shape than America. Several European countries have unemployment rates for young adults well above 15 percent.

S. Antonio Ruiz-Quintanilla, a senior associate at the New York State School of Industrial and Labor Relations, and Rita Claes, a professor at the University of Ghent, in Belgium, tell us, "Although research has indicated that, over the short term, unemployment among the young has only moderate financial and social consequences, for those experiencing [unemployment], harmful consequences of other kinds may ensue over the long term. These young adults are delayed in their attempts to become independent, to develop new work-related competencies, and to understand the domain of working in general. The delay of their full integration into the labor market adversely affects their occupational aspirations and expectations and, more broadly, their lives as citizens." Economists have concluded that early unemployment may have a sizable negative effect on later wage rates because the young people fail to accumulate work experience.

Not surprisingly, young adults report the lowest rates of job satisfaction, according to the National Opinion Research Center at the University of Chicago. People aged 18 to 24 are most likely to say they are dissatisfied with their work. Behind this dissatisfaction is the fact that many young adults are in low-paying, entry-level jobs. Similar proportions of people under age 35 say they aren't satisfied with their financial situation. Part of the dissatisfaction is also due to the declining economic position of young adults whose incomes have been eroding. Median income of recent college graduates fell during the first half of the 1990s, according to the Economic Policy Institute, a Washington research group.

The news is not all bad. Evidence shows that things get better with age. Most people aged 24 to 34 are no longer at the bottom of the career ladder. More than half perform managerial and professional work, technical sales or administrative support. They account for nearly a third of technicians and technical support and construction workers. The mid-1990s have also shown improvement for recent grads. According to the Bureau of Labor Statistics overall, the job market for the 1.2 million 1997 graduates is the strongest since the 1960s. That's partly because aggressive corporate downsizing may have caused too many layoffs among their parents' generation. Many graduates even had the luxury of choosing among several job offers months before graduation.

Photo Courtesy of Celeste Chung

CELESTE CHUNG
Director of business development, Crunch!

BODY BUILDER, EXECUTIVE

Celeste Chung is toning up her business skills as well as her body as the director of business development at the fitness company Crunch! The position was created for her when Crunch!'s management realized it needed new talent to help the company expand its line of fitness clubs. Chung's job is to capture this generation's view on fitness: "Fitness is not only the traditional going to the gym or running, but also includes mountain biking, skiing, golfing, roller-blading in Central Park, or dancing at a club until seven a.m. This generation, strapped for time, has to combine fun and fitness."

Not unlike many in her generation, Chung has held three jobs in the four years since she graduated from college—at Walt Disney, at Morgan Stanley, and now at Crunch! "Our elders tend to think that we are, perhaps, a bit irresponsible or indecisive because they have seen us angst-ridden, experimental with jobs, fashion, music. It is at times difficult for them to see that switching jobs and taking a step back could be a long-term career decision or that extra outfit you bought is offset by your mutual fund investments and direct deposits in your 401(k) plan."

Where the Opportunity Is

The first Generation Xers came out of college just before the 1987 stock market crash. The layoffs were just beginning. Companies weren't hiring. Students who graduated in the recovery period experienced quite a different scenario. The classes of 1995, 1996, and 1997 graduated to the most auspicious job market in recent memory, a product of the roaring economy, which drove the unemployment rate below 5 percent.

The surge also reflected the years of layoffs, for which many companies are now frantically trying to compensate. Many experts believe the companies laid off too many employees in the early nineties. "Corporations downsized too much," says Maury Hanigan, chief executive of the Hanigan Consulting Corporation, which advises Fortune 500 companies on how to recruit college students. Now that business has boomed beyond expectations, college students are being recruited for sales, managerial, technical, and support positions.

From 1991 to the end of 1996, 11 million new U.S. jobs were created. America was again the world's hottest job machine. Undergraduate hiring at Fortune 500 companies, on the rise since 1992, was up 20 percent in 1997. Employers needing well-educated workers are continuing an upturn that began in 1996 to increase business and operations expansion. They have experienced growth in demand for their products and services. They want to remain competitive and need support and technological advances. Competition has driven salaries upward, especially for grads holding computer-related degrees. In addition, businesses and organizations that had not recruited in years—in public relations, communications, advertising, city government, and the not-for-profit sector—began hiring in the late nineties.

High tech. The National Association of Colleges and Employers says the best opportunities for the foreseeable future are in high-technology industries—especially in hardware and software development and computer consulting. Recent college grads could expect starting salaries averaging $37,300 in 1997. Computer engineering grads with a master's degree could expect $47,080. Computer technology companies hired almost 66 percent more graduates in 1997 than they did in 1996, when computer software development employers forecast a 36 percent increase.

The business of high technology is transforming our national landscape, from Silicon Valley to Boston's Route 128 corridor to the Rocky Mountain states. "Go west, young man" is a saying from a previous century. But it well applies to the young men and women of Generation X. Despite some strongholds like Boston, the national economy for jobs is tilting toward the West. Nevada boasts the highest projected rate of job growth over the next ten years, 17 percent, followed closely by Utah and Arizona. Every state west of Kansas except Wyoming and Montana is expected to expand its job base by 10 percent or more. The key draws are high quality of life, low cost of living, and lower taxes. In 1997 the strongest reported region for hiring, according to Manpower, the nation's largest temporary staffing company, was the Midwest, where 33 percent of employers plan to expand their staffs. That compares with 31 percent in the West, 28 percent in the South, and 27 percent in the Northeast.

Banking. Wall Street is certainly prospering from higher corporate profits and an increased willingness of the average American to invest in the stock market. Bankers hired nearly 30 percent more graduates in 1997 than in 1995. Wall Street salaries shot from $16 billion a year between 1989 and 1991 to more than $21 billion every year since 1992. In 1996, the New York securities industry's 150,000 workers pulled down bonuses of more than $8.1 billion—30 percent more than the previous high of $6.2 billion in 1995. On average that's a $54,000-per-person bonus, ranging from $10 million or more for the biggest winners to a few thousand for the clerks.

Still, young adults say competition for those big bucks is fiercer than ever. A series of shakeouts, mergers, and downsizing followed the 1987 crash. New York securities industry employment shrank from 262,000 jobs in the third quarter of 1987 to 209,000 jobs in the first quarter of 1991. Today, companies know they have to produce returns for their stockholders, and working until the wee hours is as likely as partying. "It is hard to conspicuously consume if you don't have the time to consume," says Harry DeMontt, a vice president at Credit Suisse First Boston. Also, leaner staffs mean more work for everyone.

Getting Real

How are young adults perceived by those who hire them? Certainly, we have been slower to pick careers in the job market than other generations—partly a function of a tight job market. Certainly, our experience has given us different perceptions about corporate America, and we have different desires than previous generations. The one thing we do share is a desire to do something meaningful with our lives. Yes, we do have a work ethic, albeit one different than earlier ones. What are some of the notions that the older generations have about us? Are they right?

"Slackers, lazy, good-for-nothings, and . . ."   The political commentator and journalist Richard Novack remarked if it wasn't evident that this generation was stupid, just watch MTV's *The Real World*. The historian Neil Howe deemed twenty-somethings "reckless bicycle messengers, hustlers, and McJobbers in the low wage/low benefit service economy." *Psychology Today* describes us as "not knowing how to do an honest day's work." Judi Newman of ABI/ Inform, an online database for business and management information and abstracts, described us as having "little self-esteem," and being "hedonistic and risk-seeking."

Hold on a minute. Despite what some say about us, most reports and numbers show that twenty-somethings work hard. We are attending college in record numbers, starting our own businesses, and working endless hours in corporate America. "I'm told again and again that my friends and I are slackers," says Steven Rosenbaum of the Broadcast News Network. "I don't really understand this characterization, since most of the energy that is fueling the technological changes in society today are being developed by twenty-two-year-old hackers on computers in basements across the country." Three fourths of young adults are in the labor force and account for 42 percent of all workers. Also, those 24 to 35 work 3.6 percent longer each week than the national average. "When people think of Generation X, they think of people with ripped-up clothes [who] do nothing with their time," says Fran Grainger, 25, who has been planning seminars for Leadership South Carolina at the University of South Carolina in Columbia for a year. "There are also forty-five-year-olds who sit around in ripped-up clothes and do nothing. I have goals and I work on them."

Not focused?   A common myth about today's teenagers and young adults is that they're less focused than earlier generations and aren't as committed to their jobs. Contrary to current stereotypes, teenagers and young adults are focused on their futures and the majority are setting career goals before high school graduation, according to a Massachusetts Mutual Life Insurance Company publication, *Annual Survey of American Values.* The survey reveals that young people are extremely focused, motivated, and ambitious, says Thomas Wheeler, Massachusetts Mutual's chairman and CEO. "Our study found that American youth are concerned about fierce competition for employment and are willing to make sacrifices to secure a good position."

According to the survey, on average, young Americans believe they must select a career path by the age of seventeen to succeed. Three fourths already work at least ten hours a week while attending college and 83 percent want to advance into management. Two thirds believe the best way to find job satisfaction and increase their income is to stay at one company. To a surprising degree these findings suggest that young adults act on their beliefs. If companies learn to tap the potential of young people early, they could greatly reduce turnover among young employees. The study suggests that companies could offer more internships, work-study programs, and entry-level positions that directly link to a young person's career goals.

Loyalty is a two-way street. Here's some irony. Despite the fact that most GenXers prefer to stay at one firm, the majority don't plan to stay with their current employer for more than five years according to the Mass Mutual Survey. Those who plan to stay for five years or longer cite factors such as job security directly connected to their career goals and their belief that they'll be fairly compensated. Elizabeth Ouzts, a 28-year-old assistant meeting planner for Policy Management Systems Corporation in Columbia, South Carolina, says, "We just have a different outlook. I don't want to stay at a job that I don't like. Sure, I've had three jobs in the past five years, but I left for better jobs." College graduates are more likely than those without degrees to say they'll stay with their current employer longer. But having a degree also increases the odds that their job will directly connect to their career goals.

The Massachusetts Mutual Survey revealed that most young adults aged 24 to 35 are willing to work long hours; in fact, more than 75 percent who are married and have children are willing to work long hours. However, their willingness has limits. Eighty-eight percent expect to be paid time and a half for more than eight hours a day, and 75 percent expect to be home for dinner. Fifty-six percent know that job security is no longer a characteristic of the American workplace—yet they believe the best way to find job satisfaction and increase income is to stay at one company.

In fact, more than 70 percent of those surveyed would be willing to take lower-paying jobs if it brought more security. That's possibly due to the experiences of their parents, suggests Dr. Rebecca Shanok, a child development center program director in New York City and a consultant to the Massachusetts Mutual American Families Value Program. One third of those surveyed have at least one parent who is worried about losing his or her job. As Bruce Tulgan, author of *Man-*

aging Generation X, says, "Xers are not disloyal and uncommitted as so many people claim, but rather we are cautious investors in a world which has taught us to expect little from institutional relationships."

Who's not responsible? The same survey, when it posed the question "What was the most important thing your parents taught you?" found that 54 percent of the young workforce agreed with the statement that their parents taught them the importance of committing themselves to their work. These young workers said that the most important lesson about work habits that their parents taught them was to be punctual, to be reliable, and to take responsibility. Another 15 percent said that the most important work-related lesson they learned from their parents involved ethical behavior such as being honest, demonstrating respect for others, and doing the right thing.

Young people largely want jobs where they can take responsibility for mistakes or problems that occur. According to the Mass Mutual Survey, their willingness to accept increasing levels of job responsibility is evident from their strong agreement (83 percent) with the statement "I want a job where eventually I get to be the boss." Commitment, responsibility, job satisfaction, and ethical conduct are the four key lessons that young people say their parents have taught them about work.

Tulgan points out, "Dues paying is an obsolete concept for Xers who face an employment market that offers no hope of long-term job security with any one employer. Xers' impatience for short-term rewards is a quest for a new kind of work related to security based on self building." Let's not misunderstand: the American values of integrity, honesty, and diligence have been passed on, but translating them into a transient workplace has left us with a scarred reputation as workers. GenX's challenge is to turn our self-driven careers into effective tools for the economy.

Conflicting commitments. GenXers aren't sold on the idea of being company slaves. Yes, we'll work hard. We'll commit loyalty and full effort to the job. But we aren't serfs. We have family and other personal commitments. According to a survey by the University of Dallas, most young adults say they measure their success by personal happiness and not financial gain. Heather Lamm, a GenXer heavily involved in mainstream politics, says that success for her generation means "having close family relationships with husband, children, parents, siblings, and a few very good friends." *Swing* magazine says GenXers "define success as a well-honed balance of work and home." Karen Ritchie sees advantages in the Xer tendency for later marriages: "By delaying marriage until education is complete and careers have been established, they are increasing the economic stability of the future marriage." That, she said, will lead to greater financial security. All of which has to be good bottom-line news for corporations that don't have their heads in the mud.

In addition to security, our generation seeks flexibility from employers. Many of us growing up in the sixties and seventies either were children of divorce or lived in two-career households; as a result, "quality time" between parents and children was sacrificed. According to the Families and Work Institute, 60 percent of men and women under age twenty-five with children would make "a lot" of sacrifices in money and career advancement in order to spend more time with their families, versus 34 percent of workers overall. The survey found that 56 percent of people aged 15 to 31 said American workers didn't have enough time with their families. In a 1993 Roper Poll, 46 percent of our generation identified their jobs as an "expression of themselves," 10 percent less than Baby Boomers. Our generation hasn't lost the drive to work. We have just reevaluated work in light of other obligations like family, friends, community, and quality of life.

Young workers today have been deeply affected by their parents' experience. Seventy-nine percent of Americans said that parents unable to spend time with their children was a major cause of the perceived decline in American values. In the Mass Mutual Life Survey, 67 percent said loss of job security contributed to the decline in values, and 64 percent said difficult economic conditions for families has been a factor in this decline. According to the survey, 61 percent of young women and 52 percent of young men say workers don't get enough time with their families. Xer Jonathan Karl, a CNN correspondent, lists his greatest pleasure as family. "Free time is a rare and precious commodity. I have learned that it's important to break away from work. Simply, I spend free time with family and friends. And my wife and I became parents last October of a baby daughter. She commands my spare time."

These young adults know full well from the experience in their families of the stressful challenges in balancing family and work, says Dr. Shanok. For children and families this could be very good news. Perhaps our generation will eventually succeed in extracting more flexibility from the workplace. Since many of us have yet to have children, our stamp on history may well be in the area of strong family values and ties.

Half of this generation comes from divorced families. Since 1970, when Xers were growing up, the divorce rate has tripled. Wary of family breakup, our generation is marrying later, putting more time into family, and sacrificing less for the job. As Kellyanne Fitzpatrick says, "The biggest challenge is providing our own children with what we didn't have—fathers, time, attention, security. Another big challenge is to find meaning in and prioritization of religion, work, family, leisure, marriage." Employers will have to deal with the desire of Xers, men and women, to spend more time at home and on vacation with family. A majority of GenXers of age 25 say they are willing to trade more free time for lower pay. Most cite time with family and friends as their most important activity.

Corporate America is starting to wake up to this emphasis on family. At Coopers & Lybrand, one of America's top accounting/consulting firms, a "Work and Life Balance" program has been in effect since 1990. "About 900 of the firm's 17,000 U.S. employees (including one male and five female partners) now work part time, telecommute or have other flexible schedules." In September 1997 the company was included in *Working Mother* magazine's ranking of the top 100 family-friendly companies for the third straight year. That there is a list of 100 such companies speaks well for the growing corporate awareness of family concerns and how they affect the bottom line.

These GenX trends are all the more amazing in light of technology's role in opening new ways to spend leisure time. Twenty-something Christina Ohly, an on-line producer in New York, had a most illuminating comment in *Swing* magazine concerning Xers' options today: "We can travel virtually anywhere, date anyone, work anywhere. With e-mail, we can communicate with anybody. . . . Staying at home to care for your kids no longer means you have to give up your career. And even men can stay at home with the babies now without being stigmatized for it."

Tips on Managing Generation X

Given our unique temperament, how can older managers learn to deal with us and vice versa? How can corporations get the most out of their GenX employees? Targeting a population 80 million strong is a marked shift for employers, who are finding that traditional management techniques and younger workers don't always fit. "It's a need that's exploding," says Bruce Tulgan, the author of *Managing Generation X* and the founder of Rainmaker, a GenX consulting company. "It makes for a tremendous challenge, because they may look at company loyalty in a whole new way. They prefer to think of themselves as independent contractors." Tulgan has more than 3,500 subscribers to his newsletter on the GenX workforce. What techniques are managers using to attract and keep GenXers?

Leveraging the Web. The digital revolution is changing everything it touches, and the employment market is no exception. Employers are altering the way they recruit employees because research shows that a lot of Generation Xers do not read periodicals to look for jobs. Instead they search the Internet. The Conneticut-based consultant Peter Weddle said his last count showed about 11,000 Internet sites focused on employment. Forrester Research estimated that $30 million was spent in 1997 for on-line recruiting. By the year 2000, they predict, that figure will shoot up to $218 million.

College students are some of the most wired people in the country, according to a survey by Bernard Hodes Advertising, Inc. A total of 94 percent of students have access to the Web and 56 percent have looked for a job on-line. That's why the on-line recruiting market targets students. At Stanford the effort has been so successful that the university plans to create a résumé database, for access to which employers would be charged. Employers in the high-tech sector are the most plugged in. According to the Hodes survey, two thirds of the jobs in Internet postings are in high technology. Companies also are relying on video conferencing and on-line chats to screen candidates instead of flying them to an interview. Companies post jobs at their own sites, where applicants can get background information, then e-mail a résumé and cover letter with just a click.

Constant training.   Most young adults agree that the most important reason they are at their current job is "to learn." Because young adults know they will likely switch jobs, even careers, many times during their lives, they are not looking to build up corporate capital or even to get salary increases. They are looking for something more portable like training, which will give them the skills to be a valuable player. As Tulgan points out, "The U.S. economy—unpredictable and fiercely competitive—has shaped the habits and career expectations of GenXers. All they've known is a technology-based economy that moves quickly, downsizes constantly, and places a premium on change."

Many experts say younger workers need faster feedback, more rewards, and continual training to stay challenged. Younger workers don't have strong company loyalty, consultants say. Instead, they suggest that employers provide ongoing training to feed GenXers' appetite for challenging themselves. "All of our rules, policies, our procedures are based on the model of yesteryear," says Brian Stern, a managing director at SHL, a consulting group with its U.S. head-quarters in Boston. "The apprentice mentality doesn't float today." Paying your dues at one job or one company no longer makes sense to young workers.

Hands-on approach.   Training doesn't necessarily mean sitting in classrooms. Wells Fargo Bank realized about two years ago that its standard eight-to-five training sessions were not as effective as they once were, said Chris Parry, project manager in retail training. "We found that they didn't meet the needs of the people we are hiring," Parry said. A few years ago Wells Fargo tellers would have been given sixteen hours of training, with the last four hours on the computer. Today, trainees are on the computers the moment they walk in the door. "I don't know that we could have trained like this five to ten years ago," Parry said.

Kim Wilkes, nineteen, a teller at a Wells Fargo, loves her job. She said the training she received when she started three months ago was key to the satisfaction she feels. She wasn't required to read books heavy with theoretical concepts about banking procedures. Instead, Wells Fargo allowed her to learn at her own pace and style. Trainers provided her with a handbook and a mentor—and let her go. "It helps me a lot to watch," Wilkes said. She said she learned more by working behind the counter with a seasoned bank veteran than she would have by sitting in a classroom being lectured to on banking rules.

Baby Boomers who were moving into the workplace for the first time often had to endure long training periods that included videos and lectures. Hands-on instruction was a small part of their training. They were given little chance to set their schedules and goals. And they were told that they have to put in a lot of time before real responsibility would come their way. That tried and true technique worked for years—until GenXers started to come of age in the mid-1980s.

Employers didn't catch on immediately. Many companies kept pushing the same training methods onto their new workers, with limited success. By the early 1990s, employers began to change. They began to understand that employees don't want to be micromanaged.

Photo Courtesy of Johan Hueffer

JOHAN HUEFFER
Financial analyst, Morgan Stanley

FINANCIER, STUDENT

Nowadays, Johan Hueffer spends his days at the Harvard Business School, but before that he was working twelve- and fourteen-hour days as a health-care analyst for Morgan Stanley. At age twenty-three, he was part of the financial team that helped merge the health-care pharmaceutical companies Ciba and Sandoz (now Novartis). The combined company has a market capitalization of over $70 billion. It is one of the largest completed business deals in history.

What is this generation's greatest strength? "Our greatest strength, as well as weakness, is the speed with which we grew up. Although we already have more experience about the ways of the world than previous generations did at our age, we also foreshortened our childhood."

Young workers respond better to training that allows them to be more independent. High-tech, fast-food, and retail companies were the first to recognize the need for change, said the consultant Gayle Carson of Miami-based Carson Research Center—largely because that is where young workers are concentrated. In Boise, Hewlett-Packard now relies

on discussion groups and one-on-one instruction to educate new re-
cruits, their learning consultant Sue Schram said. Employees get
more opportunities to design their training and work schedules and
are allowed to work part time while taking care of a family or going
to school, Schram said.

Retail chain Mervyn's is embracing the revolution. In 1997, it
opened the Mervyn's Business Academy, targeting young workers
whom the company expects will account for 70 percent of its store
managers in the next five years. The Mervyn's program has tossed out
traditional classroom-style training and replaced it with independent
study. It partners employees with mentors and provides a system of
self-paced learning and immediate feedback. Mervyn's Business
Academy manager, Carolyn Yeats, says, "The program allows the employees to get a variety of experiences." As part of their training, most
young adults say they want feedback from their employer on how
they are doing, and some companies are responding. "Instead of the
twelve-month review, we're trying to give them feedback more
often," says Agnes Gioconda of the public relations firm Fleishman-
Hillard. Some of these changes may benefit employees of all ages.
"What people in Generation X want, everyone wants," says Sandra
Begay-Campbell, 33, of Sandia National Laboratories. "Everyone
wants feedback more than once a year. Everyone wants to feel like
they're contributing."

Quality of life.   In 1997, the consulting company Robert Half
International asked managers across the country what they thought
would be the most important change they would have to make at their
companies in order to attract GenX workers. Their answer: Employers must recognize that quality-of-life issues are extremely important
to young workers. In a similar survey by Consultancy Office Team,
more than 35 percent of surveyed executives from large firms agreed
that companies must stress quality-of-life issues to attract GenX employees. That's because young adults are rejecting their parents'
"work ethic" in favor of a more balanced life, which includes more
time with family and friends. As Roberta Maynard wrote in *Nation's*

Business in her 1996 article "A Less-Stressed Workforce", "They don't climb corporate ladders. The treadmill is not for them—except during a workout. Seeking excitement and overall fulfillment, they'll walk away from too much work or too much stress if it threatens to rule their lives."

A Future for Labor Unions?

Despite the strongest labor market in at least seven years, the average American worker has not seen huge wage gains. One reason for this, says Roseanne Cane, an economist at Credite Suisse First Boston, is that labor is poorly organized to take advantage of its scarcity. Labor unions that won wage increases for their workers in the 1960s have lost membership and clout with management. Many say that labor will organize itself to gain for workers a larger share of increasing corporate profits—that we will see a resurgence of the labor movement. Indeed, we have already seen some resurgence with the American Airlines strike and the almost debilitating UPS strike of 1997.

If unions are to reenergize they must attract the support of Generation X. So far, they have not been able to do that. Only 15 percent of our total workforce belongs to unions, and of those under 35, union membership is just 9 percent. To recruit new members, the AFL-CIO president, John Sweeney, proposed spending $60 million to boost membership. Despite this, most young people do not seem to be responding.

Why such a low response? There could be a number of reasons. Young adults are more wary of organizations of any kind than their elders. Being entrepreneurs, we tend to be pro–free enterprise and free trade. Added to that is the labor unions are seen as unfriendly to Generation X issues. They are always on the opposite end of the table on issues like Social Security and Medicare reform. The final blow is the makeup of our workforce—less and less manufacturing (a union stronghold) and more and more service-sector and high-tech jobs. So far, efforts to unionize the service industry have met with failure. High-tech workers, being in high demand, generally do not need labor unions to win good wages in the market. Since none of these trends seems to be changing, the outlook for the future of labor unions is not good.

Predictions

Generation X is going to have a profound influence on corporate America. What form will it take? How will GenXers change things? How can anyone know the answers? We can't, but we can take guesses based on our preliminary reactions to working life.

- We'll certainly impact corporations as employees—they're going to have to deal with the sheer numerical impact of Generation X's estimated 80 million young men and women. Men and women will extract more flexibility from corporations so that we can be good parents and citizens as well as employees. Corporations that downsized and depersonalized a previous generation will compromise a bit. They will recognize the family values and adopt some sensible ways of keeping a highly knowledgeable high-tech workforce happy. Why? Because competent, motivated employees are good for the bottom line.

- Our greatest impact will be from the outside, rather than as employees within companies. America's corporations will be buying a lot of what Generation X will be selling. They'll be buying high-tech companies we start. They'll be paying for the rights to technology and ideas that we develop. In the global economy, the importance of research and development will become even greater when it comes to competing for the trade dollar with Japan, China, Europe, and other players. Young adults are positioned best for providing the raw ideas, intelligence, independence, and entrepreneurial skills that R and D requires. We have already created new boomtowns like Seattle and Raleigh, and we have revitalized the old industrial cities like Boston and Chicago with new technology.

- We will gradually climb the corporate ladder, largely replacing the Boomers. By 2030 (when the last Boomers will be retiring) we will have moved into top management, entered the boardrooms, and become stockholders and company consultants. Politically we'll become senators and congressmen with powers to regulate corporations. If our entrepreneurial spirit is still alive and kicking, those corporations will be highly flexible and creative institutions. As Iris Goldfein of Coopers & Lybrand says, "I think GenXers have the potential to have an impact in the workplace as strong as women have had over the past ten years."

CHAPTER 8

Doing It Our Way

"The Most Entrepreneurial Generation in American History"

In all enterprises great or small, in all activities no matter what they are, in both peace and war, whether near or far, in all endeavors whatsoever, stands an individual, one man or one woman, a single human being, a leader. —Winston Churchill

The "X" in Generation X is the symbol for multiplication. For us this symbol strikes a chord because the most successful entrepreneurs don't win by adding dollars—they win by multiplying dollars. That is just what this generation is doing. In 1995 *Forbes* magazine called us "The most entrepreneurial generation in American history." GenXers are starting companies at a faster rate than any other age group. A study by Marquette University and the University of Michigan found that entrepreneurs aged 18 to 34 created 70 percent of all new start-up businesses in America. A study by the National Federation of Independent Businesses and Wells Fargo Bank reported an even higher percentage (77 percent). According to a *Time*/CNN poll, three of every five GenXers want to be their own bosses. Opinion Research Corporation said 54 percent of this age group are extremely interested in starting their own businesses, compared with just 36 percent of the Boomers.

Many say the high rate of entrepreneurialism is caused, at least in part, by our parents' experience in the job market. Growing up, many of us saw our parents and relatives downsized from corporations to which they had dedicated their lives. The layoff lesson taught us not to rely on one company for our well-being as our parents and grand-parents had. Our career path will not be a straight line but a zigzag from company to company. Former Secretary of Labor Robert Reich spoke of this zigzag career path when he said that young Americans can expect to have as many as five different careers during their working lives. Indeed, the average GenXer stays at his or her first job for just a year. Almost half have worked for at least three companies by the age of twenty-six.

Another major problem is that many young entrepreneurs find the rigid confines and lack of rewards in today's corporate culture a bitter pill to swallow. "Dissatisfaction with the corporate world is cited as one of the main reasons for members of our organization," says Richard Bright, marketing and communications director of the Young Entrepreneurs Organization (YEO). "Our organization grew forty percent in 1994 and sixty-seven percent in 1995." YEO is part of a global organization founded in 1987 to help young business people expand their enterprises. It has more than 1,800 members in 61 chapters who together own businesses that rack up more than $7 billion in sales annually.

The club's primary function "is to help you get to the next level in growing your business," Damon Gersh, a thirty-year-old member, said. "Its mission is to educate our members with the best resources in the world and to offer an environment of support through caring, sharing and trust." Gersh said he joined the group because "I realized that being my age not a lot of my friends could relate to a lot of the issues I was facing. Here I am, thirty years old and running a busi-ness doing several million dollars. When I joined this group I got to meet interesting people with interesting businesses and I learned from them. Essentially, it's everybody pooling their resources for the benefit of everybody. Things I've learned I've been able to apply to my company." Damon Gersh runs Maxons Restorations Inc. in Manhattan—a full-service disaster restoration firm.

YEO expects to gain more members like Gersh in the future. Motivated by the desire for individual expression, greater job security, and a larger share of the profits, Generation X may have finally found its highest calling: entrepreneurship.

Our Work Ethic (We Do Have One)

Unable to find security in corporate America, GenXers are looking to the one thing they can count on—themselves. *U.S. News & World Report* in its October 20, 1997, issue notes that "entrepreneur" is the preferred career of GenXers. "For every Xer who takes a job to pay off debt, a growing number set out to find job security by creating it for themselves." The report goes on, "In a Babson College study of 1,200 business owners last year, the highest percentage of start-ups was in the 25-to-35 age group." A report by IBM said men and women under age thirty-five account for one in five of today's small businesses.

In interviews and research, an overwhelming majority of young entrepreneurs agreed that "control of their destiny" is a main goal for their choices. Why is control so important to this generation? Perhaps the lesson of downsizing, mergers, acquisitions, and leveraged buyouts has taught us that to put control in anyone else's hands is dangerous. For us, institutions, including those of the business world, just haven't appeared to work. So we have chosen to rely on ourselves. Bruce Tulgan, the author of *Managing Generation X*, writes, "You will see that the intense attitude expressed by so many Xers is not arrogance, but rather a powerful independence, which grows out of a life experience in which we have always felt we had only ourselves on whom to depend at a very dangerous and unstable time in history."

Add to our cynicism dissatisfaction with the way our parents and grandparents have run corporations and balanced their family and work lives. Many GenXers see their parents as having abandoned the idealism of the 1960s wholeheartedly for the cash culture of Reagan's

1980s. The internet entrepreneur John Coletti says, "The Reagan era and the heavily corporate policies of the early eighties in many ways forced the hand of these flower children and Baby Boomers into the strongbox of big corporate structures. In many ways, this antithesis of feeling and philosophy encouraged others to back out of their belief systems and grasp ahold of the stock pie, and the bond pie, the AT&T pie, the Mobile Gas pie."

Jennifer Kushell, the founder of Young Entrepreneurs' Network, puts it this way: "We all grew up in the eighties with parents who were getting divorced. They were making tremendous amounts of money and then losing it. They were sacrificing their morals." She says that members of the older generation lost sight of their original goals. They got too wrapped up in money, in succeeding at any expense. "This new generation is saying, wait a minute, we don't have to screw people over money. We want to do things that are going to improve our environment, our families, our communities." This ideological about-face has led to a healthy skepticism in our generation.

According to the September 23, 1996, *U.S. News and World Report*, "Today's young business leaders, who tend to be better educated and more technologically savvy, are challenging some of the bedrock notions of entrepreneurial management and fashioning their own unique brand of corporate culture." Management experts see the biggest change to be young managers' tendency to have a more humanitarian view of running companies. They tend to be more concerned with employees and customers. They encourage workers to keep flexible schedules and bring their children, sometimes even pets, to the office for visits. Kushell says many young leaders in business will choose "to do what's right for the family, what's right for the employee, more so than what's right for their bottom line." Many say it's a reaction to the Boomer management style that has been centered on downsizing, strict rules, and hierarchies. Kushell says, "We take care of the people who take care of us, and that is our employees. That's something the older generation forgot about. Younger managers appreciate the people who work for them."

This refreshing GenX feeling leads to a different ethic. It pervades this entire generation just as the work ethic pervaded the culture of the post–World War II generation and the pleasure ethic pervaded the Boomers' culture. The Boomers' ethic emphasizes personal freedom, happiness, lifestyle choice, and financial independence. The house in the suburbs, the new car, and many other status symbols that symbolized success to the Boomer became for many young GenX entrepreneurs a quasi-enslavement. The preceding generation's rule has been called "profit-driven tunnel vision" and "management by the numbers and downsizing." That to Generation X is what Coletti calls "entirely unacceptable, unchallenging, and unwelcome." This generation's rule is based on breaking corporate molds and old ideas of success. *Flexibility, autonomy, control* are our buzzwords.

Taking It Personally

Generation X looks at work as a lifestyle. So much of our time is absorbed by work that we care greatly about what we are doing and with whom we do business. Daniel Levy of "Real Estate On-Line" says, "I'm working three, four or five times as hard [as when I worked for someone else], but at least I'm in control" (*Forbes,* May 8, 1995). Young adults "aren't just building companies or executing business plans. They're not in it for the money. They're in it for the freedom. They're not doing it because they can. They're doing it because there's no way they cannot. They—and countless others like them—simply cannot imagine doing anything else" (*Fast Company,* February–March 1997).

A perfect example of staying in control is Ted Waitt, the founder of Gateway Computers. Compaq appeared to be poised for a buyout that would give Waitt over $7 billion for the takeover, but he backed out at the last minute. "The deal appears to have fallen apart when Compaq started to project some corporate muscle, as in 'You work for us now.' Waitt bristled at his executives being treated as subordinates, not equals. Both Compaq and Gateway declined to comment. But a source close to Waitt says, 'Anyone who really knows Ted Waitt knows that there are things more important (to him) than money. Two of those things are Gateway and its people' " (*Time,* May 19, 1997). Control of one's ideas, working with the people you care about and want around you, keeping even huge businesses from spiraling into automated service—these are the hallmarks of Generation X. To be in control as opposed to being controlled. It's the raison d'être of GenX entrepreneurs and workers.

Another attraction to entrepreneurism involves teamwork as op- posed to the socially stunted and sterile environment of big business. It's difficult to be happy if you don't care for and enjoy the intellec- tual and personal worth of your fellow employees. Kim Polese had been a Java project manager at Sun Microsystems before she started the company Marimba. In an interview with on-line magazine *C/NET* she said, "I had always wanted to start my own company. It had been a lifelong dream. I always knew that the right opportunity, the right set of people, and the right product would present itself. . . . I had the opportunity to go off and start this new company with three of the best engineers on the Java team. So that was a big factor. The right people."

As former product manager at Sun Microsystems Inc., Polese took an obscure software product, code-named Oak, and turned it into Java, which has now become the most used computer language on the internet. Then at the height of the Java craze in January 1996, she sparked another sensation by beating a path away from Sun, along with three prominent Java engineers. Together, they formed Marim- ba. Their mission is to create software solutions using distribution, management, and upgrading of network applications within enter- prises and across the network.

Dineh Mohajer, the twenty-something head of the cosmetics com- pany Hard Candy, knows all about teamwork. She started in 1995 with a $50,000 loan from her Iranian-born parents, and with no time to interview job applicants, brought in her boyfriend and sister. Later

ALIZA SHERMAN
Founder, Cybergrrl

BUSINESSWOMAN, CYBER-CITIZEN

For Aliza Sherman, high tech is not just about making a buck. She has an agenda—getting more women to go on-line. In 1995 she launched Cybergrrl, a marketing company to help female-friendly companies find their markets on the net. When she launched her company, most people told her she was crazy. The thing she enjoys most about being her own boss? "Freedom. No one telling me I couldn't do something." Aliza's background isn't the norm for Silicon Valley. She's a New Yorker who worked as a domestic violence counselor, and before that in music management with artists like Metallica. She thinks that what drives this generation is a "rebellion against the things we do not like. Our entrepreneurialism is reactionary—avoiding the things we hate, creating working environments we can enjoy."

she signed on William Botts, a sixtyish member of the Silent Generation. She liked the fact that he was more entrepreneurial than corporate types, having left corporate America to start his own company, plus turn around some smaller companies. After a few years in business, in 1996 her company sold $10 million worth of nail polish and Botts said they are ending 1997 at more than double that figure. Some of her clients include Lenny Kravitz, Alicia Silverstone, and Drew Barrymore. People just go wild for Hard Candy's metallic silver, Trailer Trash, red-black Porno, Seafoam-Blue Sushi, and Candy Man, a nail polish for men. London's Harvey Nichols and Harrods have ordered Hard Candy products. "Go with your gut, and don't be afraid to delegate," she told a Yale Business and Economic Forum in 1996.

Because work takes up so much of our time and energy, Generation X entrepreneurs view their work as an expression of themselves. Perhaps that is why so many have chosen businesses that they feel will improve society, not just make money. They want to make a difference while they build successful companies. These are just a few examples:

- Cybergrrl is the name Aliza Sherman goes by on the Internet and it's also the name of her company. Her mission is to empower women through technology. Twenty-something Sherman took a one-hour, ten-dollar course in creating pages for the World Wide Web, then founded Cybergrrl Internet Media, which designs Web sites and helps companies with on-line marketing. Her on-line group, Webgrrls, has forty-five chapters worldwide. She helps women counter five basic cyber fears: it's too hard, too expensive, too dangerous, has nothing to offer professionally, and nothing for the woman personally.

- Alexander Torimiro is a GenXer who migrated from Cameroon to Canada and launched a company to provide the perfect tea from . . . Cameroon. His 1996 income was estimated at $5 million. He plans on expanding into New York with a 120-employee facility in Harlem. "When I came to this country, I was helped to get where I am. I always felt I had an obligation to help people, too."

- Kristin Roach, 22, was an avid snowboarder who grew increasingly annoyed with ill-fitting unisex apparel on the slopes. So she left college halfway through her sophomore year and founded Kurvz Extremewear, which produces more stylish snowboarding wear for women. "I'm doing this to make money, but I also have a cause here: to support women in sports," she says.

- Daniel Grossman started Wild Planet Toys Inc. in 1993 because he "wasn't interested in making violent or sexist toys," he told *Entrepreneur* magazine in November 1996. His 1996 sales were over $5 million.

Putting Life into Corporations

Another hallmark of Generation X management is contempt for bureaucracy. The way we build companies is entirely unconventional. Sky Dayton, 24, president of Earthlink, one of America's fastest-growing Internet service providers, says, "I'm young and I don't have any preconceived notions about how to run a company." At his company, executives often have their "meetings" outside the boardroom—like, at the hockey rink. His rationale is that employees will more willingly offer their thoughts when engaged in a nonjob activity.

Many say our new and often from-the-hip management style is a result of how we have built our companies—with shoestring, gum, and our own persistence. Here are a few examples:

- Jim "Mac" McNeal, 24, and his partner, Joel Sylvian, 25, have turned disrespect for corporate hierarchies into a successful business strategy. The two talent managers and founders of New York–based Bulldog Entertainment have had their clients perform uninvited in the lobbies of record companies like RCA and Electra. Their rationale? "It is important to catch them off guard," says McNeal, who calls his approach "guerrilla marketing." So far, the company is off to a good start. They grossed more than $300,000 in contracts in 1996.

- Jason Gold and Barry Swatsenbarg were barely 20 in 1993 when they came up with the blueprint for their Detroit company, Office Perfect. Their idea was simple: office space for independent lawyers. They provided corporate office space, receptionists, law libraries, and marketing services. To grab the attention of potential investors they set up four phone lines in their small apartment. Swatsenbarg's girlfriend fielded phone calls. Over time they amassed more than $2.5 million in venture capital. By 1996 the company had revenues of $4.5 million.

- Twenty-something Joseph Liemandt dropped out of Stanford University in 1990, a few months before graduation, to start a software company. Seven years later he is estimated to be worth $500 million and is the youngest self-made millionaire of the Forbes 400. That is thanks to Trilogy, his Texas-based software company. He knows the kids he hires are too smart to work for him—or anyone else—for long. "There are a lot of people here to learn how to start a software company," he says. "That's great." He prefers a few years of boundless entrepreneurial dynamics to many years of mediocre performance.

The House That Technology Built

Many argue that our generation's entrepreneurial spirit has been revived by technology. Computers, the Internet, and high tech have broken down the traditional barriers of corporate America. Today knowledge, skill, and creativity are more important in the job market than seniority. Computer technology was quickly adopted by the younger generation. As *Forbes* notes, "Just as the early 20th-century American farm boy became a mechanical whiz by playing with his Model-T Ford, so did the entrepreneurial generation become computer-literate." Michael Dell, the poster boy of the entrepreneurial generation, told *Forbes*, "People my age grew up knowing that computers are our friends."

This combination of know-how and a drive to be in control has fueled the rebirth of entrepreneurship. Randall Lane, writing in *Forbes*, says, "Older people would do well not to judge those 18 to 34 by the way they dress or talk or by the music they punish their eardrums with. This is America's first Computer Generation, and it is beginning to combine technology and human freedom in ways that promise to restore this country to economic leadership. The best of our young people share two wonderful qualities: computer literacy and a passion to control their own destinies." And many have capitalized on the technological revolution to make hundreds of millions, billions, of dollars.

Conversely, as young Americans benefit from their near-exclusive understanding of technology, a learning gap has developed that separates the tech-savvy from the tech-phobic. To succeed in this age you need to understand the speed of technology and be willing to stay on the crest of that wave. Most Americans who haven't grown up with computers have little or no desire to catch up, let alone play. Consequently, the small and large business opportunities as well as the supporting professions are being funneled to a fairly thin and young demographic.

Consider twenty-something Marc Andreeson, who wrote Mosaic, the first commercially successful graphical Web browser. From that success he founded Netscape, and he is now worth more than $70 million. About 85 percent of all browsers in use are made by Netscape. He was asked by *Rolling Stone* whether he ever wondered "Why me?" when thinking of all he has gained from this Internet boom. He replied, "No, not really. I mean, I don't think there's any reason to expect a deeper answer to it than that. I just got lucky. We have an economic system in this country now that is just tremendous in terms of opportunity for people to do new things. And we're just really lucky to be living in an age where things are relatively stable from an economic standpoint."

Then there are twenty-somethings Jerry Yang and David Filo.

While graduate students at Stanford University, they launched the search engine Yahoo! (Yet Another Hierarchical Officious Oracle). It is, as they say, a "Yellow Pages of the World Wide Web." At their initial public offering in 1996 they were each worth $132 million. With its now-famous on-line directory—www.yahoo.com—Yahoo! aims to bring a sense of order to the ever-expanding but rather disorderly World Wide Web. Yang said, "There are hundreds of thousands of things out there but no easy way to find them. That's why we have value." Yahoo!'s Web site receives so many hits (about 15 million a day) that advertisers pay huge premiums, up to several hundred thousand dollars each, to be featured alongside the company's directory. And Yahoo! has already launched a series of books and publishes a magazine.

The thirty-something quartet of Scott Dauer, Craig Gutmann, Allen Sutker, and Mark Polinsky started Vision Tek in 1988 with start-up capital of $18,000. Their company, headquartered in Gurnee, Illinois, which sells computer chips, had projected sales in 1996 of $250 million, according to *Entrepreneur* magazine. They pooled their various talents to fill a memory chip shortage in the market. Polinsky, the company's CEO, said, "We realized people buy from people. Our marketing techniques helped build personal relationships."

The market that has built up around the tech industry is phenomenal. The almost unprecedented economic growth of our post-1991 recession has been largely fueled by the tech market in much the same way that the Industrial Revolution fueled the growth of the 1920s. According to Tampa, Florida–based research company Payment Systems, sixty-four new millionaires were created in Silicon Valley each day of 1996.

The Internet has also provided enormous growth potential. Five years ago, few had ever heard of the Internet. Today more than 30 million people are on-line and the numbers keep growing. That means more opportunities for young adults. According to International Data Corporation, the transaction value of goods and services purchased using the Internet was $100 million in 1995. By the beginning

Photos Courtesy of Jerry Yang and David Filo

JERRY YANG AND DAVID FILO
Co-founders, Yahoo!

INTERNET MOGULS, CLASSMATES

Jerry Yang and his partner, David Filo, are two of the most success-ful high-tech entrepreneurs around. Just three short years ago while graduate students at Stanford, the two launched Yahoo! Yahoo! (Yet Another Hierarchical Officious Oracle) was the first online naviga-tional guide to the Web and now, in terms of traffic, advertising, and household reach, it is the most popular Internet search engine around.

Because their Web site receives over 15 million viewers a day, ad-vertisers are willing to pay big bucks to appear on Yahoo! When Ya-hoo! went public in 1996, Filo and Yang each garnered over $100 million on the initial public offering—and their stock values have been climbing ever since. Since the Internet is evolving so quickly, there is a lot of work just to keep up. "It is like running a marathon every day," says Yang.

of the next millennium, it is forecast to reach a stunning $186 billion. If the numbers reach just a quarter of that, the Internet will provide an opportunity without equal.

How do we know that this "long boom" for the Internet won't fizzle out? Listen to an autoworker's account of the car business in the 1920s, as preserved in the history archives of the Smithsonian Institution: There are certainly some lessons to be drawn. "You see, when I first started work with the transfer company as mechanic and driver, some people had made the remark that I never stuck to anything long. That automobiles were just a fad, and I'd be back on the farm before much longer. Well, I showed them. You might say that I've practically grown up with the automobile."

Despite the auto industry's expansion and entrepreneurial opportunities, the car is still a limited product with only so many parts to be made. Computer technology, on the other hand, is not defined by one platform and the sum of that one platform's parts. A *Newsweek* article (January 27, 1997) on the Web notes, "The pace of change is so fast that one year on the Internet is like seven years in any other medium. By this scheme, it has been nearly a century since the Internet was born." We are in what appears to be a state of exponential growth with huge differentiation of service, function, support, and competition.

Economic considerations will expand cyberspace by multiple factors in the next several years. Consider just one statistic: advertising revenue on the World Wide Web reached $217 million for the first six months of 1997, Cowles/Samba Information reported in *Potentials in Marketing* in October 1997, and about $340 million was projected for advertising banner space on the Internet in 1998. Twenty-something Scott Heiferman saw the light and founded the "i-traffic" agency focusing on Internet marketing. He financed the project on his credit cards. Projected revenues for 1997 were $1 million. "He's the most brilliant on-line marketer I've ever come across," says Seth Goldstein, who heads SiteSpecific, a Web design firm. "On-line advertising is well on its way to becoming a highly significant segment of the advertising industry and traditional advertising agencies and advertisers are taking notice," reports Jupiter Communications, a leading Internet-focused market research firm. Generation X entrepreneurs are at work as you read, figuring out ways to profit from this growing source of income.

Build It and They Will Come

If it was about anything, the 1990s stock market was about high technology. Intel, Microsoft, and IBM were some of the biggest movers, and then there were the new seedling companies like Netscape, Trilogy, and Yahoo!. Investors loved the high profit margins and the potential for fast growth of the high-tech industry and fed off the youth involved with many of these companies.

Not surprisingly, young traders had an unusually large role in shaping this boom. Twenty-seven-year-old managers of multi-billion-dollar mutual funds have the power to move markets and to make or break individual stocks. "There's a whole class of young MBA's who share an almost religious belief that the economy has shifted into a new mode. Communism around the world is dead. American productivity and corporate profits will reign supreme. The market cycle ended its inevitable massive downturns. It's a snarling beast that has at long last been tamed," trumpeted the *New York Times* in late 1997. Like twelve-year-olds teaching their dads tricks of the Nintendo set, the new breed on Wall Street see themselves as masters of new games, the latest techniques. "Back in the sixties the amount of information you got in a year, we get in a day," says one analyst. "You've got these old guys out here saying, 'Oh, the market's way too high,' but they're not out there digging, spending their time on the road. I think it's fabrication because they're not out there doing it." Another trader points out, "These are the same guys who don't know how to turn on their computer."

In addition to traditional forms of Wall Street funding, entire venture capital firms have been bred from the technology boom. John Doerr, who has created the "Java Fund," exemplifies the venture capitalists of Silicon Valley. With assets of $100 million, it fuels the entrepreneurial pursuits of companies looking to advance encryption technology and develop media and other new niches needed to further consolidate the media fields. Another goal says Doerr, is to further "usher in the mammoth possibility of safely encrypted and thereby insanely lucrative electronic commerce [e-commerce]."

Photo Courtesy of Jesse Milden

Bo Peabody
President, CEO, Tripod

Entrepreneur, Virtual Citizen

He was twenty and a college sophomore at Williams when he started Tripod, an on-line virtual community for young adults. Six years later Tripod boasts 375,000 members and has revenues of $650,000. Advertisers are clamoring to get on board to capture the Generation X marketer. Bo says the most attractive part about being an entrepreneur is the company: "You get to work with some of the best people around. And it is relatively easy to get started when you are young. That's because we understand the technology out there better than other generations."

But the newness of the industry does not always make things easy. Bo explains, "Creating a profitable business in an industry with no business model is difficult. We're not selling cosmetics here. As a result, I have to conserve capital and manage our growth carefully."

Silicon Alley, as New York's smaller tech boom is playfully called, is drawing young investment bankers such as Fred Wilson and Jerry Colonna, who focus on new media ventures. According to *New York* magazine, "Venture capital is being allocated in chunks of millions of dollars (in some cases tens of millions) . . . to anything with the word

Internet in its prospectus." Craig Gholston of Plano, Texas, started his own company, GenX Invest, after seven years with the Franklin Templeton Group of Funds. GenX Invest's phone number is 888-NO-SLACK. After two years, "He has $300,000 in assets and 30 young clients, most of whom find him through his Web site," the *U.S. News and World Report* of October 20, 1997, reported. These are just a few of the literally hundreds of examples of the money chasing after new technology.

Entertaining for Profit

Entrepreneurs are also active in entertainment, but it all gets back to high tech. In part these new-style artists, producers, and managers have been able to do new things because technology has made possible production of your own music, books, and films. Among these entrepreneurial efforts:

- The singer and songwriter Ani DiFranco, turned off by big record companies, started her own label, Righteous Babe, at nineteen. "I have no interest in fame and fortune," DiFranco says. However, she managed to earn more than $1 million in 1996 and has sold more than 800,000 records. "I'm more into making noise and stirring people. That's why I started my own company." She has twelve on the company payroll and has a heavy travel and performance schedule. DiFranco explains her rise: "We'd been selling primarily to people at shows and through our 800 number. But there were small stores starting to pick up on me, ones in markets where I had played. People who had been to the shows were coming in and asking for my stuff, so the owners started thinking, 'Who is this person?' They found out and began calling." DiFranco manages to put on about two hundred concerts a year.

- The GenX moviemaker Ed Burns produced the low-budget independent film *The Brothers McMullen*. It won the grand jury prize at Robert Redford's Sundance Film Festival and went on to gross $10 million, becoming one of the most successful independent films ever.

- David Mays is the 28-year-old publisher of *The Source*, a magazine dedicated to hip-hop music and lifestyle. He has watched circulation grow ten-fold since the magazine's 1988 inception at Harvard as a one-pager. It is now the second-largest title in the genre—and still growing. Not bad for someone whose entire staff walked out on him in December 1994 when his circulation couldn't break 100,000 and the company faced bankruptcy.

- Christy Haubegger founded *Latina* magazine in June 1996. It is a bilingual glossy geared to America's 8 million young, college-educated Hispanic women. She says *Latina* is filling a niche other magazines ignore, because traditional women's magazines "either didn't think people like me were attractive or didn't think that we existed." So far it seems to be working. Circulation is already up to 200,000 and growing. The magazine has also attracted advertisers to the Latin market. "We are the first Hispanic marketing a lot of companies have done," Haubegger says, citing ads from the Gap, Estée Lauder, and Ralph Lauren.

- Haley Levine had a dream job out of college. She was an associate editor for *Cosmopolitan*, which has one of the largest distributions of any women's magazine in the world. Still, she chose to leave to freelance and build her own writing career. "There is something exciting to me about running my own business. It is a real adrenaline rush."

Equal Opportunity—Made

Entrepreneurship is also a promising path for minorities who have not traditionally been afforded opportunities in corporate America. More and more minorities are founding their own businesses to climb the economic ladder. "I've seen too many African-Americans come out of college and work years [in corporate America] with no career advancement to show for it," says Sidney Warren who chose the ownership route. He is a 32-year-old co-owner of a TCBY/Mrs. Fields Cookies cobranded franchise in Cincinnati. Tariq Muhammad of *Black Enterprise* magazine says, "The affirmative action programs that gave many buppies [black upwardly mobile professionals] a boost onto the corporate ladder have sent only a few to the executive suite—and those programs are now under fire."

What is particularly important about minority businesses is that they tend to give back to their communities. Minority-run businesses tend to hire more minority employees. Warren said of one of his franchise stores, "This store was designed by a black architect, built by a black construction company and we employ black people at all levels."

The mission of Mark Winston Griffith and Errol Lewis, the founders of the Central Brooklyn Federal Credit Union (more commonly known as the "hip-hop bank"), is to provide "trust and cooperation to lending in Brooklyn." They not only provide a needed service in a poor area but also arrange youth internships and training. "We are basically community activists from the hip-hop generation who decided it was time to resume the work of the civil rights and black power movements. We believe that building community-owned economic institutions is the final frontier," Griffith says. Tariq Muhammad agrees: "Part of a nationwide trend, the move toward entrepreneurship is crucial for African-Americans." Members of Generation X have decided to take their future into their own hands rather than put their trust in faceless, heartless corporations. In so doing they are playing a leading role in the economic empowerment of African-American communities.

Building the Future

What does all this mean for the future of business? First, we are creating a business revolution comparable to the Industrial Revolution. Technology has afforded us not only the new opportunities of software and hardware design and Internet business, but also new avenues into old industries. Wall Street, the media, retail have become more accessible for us simply because these industries need our high-tech skills. Over our lifetimes we will see companies started by twenty-somethings mature and become the General Motors, the Coca-Colas and the IBMs of our nation.

CHAPTER 9

Consumer Nation

Moving Markets with Our Dollars

Money is a terrible master but an excellent servant.
　　　　　　　　　　　　　—P. T. Barnum (1810–1891).

O ne of the great strengths of our nation is our well-oiled consumer markets. We are truly a consumer nation. No one knows
how to consume quite like Americans—for better or for worse. The
strength of our consumer-driven economy has been part of the success of our democracy and the failure of centrally planned economies. The economist John Kenneth Galbraith writes in his book *The
Good Society*, "The revelation by television and other modern communications of the manifest abundance and variety of material pos-
sessions in the Western countries was one factor unsettling the
socialist regimes of Eastern Europe and the former Soviet Union. The
weakness and rigidity with which they had supplied their citizens
with such goods and services in the required quantity, styles, and
changing fashions had more than a little to do with their downfall."

The paradox, of course, is that our overspending could be the
downfall of our nation. Not just government spends too much. Personally, too, we are spendthrifts. We consume more of our income
than any industrialized nation on earth and we save next to nothing.

We love to buy and collect—and we want instant gratification. Enter Generation X with some surprisingly good news. This generation is showing signs that we save more, look for greater value in the products we buy, and invest with greater understanding than our predecessors.

Xers Vote with the Dollar

We are accused of being apathetic about using the voting booth. The truth is, we vote every day, twenty-four hours a day—with our dollars. It's Generation X democracy in action. We make and break industries by what we buy and refuse to buy. Our dollars vote in and vote out products, services, and corporate management teams. Our twelve-figure annual spending power has two sources, money we earn, and dollars we spend for others. With both parents working and often away from the home, Generation X has made more spending decisions for the family than any previous generation—when mom and dad were at work, we did the grocery shopping.

The way we use our money sends important signals to the market about who we are and how we'll guide this nation. Money gives us power in the public sphere. Advertisers, money managers, retailers, credit card companies, car dealers, real estate brokers, and others with economic interests all want control over our money. Advertising executives spend hours in conferences debating how to capture the Generation X market. Credit card companies send thousands of representatives across the country with balloons, coffee mugs and T-shirts to lure our business at college campuses. Retailers try to create a cool and hip environment to lure us to shop. Because of the money we have to spend and invest, even if it is less than our parents', we are important. It is, therefore, crucial for us to understand how we are spending and saving and what consequences that has for society at large.

For a long time the Generation X market was virtually ignored by advertisers, marketers, and the like. Some say it's because we are a poorer generation. After all, we only have 80 percent of the spending power our parents had at a similar age. Compared to the Boomers, we are currently a small slice of the economic pie. Others say we are hard to market to because of our cynicism about advertising. And others just can't "pin us down," having no idea what a Generation X market wants to buy and what messages it responds to.

As the bulk of Generation X has begun to reach adulthood, businesses have realized they cannot afford to ignore us as a market. While we haven't reached the economic prominence of the baby boom, we are the future. We are a vital market. In the coming millennium, we will buy the bulk of the cars, homes, diapers, furniture, and electronic equipment. We'll be worrying about mutual funds, CDs, 401(k)s, stocks and bonds. As a result, smart businesses (the ones that will continue to exist in the future) have started to catch on by trying to address the needs of this new market.

Our Spending Power

In 1998, those aged 15 to 35 (the broadest definition of Generation X) numbered 80 million people, representing almost $200 billion in spending power and $25 billion in new investment opportunities according to author Karen Ritchie. This age group includes GenXers born between 1963 and 1976, and part of the "Echo Boom," which began in 1977. The echo boom, says *The Baby Bust* author William Dunn, was due to the high number of childbearing-age Boomers. Furthermore, says Dunn, "After many years of postponing motherhood to finish school and launch careers, Boomer women began racing their biological clocks," triggering a jump in births in the late eighties and early nineties.

Today, GenXers aged 21 to 32 account for 28 percent of the U.S.

population—a substantial share by any standard. Thus, young adults make up the lion's share of the market for many goods and services. The number of GenXers over age eighteen will continue to grow by about 3.6 million each year until 2005. In the year 2000, there will be 79.8 million adult Xers aged 19–39. In 1997, Xers represented about half of the primary consumer target, adults aged 18 to 49, and about 30 percent of the adults aged 25 to 54.

According to the U.S. Census Bureau, GenXers aged 15 to 35 control $200 billion in income each year. Of that total, teenagers have $50 billion to $55 billion to spend, college students have $35 billion to $45 billion, and noncollege young adults have $100 billion to $115 billion. Between 1987 and 1998, that number could have increased by another $35 billion to $60 billion, which would put the spending power at $235 to $260 billion.

Teenager Research Unlimited (TRU) of Northbrook, Illinois, calculates that youngsters aged 12 to 19 spent an estimated $93 billion in 1992. Of that, $36 billion was money given to them to spend on family needs such as shopping for groceries and other errands. The remaining $57 billion was money teens spent on themselves. In 1986, by contrast, TRU estimated that teen spending totaled $74 billion, of which $29 billion was spent on household needs and $45 billion on themselves. One reason for the increase is that teens are more likely to be in dual-income or single-parent families, where they are the only family members with time to shop. Teens and young people spent more time shopping, preparing meals, feeding pets and cleaning houses than previous generations of teens. Today, kids handle more money often at an earlier age.

A higher proportion of Xers worked during their school years than Boomers. That provided us with more spending money and bigger bank accounts. *Local College* magazine calculates that the typical undergraduate in 1992 had personal buying power of $4,840 annually with discretionary spending of $138 per month. More recent estimates put discretionary spending closer to $6,000 a year.

The Bureau of Labor Statistics estimated that in 1998 there would be as many as 8.5 million households in which the household head was under age 25. Those households had an average annual expenditure of $16,518, with combined expenditures of $125 billion.

Add the three groups up, older teens, college students, and young professionals, and you get a very conservative estimate of $200 billion of spending a year. That's a considerable amount for an age group written off by the mythmakers as "poor."

Our Balance Sheet

Though Gen Xers' incomes are not rising at the rate the Boomers' did, we still have substantial net worth that we are using to finance our purchases:

Net worth.   Between 1992 and 1995, the median net worth, or assets minus debts, of householders under the age of 35 rose from $10,000 to $11,400, after adjusting for inflation. This 13 percent increase was the greatest of any age group. Among all householders, the median net worth rose from $52,800 to $56,400, a 7 percent gain. The net worth of young adults is much less than that of older householders because few are home owners (homes account for the largest share of net worth of Americans). Net worth peaked in the 55-to-64 age group at more than $100,000 in 1995. For those over 65, net worth begins to shrink as retirees spend down their wealth.

Our liabilities.   Young adults are more likely to be in debt than older householders because they have low incomes and often must borrow to make ends meet. The average recent college graduate has more than $10,000 of debt. More than 80 percent of young households have some kind of debt, compared to 75 percent of all households. Because young adults are less likely to own a home than the average American, they are less likely to have a mortgage. But those with mortgages owe more than the average household, $63,000 for young adults versus $51,000 for homeowners overall in 1995. The mortgage debt of young adults is greater than average because they have had less time to pay off their loans. Sixty-two percent of young adults have installment debt (typically, car loans) compared with 47 percent of all households.

We learned early from Wilma Flintstone and Betty Rubble that "charging" was a great alternative if you didn't have ready cash. More than two thirds of GenXers who have credit cards carry more than $1,000 in debt. The American Bankers Association reported that a record high 3.75 percent of credit card accounts were thirty days or more overdue at year's end 1996. Commercial banks wrote off 4.4 percent of credit card loans in 1996, up from 3.4 percent the previous year. The portion of direct auto loans thirty days or more overdue rose to 2.0 percent in the fourth quarter of 1996, compared to 1.9 percent in the same period a year earlier. For indirect auto loans (made through dealerships), the delinquency rate rose to 2.6 percent in the fourth quarter of 1996, from 2.17 percent a year earlier. Eighteen percent of these late payers were between 18 and 24 years of age.

Michael Geppert, senior vice president of marketing for First Data InfoSource, says that Generation X is pretty "lackadaisical about paying back debts." He adds that GenXers have no qualms about filing for bankruptcy. "Bankruptcy is being used by many as a debt-management tool, rather than a last resort. . . . They have not been taught to manage credit like the older generations." There could be a number of reasons for this. First, they are not as worried about being able to get credit. Bruce Tulgan notes that Xers have had "credit cards shoved down their throats" from the time they were 18. Credit has always been readily available. Also, GenXers do not feel the moral responsibility to pay off debts the way previous generations did. Astrid Rial, president of Arial International, a Washington-based consulting firm, noted, "Generation Xers feel like the system has let them down so they feel they can let the system down."

So how should businesses collect from us? Rial recommends the following: "Send it to the attorneys right away." She notes that many Xers are either able to pay and unwilling, or unable to pay and unwilling. In either case, she says, creditors spend far too much time holding young adults' hands. Tulgan takes an alternative approach. He says Xers are willing to make good and that creditors should not "strong-arm" young adults. It may make things worse. Instead, he said, issuers should offer young adults a range of options. "This person isn't quite sure how to manage their way out of debt. Probably the best approach is to say, 'We know you got in over your head. You do have to pay and there are good reasons why you should pay. We want to help you.' "

Our assets. On the upside, Xers seem to be building a diverse asset base for themselves. Among householders aged 35 or under, fully 87 percent had some financial assets in 1995. That compares to 91 percent for all householders. According to a survey by the Employee Benefit Research Institute, 65 percent of GenXers say they have already begun saving for retirement and 19 percent have already stashed away $50,000 or more. Compare that to the Boomers, only 18 percent of whom have more than $50,000, and they are much closer to retirement than we. Xers already make up one fifth of all investors, and that number will grow in the future. It's estimated that Generation X investments will generate $55 billion in new savings by 2000.

More Xers believe that UFOs are real than believe that Social Security will be available when they retire. Xers feel they cannot count on the corporate pension because of increased job mobility and because corporations are scaling retirement plans down. That means Xers must fend for themselves by saving now for their retirement and for rainy days. That knowledge, which Xers are surprisingly aware of, will drive this age cohort to save and invest for themselves. Dee Lee of Harvard Financial Educators does seminars for master's degree students at Harvard. "I tell them to look down at their feet; they are standing in the shoes of the person who's going to provide for their retirement." Luckily, Generation X is a comparatively sophisticated market, having been provided the opportunity to take advantage of 401(k)s, employee stock option plans, mutual funds, and credit cards

Photo Courtesy of Sigrid Estrada

BETH KOBLINER
Writer, **Money** *magazine*

MONEY MANAGER, MOM

Beth Kobliner means it literally when she says, "Get a financial life!" That's the name of her best-selling book on personal finance for Generation X. The book gives young adults advice on everything from balancing your college debt to investing in the stock market to getting a first mortgage on a home. "A few years ago it was tough to convince publishers and editors that young people need personal finance education. The general feeling was that people in their twenties and thirties had no interest in financial matters—why would they need to know about money if they didn't have money? Of course, the very fact that we have less money is one reason we need to know how to manage our money better." Kobliner got her start in the world of financial writing as the staff research associate for Sylvia Porter, the pioneer of personal finance journalism, whose syndicated column ran in over 150 newspapers around the country. Kobliner is currently a contributing writer for *Money.* When she is not taking her message to CNN or Oprah, she is managing her family, her young daughter and husband.

earlier than any previous generation. How strong is our will to save? A poll that Blum & Weprin did for *Swing* magazine gives insight: Xers were asked what they would use money for from a sudden windfall: invest for the future (42 percent); give to family (26 percent); travel (16 percent); donate to charity (8 percent); buy something (6 percent).

Retirement savings. "The people who are running mutual fund companies assume this generation is full of people who are not paying attention to their money and are sort of frivolous slackers who don't really care about investing," says Beth Kobliner, author of *Get a Financial Life: Personal Finance in Your Twenties and Thirties.* "What I found is that this generation is extraordinarily interested in the topic of personal finance and investing in particular." The numbers seem to agree; according to a 1997 poll by Yankelovich Partners, 69 percent of Generation X is thinking about retirement, compared to just 51 percent of our parents at our age. In 1995 the median value of the retirement accounts owned by young adults was $5,200, compared to $15,600 in retirement account value for the average household. Nearly 40 percent of us have individual retirement accounts or employee-sponsored 401(k) plans, up a full 10 percent from 1993, and nearly 20 percent of us have saved more than $50,000 already.

In another survey, by Roper Starch Worldwide, of nearly 2,100 middle-income and affluent Americans, 61 percent of twenty-somethings said they or their spouses had put aside money for retirement, with three out of four saying that retirement was a savings priority. The survey found that 58 percent of respondents aged 18 to 30 were participating in 401(k) plans, compared with 52 percent of Baby Boomers aged 30 to 49. The Investment Company Institute, a trade association for mutual funds, provided additional evidence of the trend earlier this year. *BusinessWeek* reported a survey of 1,200 fund participants found that those aged 18 to 30 were investing 38 percent of their savings in mutual funds, a greater percentage than for Baby

Boomers, who were investing 27 percent in mutual funds. "The results clearly identified that there had been some myths about the generations as far as savings and investments were concerned," said Sandra J. West, director of marketing and policy research at the institute.

One financial instrument that seems to be encouraging Xers to save is the 401(k), whereby employers make automatic payroll deductions to the plan to make it easy for Xers to save for retirement. From 1983 to 1993, Xers' participation in such plans more than doubled—the biggest increase of any age group. Deena Katz, a Certified Financial Planner with Evensky, Brown, Katz, and Levitt in Coral Gables, Florida, says the young people who work for her recently asked her to install a 401(k) plan in lieu of a salary increase. "Where did that come from?" she says. "My generation would have asked for the money. These kids are extraordinarily concerned about security." She attributes this concern to the fact that they are a very insecure generation—not unlike their grandparents, who suffered through the Depression. "Many are products of divorce, they are afraid of violence, and they have watched their parents forced into early retirement. They are afraid of not having enough money."

As a result of this interest, many money managers are trying to win the Generation X market. American Express Institutional Services, for example, used the phrase "What a can of pop can do for your future" in developing a marketing campaign for the 401(k) plan at Shopko Stores, a discount department store chain based in Green Bay, Wisconsin. The dimes a day spent for a soft drink, the campaign suggests, can instead be the start of a retirement program built on mutual fund investments. American Express also developed a marketing program for Toys "R" Us employees that emphasizes the tax benefits of the company's 401(k) program. The promotion played off the 1996 presidential election. A poster proclaims, "When it comes to reducing your taxes this year, you've got three parties to choose from," and shows an elephant, a donkey and a giraffe. The giraffe represents the Toys "R" Us mascot, Geoffrey Giraffe, and his message is to put money into the company's plan.

John Palombo, a senior vice president of employee education with American Express Institutional Services, said that two years ago, younger employees were generally not participating in savings plans. "We kind of wrote them off generally because we just assumed they fell into that broader, under-thirty category that believes they are going to live forever and will do it later," Mr. Palombo said. But that perception changed as the American Express unit worked with companies that had high concentrations of younger employees or that needed to increase employee participation in their 401(k) plans to meet government requirements. Though the younger employees were initially more focused on jump-starting a career than on investing, that attitude seemed to change quickly as the employees got their feet on the ground. "They began to say, 'I saw some of the struggles my parents or friends of the family were going through and I'm going to start dealing with this now,' " Mr. Palombo said.

Besides focusing on the workplace, some mutual fund companies are reducing sales charges or waiving minimum investment amounts on certain funds. At Lebenthal & Co., customers 35 and under can get a break of half a percentage point on sales fees for the company's three bond funds. While bonds remain a hard sell to a younger market, Lebenthal said, the reduced fees have attracted some younger investors. Beth Kobliner said mutual funds were offering attractive programs that allowed people to invest as little as $25 in a fund, if additional investments were made on a regular basis. Generally, minimum initial investments were $1,000 and up.

T. Rowe Price has initiated what it calls the Automatic Asset Builder program, which waives the minimum investment in virtually any fund but requires a minimum contribution of $50 a month. Steven Norwitz, a vice president with the company, said that the program was not planned with Generation X in mind but that it attracted that group because of its appeal to investors who were just starting out.

Not all financial decisions made by young people are sound. Employment Benefit Research Institute found that a full 20 percent of us have not saved a dime. Another poll, by Louis Harris, of 412 men and women aged 20 to 39 found that while 62 percent had bought lottery tickets in the last year, only 30 percent had invested money in stocks, bonds, or mutual funds. Our job is to take the message of savings to all young adults. If more young adults get serious about saving for retirement, the value of their retirement accounts could grow considerably by the time they reach middle age, thus boosting our generation's overall net worth and the country's savings rate. We are already on the right track.

Stocks. Almost 40 percent of householders under age 35 owned stock directly or indirectly through mutual funds and retirement accounts in 1998. That's only 1 percent less than householders overall and greater than the proportion among householders 65 years and over. The median value of stock owned by young adults was $5,400 in 1995, much less than the median for all households, $13,500. The median value of the stock holdings rises with age, peaking at over $28,000 for householders aged 75 and up. Stocks accounted for 32 percent of the total financial assets held by young adults; for all households the figure is 40 percent. The popularity of stocks has soared throughout the stock market boom of the 1990s. To no one's surprise, Xers like high-tech stocks. An American Stock Exchange study showed that those aged 25 to 34 with $30,000 or more in yearly income take more risks on technology stocks than the average investor (*U.S. News & World Report,* October 20, 1997).

Home buying. Purchase of a home is recognized by people of all ages as one of the surest investments to produce and increase real assets. The stability conferred by this major commitment provides impetus for other positive actions such as saving money, improving professionally, and making home and property improvements.

How are we doing with home buying? Studies from the Joint Center for Housing Studies at Harvard University found a precipitous drop in home ownership rates among the young. In 1980, 52 percent of households headed by someone aged 25 to 34 owned their own home. By 1991, the rate had plunged to 43 percent. As a result, the average age of first-time home buyers is now 32, compared with age 29 just ten years ago. Between 1970 and 1980 housing prices rose dramatically. Depending on the index used, the real price of housing rose 19–32 percent in that decade. This increase in housing prices was largely attributable to the aging of the Boomers who have with their accumulated wealth and numbers increased housing demand, according to the economists N. Gregory Mankiw and David N. Weil.

Generation Xers have also been reluctant to enter the housing market because we remember the downturn in real estate values of the late eighties. In addition, we have a different outlook on home buying. Alexander Jutkowitz, a partner with Global Strategy Group, a Manhattan market research firm, says that for Boomers, "owning a house was a dream; for Generation X it's a necessity. . . . It is a little more transactional; they look at the numbers and where they're living now and see if they can do better" owning their own home. Most who have thought about it find it makes more sense to buy. Real estate can provide equity and a tax shelter. As one recent buyer put it, "I saw I could be paying a mortgage with what I pay in rent. By buying I'm not just throwing money out the window. I will actually own something for my money."

As this realization has reached more and more young adults, housing sales have started increasing in the mid-1990s. Young adults purchased 1.53 million existing homes in 1996 compared with 1.32 million in 1991, an increase of nearly 16 percent. In 1996, nearly 40 percent of householders under age 35 owned a home. Over the next twenty years, Generation X will be in its prime house-buying years, but the housing demand may grow slowly because of our lower incomes. Some people say this will be reflected in lower real housing costs. According to Mankiw and Weil, real housing prices may well sink to lower levels than those experienced at any time in the past forty years.

Young married couples are more likely than other types of households to own a home. Home ownership rates rose by more than 2 percent between 1990 and 1996, to 58 percent for couples and also rose for young single adults heading families and for men living alone. Rates among young adults rose the most in the youngest age group, 15 to 24. Behind this rise may be the helping hand of parents who want to give their children a head start. Some are predicting an increase of sales of small houses to meet the requirements of single, older Xers who are looking for more permanent homes and sound investments.

Watch Xers Spend That Cash

Ann Clerman, the coauthor of *Rocking the Ages*, explains our spending like this: "Matures buy something because they feel they've earned it, Boomers because they think they deserve it, and Xers because they're afraid it might not be around if they wait until they can afford it" (*U.S. News & World Report,* October 20, 1997). Bruce Tulgan, author of *Managing Generation X*, takes a different view: "Younger people are not interested in plaques and trinkets. They want something they can use."

We have only 80 percent of the spending power our parents did at our age, but GenXers still spend more than $125 billion on goods yearly—a considerable amount for any age group. Although income levels for this generation are lower than for past generations, GenXers are showing a willingness to spend their money. Sociological factors such as older marrying ages have also contributed to this willingness to commit more money to materialistic pursuits rather than toward house, auto, health care, and kids. According to the 1991 National College Track Survey of Xers in college full time, 86 percent had a car, 41 percent planned to buy a new car within the next two years, 16 percent had a credit card, 70 percent had an ATM card, 55 percent had a telephone card, 63 percent had their own TV, 33 percent had a microwave and VCR, and 25 percent had a computer. That was 1991; just think how much higher those figures are today.

The growth in the Generation X population combined with its spending on big-ticket items like cars, furniture, and homes has helped spark the economy in the mid-1990s. Richard Hokenson, of the brokerage firm Donaldson, Lufkin & Jenrette, estimates that the economic stimulus provided by twenty-somethings is boosting the nation's gross domestic product by nearly a percentage point per year. Hokenson says, "The rise in the number of twenty-five-year-olds has been a major catalyst for the economy. That contribution to economic growth is especially welcome."

Building a Nest

Despite GenXers' waiting longer to get hitched, most people still marry and have children when they are in their twenties. Young adults make up a fourth of all family households and more than 60 percent of households with children under age six. Households headed by people aged 25 to 34 are average earners and spenders, but their spending far exceeds the average in categories relating to children, such as baby-sitting, child care, furniture and household equipment for babies, baby clothes, footwear, and toys and games. Most households in this age group still rent their homes. The new household generally requires a car. Households headed by people aged 25 to 34 spend 14 percent more than average on new and used cars. They also spent more than average on sound components and systems for the house, audio for the auto, and CDs and tapes.

Because they are establishing their own households, they spend more than average on furniture. Xer households accounted for 31 percent of the $45.3 billion in furniture sales in 1996—the same proportion as the more settled Boomers. Young shoppers buy an average of $1,133 worth of furniture per year, versus $899 worth bought by the same generation a decade ago. At the furniture chain Ikea, consumers under age 30 account for more than half of sales, or $474 million.

Housing values soared 25 percent between 1990 and 1995. Of course, this generation's tastes are different. "It still reverberates, how gaudy and horrible the eighties were," says the developer Bruce Mennin, whose company, Crescent Heights, is converting the former skyscraper headquarters of Paine Webber, across from the New York Stock Exchange, to a cooperative apartment building. "Already more than a thousand applicants are [seeking] the 345 units," he says. "Nowadays, there are still those jerks who go out and buy a Ferrari with their bonus checks. But a car is a car. People define themselves now by their home. They see themselves in a spacious, tasteful, fine apartment [decorated] with warm earth tones. It is just a different way to define yourself."

Still, many GenXers choose not to settle down—at least not for some time. During the 1980s and 1990s, about 18 percent of the general population moved in a given year, whereas roughly 33 percent in their twenties did, according to the Census Bureau's current population survey. About 20 percent of GenXers on the move are headed to a new state. Their mobility makes them the best market for furniture and appliance rentals, and they account for two thirds of the market for VCR, radio, and sound equipment rentals. They lead the nation in residential rentals, at 42 percent and also spend more money on Laundromats, dry cleaners, and furniture rentals.

The Cars That Go Boom

"Would I give up sex for six months for a Ferrari? I have had the last six months off from sex and I don't have anything to show for it, so why the hell not?" That's a thirty-something's response to a question in the *Swing* magazine poll (full results: 49 percent would and 49 percent wouldn't, with 2 percent not sure/no answer). Fantasies aside, the auto industry is a major beneficiary of our economic strength. According to a recent survey, 69 percent of GenXers consider buying a sport utility vehicle. Last year, we spent $395 million on Jeep Wranglers, accounting for 38 percent of its sales. And what do we want in a car? The *Swing* poll asked respondents what was the most important factor in choosing the make and model of a car. Xers answered: reliability (42 percent), the look (15 percent), cost (15 percent), safety features (14 percent), and manufacturer name (12 percent).

To woo car-shopping Xers, automakers have retooled their marketing efforts. As children, GenXers were glued to the TV, so marketers believe twenty-something consumers are turned off by excessive TV hype. When Chrysler fashioned its campaign for its new Neon, there were no testimonials from drivers. Instead viewers saw the car and heard voice-overs about its attributes. "We were actual and honest without being cynical," says Chrysler Plymouth's Steven Torok. "We made the car the star." The approach worked. Neon is one of the top five cars in the auto market. In 1994, Xers bought 39 percent of all Neons, spending about $623 million.

Volkswagen seemed to hit the right note with their urban "Drivers wanted" spots, ostensibly geared toward Generation X. These ads are some of the most talked about in the advertising industry. One of the most popular of the ads featured two young guys driving through the city—just cruising to the popular tune "Da Da Da." The ad debuted on ABC's *Ellen*, on the "coming out" episode in April 1997. Within a week, it was being parodied (a sign of its success) by others, including by the ABC sitcom *Spin City*. Volkswagen is trying to position itself to reflect the literal meaning of its name: "people's car." Volkswagens are not the fastest nor most expensive cars on the road, but they offer utility, they are reliable, and they are well made. Young adults respond to this. Sales figures in 1996 were the company's best since 1990.

You Look Faaabulous!

Twenty-somethings spend a lot of time and money on clothes. About 6.1 percent of Generation X expenditures go for apparel, compared with the national average of 5.5 percent. Urban Outfitters, a Philadelphia-based apparel retailer that targets Generation X consumers, recorded a sales increase of 42 percent in 1996, almost ten times the industry average. According to the International Council of Shopping Centers, 18-to-24-year-olds shopped more often in malls than other groups—an average of seven visits per month. That's at least one more visit than Boomers made. The average number of visits for all age groups was five per month. Eighty-three percent of these young adults' shopping trips are to full-fledged enclosed malls, as opposed to shopping strip centers, and only 19 percent preferred traditional downtown shops. There are 31,500 shopping centers across the country, of which 2,500 are enclosed malls, according to the Gallup survey. GenXers like to shop, and more than half describe their shopping trips as recreation, unlike Boomers, who must shop for their children as well as themselves. Xers, most of whom are still unmarried, often shop by themselves.

The five-year-old million-dollar-plus active-wear company No Fear may be a quintessential GenX marketer. Its TV commercial on the 1995 Super Bowl didn't even mention what the company sells. No Fear, which splashes impudent slogans like NO CURE FOR DEATH and HOODLUM on its apparel, denies making any specifically generational appeal. "We don't even allow that word, 'Generation X,' to enter our building," says Jim Hancock, the marketing director of the privately held Carlsbad, California, company. "We tend to market to people's lifestyles—those attracted to the psychological challenge of sports. They could be fourteen or fifty, but most sales are to Xers and Boomers." The company has meticulously crafted its mystique through intensive research and methodical niche marketing on billboards and enthusiastic magazines for surfing, cycling, and motor and bike racing.

Working Out

Looking fit is easy for those of us in our late teens, twenties, and early thirties even if we don't work out at a gym or at a fitness club three or four times a week. We simply enjoy the glow of youth. In fact, health club operators report that it's the Baby Boomers who use health clubs to work on their bodies. GenXers often use the facilities just to have a good time. *Swing*'s poll asked Xers whether they would still work out if they didn't have to worry about their weight. Sixty-nine percent said yes.

Douglas Levine, of Crunch! fitness centers in New York and Los Angeles, says the centers are really competing with entertainment such as nightclubs, movie theaters, and even the Internet. So they have to provide an entertainment and social environment as well as a place to get in shape. To lure Xers, Levine's clubs have added elements such as aerobics classes led by a transvestite, a gospel choir brought in for dancing class, and aerobics combined with collegiate-style wrestling training. Crunch! has three to five new programs a year, Levine says. Similarly, the Zoo Health Club in Fort Lauderdale, which is located by the ocean, has its exercise biking equipment on the roof so bikers can get an ocean view and tan at the same time.

In short, Xers don't exercise the same way as their Boomer parents. GenXers, most say, want to look better, not necessarily feel better, and they want to have a good time. We are a terrifically active generation, as evidenced by the amount of money we spend on equipment for golf, tennis, jogging, sailing, skiing, skating, equestrian pursuits, bicycling, swimming, and just plain walking.

Almost two thirds of teens are involved in some kind of sport activity, but this figure drops off sharply after high school. Some of the decline is due to lack of opportunity available to young adults. Of course there's a time factor, as young adults are involved in the working world. *Swing* magazine reported that two of five 18-to-24-year-olds regularly participate in sports or fitness activities. The total drops slightly to 36 percent in the 25-to-34-year-old group. People 25 to 34 are beginning to slow down a bit. And preferences change with age. They're only half as likely as the average to play basketball, but still more likely than the average to participate in aerobics. As they get older, they add golf to their sports repertory, a slower game more associated with business activities.

More than half of those who participate in regular and low-impact aerobics are aged 18 to 34. They are also more likely to run or jog and play basketball, beach volleyball, and fast-pitch softball. They are nearly twice as likely as the average American to downhill ski. About 77 percent are more likely to play tennis.

Food, Drink, and Stomach Pumps

When it comes to eating and drinking, Generation X quickly outdistances other generations. Our solid/liquid consumption habits aren't always what the doctors and health experts recommend. What can I say? We're young.

GenXers exist on a vast array of fast foods ranging from hamburgers to tacos to pizza. We admit we formed these habits in high school and even before that, when working parents were unable to put full-course meals on the table every night. Young adults, especially those 18 to 29, are less likely than the average American to work at maintaining a healthy diet. According to the Center for Science in the Public Interest, only 65 percent of people 18 to 29 say they usually eat a healthful diet compared with 79 percent of all adults. People in their thirties are more health-conscious than those in their twenties, with 77 percent eating a healthful diet. Adults under age thirty are also less likely than the average to worry about the fat and cholesterol content of their foods. Younger people are less likely to choose whole-grain over white flour. For sure we are less likely to skip our favorite foods in favor of healthier ones.

"The one thing that is distinctly different about Generation X is that it eats more fast food than any other age group," said Carol Blindauer, the manager of Kraft Creative Kitchens in Glenview, Illinois. Kraft's network of kitchens has been meticulously tracking food trends for the last few years in a study called Foodcast. The eating style of Generation X makes up a fascinating chunk of its latest report. The snarfing of burgers and fries might seem odd for a group that is perfectly comfortable with vegetarian food. Not so strange, said Blindauer. "The interest in vegetarianism is based on many different drives," she said. "Some have to do with health, but some of it is convenience; it can be more convenient to cook something without meat, and in some cases, it's just because they like that particular food."

In general, nutrition is not a strong concern with this group, she said. "They're young, they're invincible, they haven't had any health problems." Pizza is revered. In fact, it is the number one cafeteria food choice among students of all ages, said Blindauer. "Make-your-own" bars for pasta, baked potatoes, hot dogs, etc., are a huge hit on college campuses. More intensity of flavor and spices defines the flavor preferences of this group. "This is primarily because of their broader exposure to ethnic cuisine," Blindauer said, "and America in general is using more spices."

Xers are on the go. "They eat a lot on the run. We know a lot of people who eat their breakfast over the bathroom sink or in the car. This is every day," says Blindauer. Forget that cup of coffee their parents or grandparents required to start their day. This is the water-tea-juice-soda crowd, with the possible addition of smoothies, those yogurt-based shakes and drinks. Specialty coffees and teas make their mark in the coffeehouse movement. "But in general, this is a group that will have a soda for breakfast."

GenXers also follow nontraditional mealtimes, said Blindauer, referring to this phenomenon as "meal blur." The older generation had lunch at noon and dinner at six. For this bunch, the slogan could be "Anytime, anywhere. They may have a main meal in the middle of the day, and then popcorn or noodles when they get home at night." Eventually this changes. "Once people have children, there is strong interest in having the bonding and family time around the table," she said. "The meal is simpler, less effort goes into it [than for older generations], but regardless of the age group, there is always that interest in sharing family meals."

Encouraging news, but what about home cooking? Is Generation X the test group for whether this life skill will thrive in the next millennium? Blindauer answers. "What you grow up with is what you know," she said. "This generation grew up with more options, so they are definitely less connected to making homemade meals. They had some homemade meals, some takeout, some in a restaurant, and some meals made in the microwave. It's very clear that Generation X doesn't know how to cook like the older Boomers, and the older Boomers don't know how to cook like the mature market."

One reason, we know, is that the primary teachers of home cooking, parents, are too busy earning a living. Fifty-seven percent of us had working mothers. On the other hand, that also meant that we learned how to cook for ourselves. A survey sponsored by Reynolds Corporation found that 17 percent of GenXers learned how to cook before the age of 12. By age 17, 63 percent had started to cook. Those who didn't learn to cook at home find other avenues, including TV cooking shows and the Internet. "Though I do believe this group will not learn how to cook the way Grandma did, they will learn how to put a meal on the table using the strategies they need," Blindauer said. One thing that hasn't changed is that women still do the majority of cooking in the household. Seventy-four percent of young women who work outside the home still cook for their families. However, 40 percent say they get at least some help from family members—most often their husbands.

Hard Liquor, Light Market

Generation X may be recreating the marketing of liquors. For instance, marketers say they are catering to tighter budgets by bringing out single-serve portions. In many regions, for example, Hiram Walker sells a four-pack of Kahlúa for about the price of a six-pack of premium beer.

Given the generally harsh taste of distilled spirits, though, image isn't everything. To deal with taste, marketers are bringing out fruit-flavored spirits and developing lighter-tasting mixed drinks. For example, Seagram & Sons is marketing Absolut vodka in citrus and currant flavors and has had success with its Captain Morgan's spiced rum. At bar parties, Dewar's works up such concoctions as scotch margaritas, and Tanqueray gin mixes up cranberry sours. And we like our beer; we spent 26 percent more than the average household on beer for home consumption and 52 percent more for beer consumed away from home.

Pop Goes the Soda

Generation X is putting a "rush" on the soft drink market like no previous generation. Householders under 25 spent far less than average on coffee and tea, preferring instead colas and other carbonated beverages.

Ian Murphy of the American Marketing Association describes marketers' reaction to the new market segment: "Beverage marketers are putting more pep into pop and more 'spring' into spring water, and they're adding a jump start to juice. The devil didn't make them do it—Generation X did."

Large and small, soft-drink marketers see a bright future in bottling products enriched with caffeine and other stimulants—and selling them for their energy-enhancing properties. The drinks "satisfy the needs of a demanding lifestyle," said C. J. Rapp, the president of the Rochester, New York–based Global Beverages; its Wet Planet division markets Jolt Cola, caffeinated spring water called K_2O, and herbal "elixir" XTC. "The world has become more complex and demanding, so there is a greater need for drinks that provide stimulation."

As if you didn't know. The most popular and accepted stimulant of the plugged-in information age is caffeine. "Caffeine is the country's drug of choice," said Tom Pirko, president of Bev-Mark LLC, a New York–based industry consultant. "It isn't seen as a gross evil anymore. With young kids drinking caffeinated soft drinks and designer cappuccinos, it wasn't a big step from there to caffeinated juices."

Jolt was the first drink to capitalize on caffeine, when Rapp introduced it in 1985, at a time most marketers were draining sodas of sugar, caffeine, and color. At 71.2 milligrams of mild stimulant per twelve-ounce can, it was just shy of the FDA-mandated limit on caffeine content for soft drinks, according to the National Soft Drink Association, an industry organization in Washington, D.C. With the help of a cult of computer programmers, students, and other regular buyers, Jolt became a moderate success and marketplace fixture. But few soft-drink marketers succeeded in pitching pops as pick-me-ups, despite Starbucks outlets' offering high-test lattes from every corner, and lessening health concerns about caffeine use. PepsiCo's morning beverage Pepsi A.M., sank, despite the popularity of Mountain Dew and Diet Coke as de facto caffeine-delivery vehicles. Even today, Coca-Cola denies that Surge, its answer to Mountain Dew, relies on caffeine as a selling point, despite the product's name and its "Feed the rush" slogan.

Niche marketers haven't been as shy about placing the wake-up call. Water Concepts LLC of Lake Barrington, Illinois, created an instant buzz among fans and the industry last year when it fortified a plain spring water with caffeine, marketing it as Water Joe. The brand quickly defined what Pirko called a new "hot spot" in the marketplace. In less than a year, Water Joe spawned a spate of similar products, including Global's K_2O; $Edge_2O$, from Beverage Alternatives, Fort Lee, New Jersey; and Aqua Java, marketed by RJ Groux of Santa Ana, California.

The frenzy to add caffeine accelerated when caffeinated water marketers found that buyers—typically, students, athletes, and people who just don't like the taste of coffee, according to RJ Groux president Bob Groux—often used the product to mix orange juice from concentrate. A new wave of ready-to-drink caffeinated juice products is the result. RJ Groux was first out of the gate with Java Juice, marketing it in California markets in March 1997 with the tags "Not your mama's juice" and "Juice with a boost." Beverage Alternative's $Edge_2O$ and West End's X-treem Caffeine line aren't far behind. Java Juice will target "anybody with a tongue," Groux said. "Younger audiences want to be stimulated," Bev-Mark's Pirko said. "And the more you want to be stimulated, the more you want a drink that supercharges."

The name Surge is appropriate for Coca-Cola's latest entry into the $31 billion soft-drink market. That's because the beverage aims to compete with rival Mountain Dew's dominance in the carbonated citrus soft-drink arena. For years, the Atlanta-based beverage giant Coke has searched, albeit unsuccessfully, for a way to combat Pepsi-Co's Generation X marketing of Mountain Dew with the "Been there, done that" slogan and spokesmen like André Agassi. Mountain Dew is the only Top 10 soft drink to grow at a double-digit clip at least three years in a row through 1996, its sales of more than $3 billion being roughly 60 percent of the so-called heavy citrus soft-drink category. Other citrus drinks like Sprite and 7-Up have fewer calories and thus are not included in the "heavy" drink category.

In the past, Big Red pushed Mello Yello on the same young crowd. A 1994 Mello Yello campaign commanded, "Make some noise," but a NASCAR tie-in and new hip-looking graphics didn't. A more recent slogan has been "Let it out." Mello Yello sales are about $300 million.

"Surge is one more ingredient in our recipe for capturing the growth in the industry," said Jack Stahl, president of Coca-Cola's domestic operations. Coke wants to control half the U.S. soft-drink market by the turn of the century. Now, it's at nearly 42 percent. A soft-drink industry analyst at Robinson-Humphrey, David Goldman, estimated that Coca-Cola would spend $60 million on Surge's rollout in 1997, mainly on ads. That's more than the company spent advertising Sprite, its fast-growing lemon-lime drink, in all of 1995. By comparison, PepsiCo spent $27.5 million advertising Mountain Dew for the first nine months of the year, according to Competitive Media Reporting. Coca-Cola spent $1.4 million on Mello Yello.

Like Mountain Dew, Surge targets the 12-to-34 age group. With extra carbohydrates, Surge is also marketed as a sport drink; Gatorade now dominates the category, said Goldman. Coca-Cola's sport drink, Powerade, owns 10 percent of the market. Mountain Dew also targets sports-oriented consumers. Success isn't guaranteed. Coca-Cola's OK Soda, another carbonated soft drink targeting a young audience, never made it out of test markets. Fruitopia, a line of fruit and tea drinks introduced in 1994, has had mild success. Tab Clear and Nordic Mist, both introduced in 1992, also flopped.

One company that targets young taste makers, Vancouver, Washington–based Jones Soda, warns against selling product on the basis of caffeine content. Although many Jones flavors contain Mountain Dew levels of caffeine (about 54 milligrams a serving), they don't exploit it, says Rob Wells, vice president of marketing.

"Mainstream America wants to target this group, Generation X, so they use alternative sports and music as tools, and they say, let's put 'extreme' or 'maximum' caffeine in this product," he said. "But Generation X, for lack of a better term, supports companies who support them. If you're just trying to market to them, it's not going to work." Instead, the company puts its products in skate shops and tattoo parlors, where teens and young adults spend time.

Vote for Generation X

Generation X is a $200 billion-plus spending market that is growing. The soft-drink industry is an example of how manufacturers woo us unashamedly. They understand our tremendous economic power. They have a major stake in our generation.

Simply put, we vote with our dollars and dictate the terms concerning many, many products and services in modern America. Many industries are jumping on the bandwagon. Fast-forward to the next chapter for just how they are targeting us.

CHAPTER 10

A Bull's-eye Marked X

Changing the Face of Marketing

It used to be that people needed products to survive. Now prod-
ucts need people to survive.
—Nicholas Johnson, Center on Budget and Policy Priorities,
Washington, D.C.

It is hard to market to a generation that you can't focus in on long enough to hit the bull's-eye. Collectively, the marketers can't hit the bull's-eye. Their sharpshooters hit the perimeters a lot. Sometimes they miss the target. That's how the game is played when marketing's best minds try to figure out what sells to Generation X. You ask, what's to figure out about those lazy slackers? Before going into the ingenious methodology of marketers, I'll let some GenXers put up the targets.

"We all are more willing to take risks."
—Rachel Bell of JobDirect

"GenXers are thought of as cynical, nonconformist nonjoiners, as people who tend to want to stand out from the crowd. That's true."
—Steven Rosenbaum of Broadcast News Network

"We are an extremely motivated and concerned group of people who are doing a lot to make the world a better place."

　　　　　　　　　　　　　　　　　　　—Erin Potts of Milarepa

"I think that it is true that we are cynical, aloof, and detached from our nation in a significant way."

　　　　　　　　　　　　　　　—Heather Lamm, political activist

"We are skeptical but hopeful. I don't feel a culture of cynicism."

　　　　—Jason Brown, a Stegner Fellow at Stanford University

"The soul of GenX is amorphous. That's why I like the term X. Fill in the blanks."　　　　　　　—Richard Thau of Third Millennium

"If there is a defining characteristic of our generation, it is the rejection of the notion of a defining characteristic."

　　　　　　　　　　　　　　　—John Karl, CNN correspondent

Let's see, that's seven folks with seven different descriptions. I could go for seventy different answers and not scratch the surface. You get the point. But marketing people? They are optimists by nature. They make fortunes by hitting the perimeters. Not satisfied, they keep trying for a bull's-eye. Wow, do they keep trying.

Some Misconceptions About Us

The stereotype of Generation X as lazy, clueless, underemployed, living in their parents' basements isn't a good inspiration for advertisers and marketers. A *TV Guide*-MTV poll concluded that GenXers may profess to be fun-loving, but they're also conservative and cautious with their money: "They aren't the people you saw in movies like *Singles* and *Reality Bites* or read about in books like Douglas Coupland's *Generation X*. They are a maddeningly heterogeneous group full of contradictions and surprises." Ironically, Generation X is one of the best-educated and hardest-working generations in American history. Bureau of Labor Statistics data clearly document that a higher percentage of the young are earning degrees at all levels than before. Other statistics show that GenXers work longer hours than previous generations and are serious about saving and investing.

Broadly branded as pessimistic slackers with a bleak financial future in an economy marked by corporate downsizing, GenXers are perhaps the most misunderstood consumers in the marketplace. "Many retailers make the mistake of treating Generation X shoppers as if they don't have money to spend," says Karen Ritchie, the author of *Marketing to Generation X* who also oversees the purchasing of all General Motors broadcast and print advertising. She says GenXers are "generally well educated, and many have a substantial stash of cash, if only because many live with their parents until their late twenties and delay starting their own families."

According to some estimates the average GenXer sees over a hundred advertising images a day and has watched more than 160 days' worth of television advertising by his or her twenty-fifth birthday. Dealing with this advertising-saturated market can be tricky. Exposure to pop culture has provided Generation X with more than just the media savvy to avoid being influenced by advertising. For instance, Jerry Hirshberg, the president of Nissan's Design International told *Advertising Age* (April 1, 1996) that, unlike with Baby Boomers, sexiness isn't enough to sell a car to Generation X, because "this far more conservative group is looking for value, more subdued expressions, and more practicality" in its purchases. Eric Liu, founder of the *Next Progressive Quarterly*, draws a corollary for the publishing industry: "Flashy graphics and snappy stories won't necessarily work. A lot of young people would rather just have intelligently written pieces."

Our generation doesn't hand over hard-earned cash to just anyone. GenXers are practical, value-oriented, and risk-averse. "Our generation is the most educated one in history," says *Get a Financial Life* author Beth Kobliner. "And for all the talk about how consumerist we've become, we're pretty smart consumers. We don't fall for hype, at least for long, and we have good radars to weed out what's real from what isn't."

Perhaps the toughest thing about Generation X is that it is difficult to talk to us as "one group." According to an MTV survey, less than 10 percent of Generation X are willing to recognize that Generation X even exists. David Watkins, a 26-year-old VP of the urban marketing company Dastreetz, reports, "If anything, we should be called the hip-hop generation. We are a generation that buys eight hundred dollars worth of alternative music records each year, has gotten into snowboarding and skiing, likes earth-tone packaging, and has created a hip-hop fashion industry that has gone off the charts." Of course, there are other views. Some want to call us "generation green" for our love of environmentalism or "computer babies" for our high-tech skills.

Unlike previous generations, Xers don't have clear defining historical moments, so companies who are wooing them have trouble finding the handles. But representatives of the advertising agency Saatchi & Saatchi say they "have a handle" because they have broken the generation down into segments. The agency conducted an intensive study of the generation in which they employed teams of psychologists and cultural anthropologists. The research produced four key segments: (1) "cynical distillers," the most pessimistic and skeptical and the group that has got the most press; (2) "traditional materialists," those most like the Boomers—positive, optimistic, striving for the American Dream; (3) "hippies revisited," who replay the lifestyle and values of the sixties and express themselves through music, fashion, and spirituality; and (4) "fifties-machos," the young Gingrich Republicans who still believe in stereotypical gender roles and are the least accepting of multiculturalism.

So does generational marketing work? Peter Kim, vice chairman of the ad agency McCann-Erickson, says, "Most companies are still organized around a mass-marketing concept. Very few people in research and marketing departments even understand the concept of cohorts or generations." Some argue that generational marketing won't work. Many say it's ineffective to divvy up a market according to age. Ross E. Goldstein, a consultant at Tome and Kenney, in San Francisco, says, "It used to be that when you knew someone's age you knew a lot about him because the population went through life stages like marriage and having children at fairly predictable times. Not anymore. My older brother is fifty-two and has a one-year-old daughter." However, more and more companies are willing to give it a try anyway. Generational marketing as a strategy is supposed to reach consumers by taking advantage of the important external events that occurred during the generations' formative years.

Most companies are choosing to market this way. *Fortune* reports, "Because age is the universal currency in the high-stakes world of advertising and media, it is how rating services like Nielsen, Arbitron, and Roper Starch categorize the viewers and listeners and readers they count." So when marketers spend their dollars for television spots, the orders go out to place them on shows appealing to males 18–49, or women 25–54. Steve Goldstein, the head of marketing of Levi's men's jeans at Levi Strauss, says a good way to do generational marketing is to understand the values of the generation you are targeting.

Tactics Used to Woo Us

Marketers' techniques are fascinating. They're original, sometimes good, sometimes bad, sometimes out in left field, and at times even corny. They are hardly ever boring. Take a look for yourself at how the marketers try to zero in on Generation X.

Competitive generationalism. These are not your parents' advertisements—or so GenXers are told over and over (and over) again. Advertisers targeting GenXers seem almost in pain over their desire to share their acknowledgment of the legitimacy of Generation X.

It's an ironic idea, considering the fact that the majority of GenXers disdain the label and abhor the slacker stereotypes associated with it. So how do they try to give us legitimacy? They allude to our distaste for the current state of societal affairs, pitting us against the Boomers. It is evident in Kool's "Now it's our turn" ads—since previous generations screwed everything up. Or how about Beefeater's "Generations will come and go. Some will just be a hell of a lot cooler than others." Or Camaro: "If everyone owned one, maybe we could have prevented disco." And then there is the "This is not your parents' hangout" image. Many of the friends we see in group-themed ads represent a variety of ethnic backgrounds appealing to our greater diversity. This is particularly true in CKOne promotions, Tommy Hilfiger ads, and the famed Benetton commercials.

Ever edgier.   Weary of white-bread suburban upbringings, many GenXers seem to respond to urban, hip, and progressively dangerous images of a post-Reagan, postcocaine cityscape. This is GenX as the chemical generation, a part of the Prozac nation welcome to the mind-altering effects of antidepression drugs while also becoming more open to nonprescription "street" drugs (Ecstasy, Special K, and of course, heroin).

Although some of the modeling world's icons of beauty have recently begun to reflect a more athletic image, the superstars of the industry spent much of the nineties doing their best to look like heroin junkies—which, according to some insiders, was more an extension of reality than an acting job. The waif look incorporated the painfully thin frame, empty eyes, and dirty, scraggly hair of heroin shooters into advertising campaigns offered by such mainstream institutions as the Gap and Calvin Klein. When not flirting with drug addiction, advertisers devoted an interesting amount of attention to the younger female body, as seen in the Guess "Lolita" ads and the famously denounced Calvin Klein "kiddie porn" promotion. Danger was courted with an eye to marketing.

As noted, however, images of beauty are changing to include a wider variety of body types. The most notable is in Calvin Klein's

Photo Courtesy of Mark Finkenstaedt

DAVID LAUREN
Editor-in-chief and founder, **Swing**

GENX GURU, EDITOR-IN-CHIEF

David Lauren, the son of designer Ralph Lauren, is making his own way with *Swing*, "the magazine for people in their twenties." After graduating from Duke, Lauren began the magazine as a venture that sought to fill a void—news for young adults. "The current media doesn't address the issues that are important to us. There are niche magazines that appeal to our specific interests, but not magazines that appeal to us as a generation." Why *Swing*? Because, he says, "we are the 'swing' generation, a generation capable of making great changes in this country."

1997 jeans campaign, featuring relatively robust models hawking the kinds of jeans that only rail-thin models would have been seen wearing in the past.

Slacker/philosophical. In an apparent effort to cash in on one of the more pervasive GenX stereotypes—the disaffected slacker, the unemployed philosophy major sitting in a San Francisco coffee house reading Jean Genet—advertisers seem to enjoy presenting ads that address either GenXers' love of recreational time or their need to question the "meaning" of life. Advertisers are aware that many GenXers are apprehensive or simply unwilling when it comes to dedicating as much energy to their jobs or careers as their parents. We see that reflected in ads such as that for the Chevrolet Cavalier: "Funny how much free time costs these days." A generation's indecisiveness seems especially apparent in campaigns geared specifically to college students, such as MasterCard's "Where do you want to go?" ad.

Extremism.   *Extreme, optimal, ultimate*—such superlatives are sprinkled literally throughout GenX-based advertising. Even as staid and proper a product as a fabric cleaner can work in this theme. In a print ad, Woolite advertisers promise consumers "optimal maintenance." ESPN2, the three-and-a-half-year-old ESPN spinoff geared specifically to the 18-to-34 age set, spotlights yearly Extreme Games, which feature a collection of progressively wild sports that has come to include bungee jumping, snowboarding, and the luge. Apparently, GenXers have yet to become desensitized to the number of products that all proclaim themselves to be the best, the edgiest, the most extreme. The more dangerous the better—to the point where even a video game company (2 X TREME) warns players that it refuses to "take responsibility" for any injuries occurring during its use.

Independence.   "Even advertisers have recognized the younger generation's self-reliance," writes journalist Mark Johnson of Media General News Service. "Prudential altered its slogan from 'Get a piece of the rock' to 'Be your own rock.' An ad for the Honda Accord says little about the car and, instead, uses the vehicle as an example of maintaining control of your own life."

Offbeat.   There's a certain connoisseurship in the appreciation of advertising among GenXers. It crops up in our reactions to contemporary advertisements. There's no other way to explain the cult status achieved by Mentos Freshmakers commercials. As a *Hartford Cour-ant* reporter said, "The ads are so bad that they're good." Specifically, they're so hypnotically amateurish, so clearly European and laugh-ably detached from the American culture, that Xers love them. The popular Seattle grunge band the Foo Fighters even pays homage to the campaign in one of its videos.

Another set of notable ads were produced for Levi's wide-leg jeans. Robin Givhan of the *Washington Post* describes the offbeat commercial: The commercial begins with a poor battered guy stretched out on a gurney being wheeled into an emergency room. His body is bandaged. His bloodied eyes are ringed by huge purple bruises. He is on the edge, barely hanging on. The emergency-room staff gathers around to survey his injuries as a heart monitor beep, beep, beeps in the background. The patient stares anxiously upward. Slowly, the trauma team, dressed in faded aqua scrubs, begins a le-thargic, off-key rendition of Soft Cell's fabulously synthesized "Tainted Love." The heart monitor keeps time. If *ER* were a music video, this would be it.

The idea is to grab the attention of a youthful market that is over-whelmingly blasé about television and advertising. "Youth are desen-sitized to what adults are sensitized to," says creative director Chuck McBride of Foote, Cone, Belding advertising, which produced the wide-leg ad. "If everything is farce, how farce can you go? With the Calvins of the world doing what they're doing, you almost have to stay comfortably close to that edge; otherwise you're a wimp. You look like you're selling clothes for old people," McBride says.

The "Tainted Love" spot, titled "Doctors," was directed by the video auteur Spike Jonze, who found MTV fame with an award-winning video for the band Weezer. Jonze's basic approach to the ad was to "make it like something I like, to not treat it like a commer-cial." Which is one reason the jeans get scant airtime. Before the three-day Los Angeles shoot, some Levi Strauss executives worried that the product was being given short shrift. They also worried that the "patient" actually dies, if only momentarily, while wearing their pants. "But the commercial isn't so much about seeing the pants,"

Jonze says. "Its about what could happen when you're wearing the pants. We shot some pant shots, but once we started to edit, they saw that what was best about the commercial were not these jump-out-at-you product shots."

The ad's strength is its bizarreness, the way it stands out from everything that surrounds it. That strong personality works when the target audience is relatively minuscule, as it is here: men and women 20 to 24, says a Levi's spokeswoman. The campaign, which includes other spots titled "Elevator" and "Skyscraper," is supposed to be about "wide-open" possibilities.

Amstel Corporation is trying for the same kind of shock value. Passersby in the Times Square area of New York City are scratching their heads these days when they look up at billboards directing them to KEEP 42ND STREET PURE and WAKE UP! The billboards, supposedly paid for by a public watchdog group called Americans for Disciplined Behavior, direct onlookers to resist the temptation to try Amstel beers. The billboards, on Forty-second Street between Seventh and Eighth avenues, are interspersed among billboards for Amstel. The signs are part of a humorous new Amstel campaign poking fun at the serious nature of so-called morality watchdogs. Getting onlookers to scratch their heads is just the point, as it has been with other campaigns of this type that seek to portray products as forbidden fruit by inventing opponents who rail against them. The purportedly anti-Amstel billboards were part of a $20 million campaign to promote two new Amstel beers, Amstel Bier and Amstel 1870 Pilsner.

Labels. Generation X is swooning for designer gear with name-brand cachet. The new status dressing is T-shirts, baseball caps, sweatshirts, and jeans—no news here—but this time around, they'd better show a label. Some of the biggest monikers of the moment among teens and twenty-somethings are Calvin Klein, Mossimo, Ralph Lauren, and Tommy Hilfiger. Logos, last seen as the badge of eighties-style conspicuous consumerism, are rampant in the 1990s. Everyone from hip-hop groups to kids on the street is sporting designer tags. "It's a fashion statement," says one teenager. "I guess I just like it. I'm not going to wear a crummy shirt. If I could, I'd have everything Polo." T. J. Kosick, 17, would likewise indulge his passion for logo'd fashion if he could. "I have a Mossimo baseball cap and skateboarding shoes that say Mossimo," says Kosick, appropriately decked out in a shirt from the designer. "We used to wear a lot of Mossimo shirts in Indiana before I moved here. Once I get a job, I'll get more."

To be successful today, many fashion ads try to appeal to the consumer by glorifying a lifestyle. Perhaps that's why the images Calvin Klein's ads conjure up may be more compelling than the perfumes or clothes they are touting. In black and white, often with scantily clad youth in candid poses, they scream attitude. It's evocative. And often provocative. That was the strategy behind the newest Calvin Klein fragrance, "cK be," created for men and women. "Be single. Be plural. Just be," the ads for Klein's eighth fragrance say. Or, "To be. Or not to be. Just be." And it seems to be working. One teenager says, "Just about everyone [I know] wears Calvin Klein. The people I hang out with wear Calvin Klein at last once a week. At school, on a daily basis you see it everywhere, on both guys and girls."

Friends as family and the defining social unit.   GenXers have seen enough divorce and family strife to look for support and affection in a different social structure—the kind of circle of friends depicted in such programs as (duh) *Friends* and immortalized in photo spreads for Benetton. Whether the groups appears to be a set of white careerists (the former) or a diverse assortment of East Villagers (the latter), advertisers continually reinforce the notion of friends as a package with all the benefits of a family and without the messy custody suits.

Serialization.   GenXers who were denied the serialization of their lives—uprooted from weekend to weekend by divorced parents, for example—looked for continuity in other sources. We can see serialization in everything from the latest episode of *ER* to the newest installment of Dewar's panels illustrating the trials and tribulations of everyday postcollegiate life. As twenty-four-year-old Jennifer Marvel put it, "When you couldn't count on your own family there were always television families—like the Brady Bunch—to provide consistency."

New media. It isn't just our outlook that's different. GenXers get their information from different media than other consumers. Young adults represent only 7 percent of total newspaper readership, turning instead to radio, TV (especially cable like MTV and Fox), and magazines geared toward them, such as *Spin, Vibe,* and *Mademoiselle.*

The Internet offers a host of advertising possibilities. Although critics say the Web has failed to exert the commercial influence expected, Net-based advertising has provided companies with another method of communication. Company home pages have become almost fashionable for GenX-based companies, which count on GenXers' Net savvy for effect. Advertisers see ways to encourage readers to interact with the product image on company Web sites. Macintosh does a promotion offering readers a space to fill in a line requesting "your dream." This asks readers to think how they would respond to a particular question. Gatorade asks readers to complete the statement "Life is ―――.'' Furthermore, maintaining Web-based advertising and a corporate home page—the more shockwaved the better—reinforces the idea that Web-literate GenXers are experiencing something unavailable to their less computer friendly parents.

Diversity. Generation X is more diverse—ethnically, culturally, and economically—than any earlier generation. Today 25 percent of 10-to-30-year-olds are nonwhite. With immigration, that percentage will grow, and by 2020, non-Hispanic whites will make up only 64 percent of the population. While U.S. population growth slows, growth rates for all minority groups are higher than the average. During the 1980s, the nation's population grew 10 percent, but the non-Hispanic white population grew only 4 percent. By contrast, the African-American population increased 13 percent, to 30 million.

Hispanics increased 53 percent, to 22.3 million, and Asians 8 percent, to 7.3 million.

By virtue of our increasing black, Hispanic, and Asian populations, we've become more inclined to talk about our differences. Under the banner of multiculturalism, companies like Tommy Hilfiger, Calvin Klein, and Ikea have used ethnicity in their advertisements. This newfound respect for diversity has made a person's origin much more worthy to the whole of society. The demographic marketing analyst Peter Doherty told *Nations Business* in a July 1992 article "that minority consumers want to see representation of their people in the ad message. When you are trying to send a message to, say, a Cuban consumer in Miami, don't have a generic Hispanic that Cubans cannot relate to." Some marketing efforts to minorities include:

- Michael Ghafouri in 1989 launched Kayla Beverly Hills, a cosmetics firm that creates makeup and lipsticks specifically for skin tones and textures of Asian-American women. In less than two years his annual sales hit $8 million.

- Gulf Atlantic Insurance Company, the first Hispanic-owned insurance company, was launched in 1991. Its strategic advantage is selling policies to Hispanics through a Spanish-speaking sales force, and its ads in Spanish feature prominent Hispanics and are run in Hispanic media.

- Revlon and other major cosmetics firms now market products reformulated for the skin tones and textures of African-American, Hispanic, and Asian women.

- FritoLay, the potato chip giant, has introduced Platanitos, which are aimed at a growing Hispanic population.

- Gerber products has expanded its baby-food offerings to include a line aimed at Hispanics, made from tropical fruits.

Listening to our causes. For young adults, environmental issues are almost as important as economic ones. According to the Sierra

Club a plurality of adults (except those aged 55 to 64) say they would pay higher prices to protect the environment. People aged 18 to 24 are more likely than older age groups to say they would pay higher taxes and prices. Under 40 percent of those aged 18 to 34 feel that Americans worry too much about the environment and not enough about prices and jobs. McDonald's has capitalized on the issue by switching from Styrofoam to paper, and the company now puts pamphlets in their outlets about how they help the environment.

American Express pioneered cause marketing in the early 1980s, when it raised $1.7 million to restore the Statue of Liberty. Since then, cause marketing has been embraced by the likes of Ben & Jerry's, Kimberly-Clark, Coca-Cola, Target, Home Depot, Avon, and toothpaste maker Tom's of Maine.

Taco Bell put together such a promotion targeting the musical tastes of young adults. Customers who purchased any Taco Bell food or beverage could buy a ten-song compilation of chart-topping hits called *Do Something* for $4.99. The recording was developed in conjunction with the Do Something organization, a national nonprofit group that encourages people under the age of 30 to take problem-solving action in their communities. A share of the profits was donated to Do Something.

Marketers use event sponsorships to enhance their image and show how they fit into the Generation X lifestyle. Carillon Importers' Stolichnaya has backed skiing and snowboarding competitions. Dewar's hosts monthly acid jazz concerts in New York. Tanqueray has sponsored an AIDS bike-a-thon in Los Angeles and other cities. Tanqueray "got enormous emotional mileage" from that summer event, which generated a buzz in bars, said the brand manager, Deborah Callahan. "Whether it translates into sales mileage, we don't yet know. Attitudes come first and volume comes second."

High on tech, low on time. The Dime Savings Bank, a $20 billion institution serving the New York metropolitan area, initiated a program called "access checking." The program is aimed at attracting

GenXers who place a high value on their time and favor the ease and convenience of automated services. The program waives all fees, including minimum balance requirements and ATM charges, for one year, as long as the customer uses alternative distribution systems, ATMs, and telephone voice-response units. Customers may use live tellers when needed. Free telephone cards were offered as sign-up incentives. "This is an attractive account for Generation X because this segment tends to be more in tune with [technology]," says David Totaro, Dime's executive vice president and chief marketing officer. Since the program started, balances have increased 21 percent and the number of accounts has tripled. The Dime has expanded to offering other products for Generation X, like mortgage loans. "We know that Generation X is a very loyal customer base. Wherever they hold their first line of credit, whether it be a credit card or an auto loan, they typically remain at that institution for a long time."

Time is of the essence. Don't expect Xers to tolerate shipping delays. "They know that if they need a new shirt, they can go to the mall and get a shirt," said David Morrison, the president of the Collegiate Marketing Company. The Chevy Chase Bank of Maryland is trying to lure young adults with added technology like home PC banking, which offers banking services via the customer's personal computer. The People's Bank of Bridgeport, Connecticut, has a similar program in place called "e.Plus." The *e* stands for *electronic*, *economical*, and *evolutionary*. "The program meets the needs of people who are very time-stressed," says Bryan Huebner, executive vice president of consumer financial services at the People's Bank.

Choice. Xers are less loyal than Boomers to designer labels or other brand names, says Sean Keller, an associate director at Yankelovich Partners, a firm that tracks consumer trends. Instead they thrive in environments where they have choices. They seem to equate choice with power.

Some retailers who serve a broad range of patrons lay out their stores so that the customers are presented with many options and a lot of product information, an approach they have found to be particularly appealing to Generation X. At Ikea, a chain specializing in inexpensive furniture that customers assemble themselves, stores are designed to showcase an array of very similar items that differ slightly in price and quality. Tags on each item provide some detail about the product for use in making comparisons. Younger shoppers respond enthusiastically to this retailing environment because they like to make the ultimate decision about what value means to them, says Pamela Diaconis, a spokeswoman for Ikea. "The important thing, though, is that you have to offer a quality product at each price level." Another retailer that focuses on choice is the Borders chain selling books and music. The store offers customers earphones so they can sample up to 500 CDs, and they can use video kiosks to find all the titles of a favorite recording artist, for example, or to read music reviews of the popular sellers.

Subtlety. Some successful Generation X marketers find it pays not to advertise at all. Urban Outfitters relies entirely on word of mouth. Catalogues like Delia's are passed among high school girls but are virtually unknown to their parents. Many other popular catalogues, while they may welcome GenX customers, deliberately avoid targeting them. Patagonia's intent, says spokesperson Lu Setnicka, "is to make high-quality products for use outdoors." Tweeds declares its purpose as creating value-priced fashion with an edge. "We did not sit around and say, 'This is Generation X, and this is who we want to target,'" says Mark Friedman, vice president of marketing for Hanover Direct, which owns Tweeds.

GenXers, more than members of other generations, are astute about sales tactics and can be turned off by sales clerks who try to push them. To appeal to a Generation X market, says Wendy Liebmann, president of WSL Strategic Retail, a New York–based retail consulting firm, you have to train sales clerks to act as information resources for shoppers instead of as salespeople. At CompUSA, a national chain of computer product stores, managers have phased in satellite training seminars to acquaint salespeople with developments in software products. Software manufacturers can communicate with clerks at all stores to help them learn how to answer customers' questions about products.

We can handle the truth. *American Demographics* wrote of us, "While they are not anti-advertising, they are repulsed by insincerity—and they are experts at spotting it. . . . They dislike overstatement, self-importance, hypocrisy." Michael Robinson, a managing partner at the Chicago-based EURO RSCG Tatham advertising agency, says, "Their antennas go up when they hear BS—they see right through it." He says GenXers appreciate a more straightforward approach. Karen Ritchie, author of *Marketing to Generation X*, writes, "If you wish Generation X to adopt your product, it must be perceived as a useful product—not one to be purchased for reasons of status or to make a statement, but one that fulfills a genuine need." She says that Generation X is less likely to be brand-loyal.

Relating to our pressures. Many commercials seek our response by portraying a young person who is trying to work his or her way up and is often stretched for resources. The Dime Savings Bank has created a thirty-second television commercial that targets Generation X by portraying a believable real-life scenario that focuses on telling a story about a typical young professional. The story could relate to either a male or female, but in this case it focuses on a young professional woman. The ad depicts the woman's busy life, moving from scene to scene in which she is visibly spending money, possibly more than she earns. She lives day to day, using the ATM and her checking account. She sees a pair of shoes she just has to have, plans a weekend trip with her friends, and encounters unexpected everyday expenses. David Totaro, the Dime's executive vice president and chief marketing officer, says the commercial's purpose is to appeal to GenXers who may find themselves in a similar situation—working their way up in the real world but still not having the resources to pay for the things they want and need.

General Motors' Saturn division also hit the right note in its commercial featuring a young lady who visits many automobile showrooms and is treated shabbily by salespeople, presumably because of her age and limited budget. Then she walks into a Saturn dealership, where she's greeted warmly and the staff is attentive. "This ad is always mentioned as a favorite in the focus groups I conduct," says Rachael Martin, President of The Milo Group, a GenX consulting firm. "If I were buying a car I would look at Saturn simply because of the ads. I identify with that girl."

Don't judge! Crunch! is all about not being judgmental. It is the hot new chain of gyms that "warmly welcomes and accepts people from all walks of life, regardless of shape, size, sex, or ability. You don't have to be flawless to feel at home in a Crunch! gym. We don't care if you're 18 or 80, fat or thin, short or tall, muscular or mushy, blonde or bald or anywhere in between." Their instructors are from all kinds of backgrounds and include a drag queen, a neurologist, a corporate attorney, a comedian, and numerous actors. Classes include "Hip-hop Aerobics" with a live rapper, "Gospel Aerobics" led by a soul-church choir from Harlem, and "Action Wrestling," a co-ed wrestling-conditioning program designed to improve agility. They developed "The Heart Attack," a class utilizing polar heart rate monitors in alliance with circuit training, and "Cyked," a revolutionary new yoga class taught on stationary bikes in a candlelit room. Now that's alternative.

A New Industry Is Born: Analyzing Xers

A cottage industry of sorts has sprouted up to analyze Generation X. The going rate for a "Generation X explainer" can run about $1,000 a day. Douglas Coupland, the fellow who popularized the term "Generation X," commands an estimated $8,000 to $10,000 as a speaker. Lower down the pay scale is Deroy Murdock, a former

Photo Courtesy of Deroy Murdock

DEROY MURDOCK
President, Loud and Clear Communications

MASTER MARKETER, CONSERVATIVE VOICE

There is no doubt that Deroy Murdock's first love is politics. He is a freelance writer for conservative magazines and an MSNBC contributor. His big issue? Fiscal responsibility. He uses research he has done in Chile and in Argentina to convince politicians that privatization of programs like Social Security and Medicare is the way to go.

But that doesn't keep him from having a successful marketing and media consultancy. As president and founder of Loud and Clear Communications, Deroy advises companies on how to market to Generation X by focusing on no-nonsense, content-driven messages to a generation that has "seen it all."

Ogilvy & Mather account executive who runs his own X-focused consulting firm, Loud and Clear Communications. Murdock bills up to $500 a day. "I'm not making money hand over fist, but I'm sitting here working in shorts and no shoes. That's another kind of compensation."

Suzi Chauvel quit her job as an executive vice president at Ocean Pacific Sunwear three years ago to form Popeye Chauvel, a consulting company whose mission is to convey the qualities and characteristics of Generation X to businesspeople who are aging Baby Boomers. Chauvel carts a video camera around and tapes Xers in their haunts, selling three tapes for $3,800 to clients like Liz Claiborne and Mattel. To help convince marketing people that Xers are a different breed, she shows them the scene from an art show called the Poverty Pop Exhibit at Exit Art in New York, featuring artworks like a collage of sponges and a towering sculpture made entirely out of found shoes. "I basically appeal to the Baby Boomer mystification [with Generation X]. Our angle is total submersion in the culture."

Many ask, who wants to know things like this? Try Chrysler, for one. When Chrysler's ad agency, BBDO Worldwide, launched the Neon, a car aimed squarely at Xers, a user panel of experts included Murdock. BBDO felt it needed to run some forty focus groups of Xers, far more than it would normally conduct for a different target market. Among other things, the research convinced BBDO to tone down any hype in favor of straight talk, since GenXers have unusually acute hype radar. It also prompted BBDO to list the price of the car fully loaded in the ads.

The Greater Talent Network runs day-long seminars called "X-Fests" that feature youthful experts. Among the speakers are Richard Linklatter, who directed the movies *Slacker, Dazed and Confused*, and *Before Sunrise*, and Mark Leyner, the author of *My Cousin, My Gastroenterologist*. The network charges anywhere from $20,000 to $100,000 per seminar, depending on how many presenters a marketer wants to hear. The X Fest idea was launched in 1994 and has received much attention as well as corporate interest.

Twenty-something Steven Grasse is the founder of a GenX ad agency and consulting group called Gyro Worldwide. He says, "If anyone thinks Generation X has no buying power, they have no idea of this generation. They're savvy at a younger age. They drive about thirty percent of computer sales. They have some of the most major impact on book superstores, and they single-handedly destroyed the mall-based music stores by buying in free-standing stores." Clients for Gyro typically pay the agency between $20,000 and $50,000 to market products to a twenty-something audience. Gyro's accounts include RJR Reynolds Tobacco, a unit of RJR Nabisco Holdings; the Paddington Corporation, which sells several brands of alcoholic beverages; and Reactor, a clothing company. The theory behind the agency is hire people in their twenties to consult on how to sell items to other people in their age group.

Other agencies similar to Gyro include the Collegiate Marketing Company and Tattoo, Inc. Gyro has gained attention because of its very bold and sometimes offensive advertising. In 1993, for instance, it proposed a campaign for a local clothing merchant, Zipperhead, that featured a picture of Charles Manson with the tag line "Everyone has the occasional urge to go wild and do something completely outrageous." Some Gyro clients, like Comcast Corporation, weren't amused by the idea and fired the agency, whereas other clients were attracted to the controversy. In 1996, Gyro was responsible for RJR Reynolds's most successful product launch in twenty years—Red Camels. The product's edgy look is targeted to young adults. Grasse says the product works because "we don't know anything about selling cigarettes. The regular and lights packages don't match—that's breaking the ultimate rule!"

Other rule-breaking strategies are employed by Sputnik, a GenX consulting group. Calling their strategy reverse marketing, they tell their client to deflate the claims they make about their products instead of inflating them. Generation X has been saturated with "more" and "better." To get our attention and throw us off guard you have to downplay what you are selling.

Rewriting the Book

As you can see, marketing professionals are trying to relieve GenXers of their money in any and every way. Their aim is good on the perimeters and we're forking over a lot of economic welfare to their clients. Still, they haven't been able to pull the trigger and hit the

GenX bull's-eye. It could be that that's because we're just not a central target.

We're making them rewrite the book on marketing. The problem with that is in the focus. They'll continue to shoot away at the perimeters. It's a good living. For our part, Generation X is having fun. I think we'll keep 'em guessing for quite some time. After all, we know how to move the target.

CHAPTER 11

Our Collective Soul

Molding the Media

America is vomiting its media-soaked culture all over the world.
—Laure De Marcellus, opera singer

If America is vomiting, the rest of the world has its mouth wide open.
—Leslie Lewis, independent film producer

No other generation in history has been more overstimulated by noise, visual motion, and electronic signals than Generation X. In a constant state of ambivalence, Americans voraciously consume more TV programming and printed words than any nation on earth. We are hopelessly addicted to twenty-four-hour news, tabloid gossip, TV sitcoms, computer chat rooms, e-mail, and digital phones. We depend on the media to be shocked, thrilled, entertained, informed, developed, befriended, analyzed, relieved, spiritualized, transformed, and transported.

It started early for this generation—in our cribs—with everything from singing baby rattles to twirling motorized over-the-crib mobiles. We were conditioned to search out every electronic device invented, including CDs, videos, VCRs, stereos, computers, television, audiotapes, and more. Our rooms and apartments are warehouses for storing receivers and software. Our voracious appetite for gadgets that soothe, stimulate, pacify, and please our senses has spewed forth new markets that dominate vast stretches of America in the likeness of

McDonald's. These high-tech centers include Blockbuster, Computer-Land, Radio Shack, Circuit City, and more. Because of the buying, viewing, and listening habits of my generation, whole new categories of products, real estate, and employment have been born. The trickle effect to the gross national product, to federal, state, and local taxes, and to export and import trade alone measures in the hundreds of billions of dollars.

The media—which now encompass equipment manufacturing; the assets of film, TV, and radio programming; publishing; advertising revenues; and sales of related products—are America's biggest business and our largest export aside from weapons. We are hit by every conceivable carrier of sound and sight, from radio to Walkman to digital phones to the Internet with stereo and 3D—it's instant playback and never-ending communications everywhere. We have come to rely on the mass media for a sense of community. That's because for all our technological and industrial progress, we are isolated as human beings, locked away in Dilbert's cubicles in tall buildings or in suburban boxes.

Nailing down the term "media" is difficult. It has expanded way beyond its original meaning, when it referred to the relatively limited mass communications mediums by which we receive information. Today three generations of media are alive and well in our nation. The first generation is print media: newspapers, magazines, and books. The second generation arrived with moving pictures, radio, and television. The third media generation—"the next generation"—is driven by computers, the Internet, and interactivity. To understand where the media are headed next, we should take a look at how America's next generation is creating new media and revitalizing the old ways.

First-Generation Media: Newspapers, Magazines, Books

The paper. Newspapers have never had an easy time grabbing young readers, but today the stakes are higher. About half of all young people read the daily newspaper today compared to about two thirds in the early seventies. That's devastating. It's no longer certain that the twenty-somethings will develop a newspaper habit as they age. Most regular newspaper readers are people about age 55. Younger people and their parents are turning increasingly to competing media, some of which, such as cable TV and cyberspace, didn't exist twenty years ago. This is scary for news executives because the twenties has long been seen as the last chance in which to establish a person's reading habit.

Newspapers have to change to be relevant to young readers, says Al Gollin, research director for the Newspaper Association of America. One of the first to try was the *New York Times*, using its "Style" section. Its experience shows the pitfalls in reaching an entire generation via a special section. The "Style" section started appearing in the Sunday edition in 1995. It featured such overtly striving-to-be-hip topics as body piercing and the arm as a fashion instrument. The section was sniped at as a hokey attempt to spiff up the old gray lady. Four editors in two years failed to improve sluggish advertising, and the section was scaled back and lost its color pictures in mid-1997.

Smaller papers started similar sections. The Fort Wayne *Journal Gazette* (circulation 64,000), a daily, began publishing a thrice-weekly page in October 1996 called "Next." The stories are intentionally eclectic, featuring everything from how to handle a mortgage to a first-person account of getting tattooed, a favorite topic in many newspaper sections geared to younger readers. Steve Burn, the twenty-something editor of "Next," said the section doesn't want to be the arbiter of cool nor does it aspire to write stories that will appeal to everyone between 18 and 29. "We don't want to be the grunge record review page and we don't want to be the business page either," he says. "We just throw scraps out there and see if the dogs chase them."

Some papers are raising their hipness quotient more cautiously. The *Macon Telegraph* in Georgia carries a weekly youth-oriented column, "After the Boom," written by staffers in the target age group. Each month the paper runs a special page, "Telex," which has included articles on interracial dating, the 1970s, retrofad, and a statistical look at Generation X, all displayed in fashionable snazzy layouts.

Certain newspapers have decided that a few pages or stories will never attract young readers in large numbers and may actually turn off regular readers. Instead, they have decided to go after younger readers with separate publications. In Fort Lauderdale, the *Sun Sentinel* created "XS," a free weekly tabloid distributed through movie theaters and stores. According to the editor, Steve Wissink, the company concluded that the *Sun Sentinel* is a fine, successful paper, but the tabloid is not much of a success. The Knight-Ridder newspaper chain is also considering a newspaper-magazine hybrid for younger readers, says Gregg Bragonier, the chain's special publications director. He said they may not gravitate to the newspaper, but at least they are reading something.

Maybe newspapers shouldn't give up so soon. Eric Liu, the founder of *The Next Progressive*, a twenty-something–oriented magazine, argues that flashy graphics and snappy stories won't necessarily work. A lot of young people would rather just have intelligently written pieces. GenXers know when they're being put down. The media critic John Katz, writing in *Wired* magazine, says the newspaper industry's relentless alienation of the young is the corporate equivalent of a scandal.

Declining circulation, aging readership, and weaker ties between the public and their papers are all aspects of a weakening newspaper industry. From coast to coast, in big cities and small, newspapers are embracing color, drama, and intimacy in hopes of better connecting with increasingly distracted and time-pressed readers, many of them young. These efforts are squarely aimed at reversing the grim trends faced by nearly all newspaper editors and publishers.

Some of the largest dailies, like the *New York Times, USA Today,* and the *Wall Street Journal,* strive to satisfy an affluent readership, reaching a national audience by publishing from distribution centers across the country and launching new Internet sites. Such papers have retained their focus on national and international events, business news, news analysis, and the arts. But editors and publishers of more locally oriented papers are more constrained and have to appeal to a wider variety of folks.

Ivan Peterson of the *New York Times* says that in the audience-targeting process, papers have begun to question one of the basic principles of journalism: that hard news trumps soft features. In the new world of adaptive journalism, readers and newspaper marketers are getting a bigger say in what goes on in the paper. Like it or not, editors and reporters are being forced to do the listening. "We are trying to get out of the business of being mediator between our readers and the news and into the business of listening over the back fence while people talk," says Jerry Ceppos, executive director of the *Mercury News,* a San Jose newspaper.

Overall, the percentage of adults in America who read a daily paper declined to 64.2 percent in 1995, from 77.6 percent in 1970, according to the Newspaper Association of America. Sunday newspapers have recovered some readership in part because of the advertising supplements and discount coupons.

All the tinkering seems aimed at the common objective of a more emotional, intimate and wider relationship with readers. Tom Koenninger, the editor of *The Columbian* in Vancouver, Washington, is working his way down a list of thirty-two community groups, from real estate agents to conservative Christians, in an effort to make closer connections. Representatives of each group are invited in for coffee and conversation. "We had the medical society in and we found out they were mad at us for an article we did on managed care in 1984. They were still mad and we didn't find this out until we asked them to come for a visit." The idea is to open up reporting to all points of view in the community.

The *Sacramento Bee* closed its Mexico City bureau during the recent West Coast recession, reduced its San Francisco bureau from four to one reporter, and has delayed plans for a Pacific Rim bureau until business improves. Editor Rick Rodriguez says a high priority is hiring a second pop music critic. "I think all newspapers have to be interested in getting young people as readers, and in Sacramento we do a good job of it. But we have to do better, and getting younger readers might mean some changes in the staffing emphasis."

It pays to be **Wired.**   In the 1950s magazines were mass media. Magazines such as *Life, Look, Collier's,* and the *Saturday Evening Post* achieved and maintained huge circulation bases. The seven sisters—*Good Housekeeping, Redbook, McCalls, Homes & Gardens, Ladies' Home Journal, Women's Day,* and *Family Circle*—had a combined circulation of 27 million in 1955.

Like network television ratings, newsstand sales of magazines have been in gradual decline since 1980. As GenXers moved into the buying market and their grandparents moved out, a reliance on magazines in general decreased. GenXers get their news and entertainment from other sources—cable, late-night talk shows, the Internet. So magazines have had to slash subscription prices, reduce staffs, and bombard the readers with renewal pleas.

GenXers' interests have become increasingly differentiated, which is reflected in our magazine subscriptions. Not surprisingly, the most successful magazines are those that cater to specific interests such as *Working Woman, Martha Stewart Living, Spin, Seventeen, Wired,* and *Entertainment Weekly.* Each has a specific target audience—young professional women, music-crazed young males, fashion-crazed young girls, male computer entrepreneurs, or pop culture–obsessed women. These magazines feed the specific obsessions of their target audiences. People turn to newspapers, CNN, CNBC, and the Internet for general news. The magazines that are doing the best are increasingly visual—but that doesn't mean a return to the type of format *Life* gave us. We have television for all the visual images we need. Rather, youth responds to text that is enhanced with pictures, illustrations, bullet points.

Wired is one of the few success stories in magazine start-ups. A virtual unknown in 1994, *Wired* sprang up to be the leading magazine on Internet and technological culture. With a circulation of 320,000, it has beaten its main competitors, *Home PC*, *Purchasing*, and *Information Week*. The reason? Its publishers know its audience: high-income, self-employed, graduate-degreed males interested in the world of high tech. As a percentage of readership, it has more young adults than *Fortune*, *Time*, *Newsweek*, and *BusinessWeek*.

And there are other start-up magazines, like *Jane*, a magazine for women in their twenties created by Jane Pratt, the founder of *Sassy*. Or *Curio*, launched last year for men and women 25 to 35 who like the feel of 'zines and care about art, culture, and politics. These new magazines compete with fledgling Generation X publications like *P.O.V.* and *Swing*, not to mention the already established *Details*, *Men's Health*, and *Men's Journal*, plus spruced-up oldsters like *GQ* and *Esquire*.

The editors of the new magazines are young, smart, energetic, and convinced they've found an untapped niche in an otherwise crowded, competitive market. "We're an old-fashioned general-interest men's magazine, like *Esquire* was in the sixties," says *Men's Perspective* editor Trevor Miller, a 31-year-old Brit. *Icon* "celebrates the individual" and his search for a personal definition of success, says editor David Getson, 24. His ideal reader "doesn't want to be told what to do or how to do it." Getson fiercely rejects the fashion and lifestyle advice now pervasive in men's magazines. "The whole concept of 'lifestyle' is demonic—from hell or from the government," he declares. *Curio* editor Teresa Lawrence, 31, a corporate lawyer by day, says she hopes to attract "smart, media-savvy" readers "not limited in what they want to know."

Cynics may have a different take on these magazines' thrust. What the new Generation X magazines have in common, writes Ron Radosh in *Icon*'s prototype issue, "is the deep conviction that there is nothing people in their twenties find more fascinating than themselves. Or, more specifically, people who are just like them, only more so. More successful, more artistic, more dedicated, and-or better snowboarders."

Not only new magazines are trying to capture GenX's attention. Some older magazines are trying and succeeding in making the generational transition. *Glamour* maintains a readership of 10.5 million. More than 60 percent of their readers are GenXers. *People* magazine reaches 34.5 million Americans and has almost 30 percent Generation X readership. Holding up respectably are *Premier, Details, Spin,* and *Entertainment Weekly*, magazines that cater to GenXers' obsession with television, film, and music. The lesson here seems to be that magazines of the future will cater to specific interests rather than impart general information. By the time you receive *Time* and *Newsweek*, all of the information in them is outdated. That's why they too are retooling their focus by doing more investigative reporting and feature pieces and jazzing it all up with pop-culture images.

Books.   Doreen Carvajal of the *New York Times* wrote in 1996 that "the publishing industry is struggling with record-breaking returns of unsold copies, a steady decline in adult trade sales and a shelf life for new titles that has compressed to 'somewhere between radicchio and active culture yogurt.' " After a book boom in the early nineties, sparked by the opening of megabookstores like Barnes & Noble and BookBinders, book sales leveled off in the mid-nineties. HarperCollins, one of the oldest and largest publishers, canceled at least 100 titles in 1997, deeming them unprofitable and unpublishable. HarperCollins posted a loss of $7 million in the first quarter of 1997.

Nothing can be more difficult than getting a book published, especially today. Nevertheless young adults are making inroads in fiction and nonfiction by taking advantage of the alternative media and by forging into the mass media by relying on their youth culture.

A notable volume is *25 and Under Fiction*, edited by Susan Ketcin and Neil Giordano, a collection of the best short stories by authors born since 1972. The Harvard professor and Pulitzer Prize–winning psychologist Robert Coles observes in his introduction to the work: "If this is what men and women can give us when they have yet to turn twenty-five, we can only speculate on what will be forthcoming from them in twenty-five years or fifty."

"There is a renaissance of youth culture in this country," says John Davis, the key accounts manager for Koen Book Distributors in Moorestown, New Jersey. "Some stores recognize this and are excellent at luring these customers, and some stores are missing the boat." In order to help more stores target the alternative audience, Davis and his partners created "Bibliopalooza: Reaching Generation X," a road show with tour stops at several regional bookseller shows. He spearheaded an alternative books and small press catalogue at Koen and has organized the Firecracker Alternative Book Awards.

GenXers will come to a bookstore, says Suzy Staubach, director of University of Connecticut's co-op, if you hold special events such as poetry readings or musical entertainment. Having done this she writes, "It was a wonderful night, filled with creativity and good feelings. No one stapled any body parts." The key to success in marketing to this generation is specificity. Rob Haley buys for his small bookstore, Farley's Bookshop, in New Hope, Pennsylvania. He has identified no less than a dozen subcultures, including punks 14 to 50 years old, pagans, gays and lesbians, Deadheads, neo-bohemians, amateur UFOlogists, and *X-File* types. He says he makes money by tailoring his selections to their demands. Across the country these types of categories get discovered by other bookstore managers and distributors. The national chain Tower Records, which sells books in many of its stores, has a special section for these types of niche books. The division is called "Outposts" and is expected to have sales of $20 million in 1997.

Small presses have always been the mainstay of niche books. Last Gasp, Serpent's Tail, City Lights, and Manic D Press are some of the small presses that have done well in the past. Now, the major presses are following suit by publishing alternative books as part of their regular lists. They include St. Martin's (with its Griffin imprint), Simon & Schuster (Pocket Books's MTV Books), and Random House (its Ballantine Books is paying $1 million for titles by GenX spokescomedians Janeane Garofalo and Ben Stiller), and Macmillan. GenXers aren't limited to new alternative books. We are recycling older authors such as Beat Generation writers like Kerouac, Ginsberg, and Burroughs and Lost Generation giants T. S. Eliot, Fitzgerald, and Hemingway. Movies have revitalized Jane Austen, whose books have never sold better.

Henry Rollins has a twelve-year-old publishing company called 2.13.61—it's his birth date. Having given up on the traditional methods of publishing, Rollins chose to go it alone. "I never tried to get published by anyone else. I figured that no one would publish me; I think I'd just have been laughed out of the room. There really was no hope for a guy like me other than to do it on his own." Rollins says it took a long time to get into bookstores but now his publishing company is profitable. His titles include collections of Led Zeppelin and Metallica photos, a David Lee Roth autobiography, his own musings, and the writings of an ex-lover of Henry Miller.

Larry Daniels, director of information technologies for the National Association of College Stores, provides an overview of technological and demographic trends that will change the face of book retailing. He focuses on the college store, where many of the trends that spread to the trade first surface. The college market has total sales of about $7.6 billion a year, more than home TV ($3.2 billion), infomercials ($1.3 billion), and the Net ($200 million). Sales are rising in the area of custom publishing, print-on-demand, and computer hardware and software. Half of wholesalers' sales to college stores are software.

Photo Courtesy of Leslie Lewis

LESLIE LEWIS
Producer

AUTHOR, INDEPENDENT VOICE

In her twenty-four short years Leslie has been everything from a waitress to a travel guide. But now she seems to have found her passion and the media is where it is at. She is the author of a GenX waitressing guide (*Waiter, There Is a Fly in My Soup!*), is the host of *Independent Eye*, a television special that showcases independent films, and has produced two upcoming independent films.

Born of an African-American father and an Asian mother, Leslie says she has always had to battle stereotypes. The media industry is no different. "My entire life is an anomaly. I know that anything I do, I will be the first to do it. I got comfortable with breaking the molds a long time ago. It just means I try harder." And what does she dislike most about what our elders say about us? "That we are sitting on our collective ass. We work hard."

Second-Generation Media: Radio, TV, and Film

Radio.   Radio, the first medium to simultaneously unite us on this planet, isn't forgotten to my generation. While radio was a talk medium from the 1920s to the 1950s, to us it's a music master. We relish FM formats because of their superior sound quality. Boomers discovered how well rock and roll could vibrate, and they literally took over the FM dial as 815 stations in 1960 grew to 2,169 in 1970 to 3,282 in 1980. Gradually album-oriented rock became the dominant FM format. Today FM continues to be the dominant force in radio, accounting for 75 percent of radio audiences, according to the Radio Advertising Bureau. Radio talk shows—which have become more lively, in-your-face, and irreverent—are part of our daily lives as we drive to work or study for exams.

The TV hearth.   Still at the center of our media universe, though, is the ever-present tube, the hearth of the modern world. We were the first generation literally to be raised by television. Most of us knew television before we knew real people. To GenXers, television is a surrogate parent, baby-sitter, friend, remedy, tranquilizer, boyfriend, girlfriend—yes, TV is where we go on dateless Saturday nights. Our attachment to TV made fortunes for cereal and toy companies, not to mention the lucre we put in the pockets of producers, actors, and media moguls.

Our first neighborhood was *Sesame Street*, and our first buddies were Bert, Ernie, and Kermit. Yes, we have had a long history with the tube, from reruns of *I Love Lucy* to *The Addams Family*. When they canceled *Welcome Back, Kotter* we moved to the suburbs with Tony Danza in *Who's the Boss?*, and we got our first taste of corporate America through Maddy and Dave on *Moonlighting*. Still, we are faithful as ever to our *Friends* whether in *Beverly Hills 90210* or in the *ER*. When all is said and done, many of us probably spent more time with our network family than with our real-life relatives.

"People raised on TV have a real vocabulary for TV tradition," Amy Lippman, the thirty-one-year-old co-creator of Fox's hit series

Party of Five, said. During the second season of *Party of Five* the name of the band fronted by Bailey's girlfriend, Sarah (Jennifer Love Hewitt), was The Nielsen Family. Erin Smith, a twenty-three-year-old TV connoisseur and editor of the 'zine *Teenage Gang Debs,* says that TV is now at the center of popular culture: "You lose a tremendous amount not knowing about TV. It permeates the culture. Anything that is ever-present in anyone's life should be taken seriously. You can't go to the movies every day, and a lot of people I know don't subscribe to a newspaper, so TV is the common thread."

David Poltrack, executive vice president for research and planning at CBS, said the lives of the *Friends* cohorts have been more culturally shaped by television than previous generations. "If you watch *Friends* and the sitcoms done by Generation X writers for the Generation X audience, they're totally filled with allusions to TV," Poltrack said. "The utilization of TV series as time stamps are much stronger than they are in the earlier Baby Boomer programs. This may be the true television generation. For the Baby Boomers it was a transitional medium. We watched a lot of TV, but we didn't have TV in our classrooms, we didn't have computers with TV screens."

When the Boomers were young, the three networks that dominated TV claimed to reach 95 percent or more of American households in a single night. Adults and children were part of a massive simultaneous viewing audience, and programming was most often designed to appeal to both adults and children. Today's generation are more active viewers of TV. We surf with our remote controls, searching among hundreds of options within a matter of seconds. The average household has dozens of channels available; houses with satellite dishes have hundreds. The networks are feeling the competition. Despite network effort, over the past ten years Generation X has drifted away from traditional programming, fueling entire new stations like Fox and MTV.

Karen Ritchie, the author of *Marketing to Generation X,* points out another difference between Boomers and Xers. "Xers watch TV differently, and they're a lot more comfortable with the technology that allows them to tape and time-delay and switch channels. They can watch several programs simultaneously or surf ninety to a hundred channels without viewing it as a waste of time." Generation X is the first generation to grow up with VCRs and multiple remote controls, so it should come as no surprise that the most often taped TV shows are *The X-Files*, *Melrose Place*, *Beverly Hills 90210*, *Party of Five*, and *Frasier*, all programs with a high number of GenX viewers.

Despite a distrustful nature, cynicism, and resistance to marketing, there are things Generation X holds dear. Television executives have figured those things out, and they're now appearing with greater regularity in TV shows in an effort to lure Xers. With the rising divorce rate, young Xers turned to their friends more often than their parents or relatives. Male-female relationships were just as likely to be based on friendship as on romance. To Xer youths, a group of friends often became more important than their families, especially when their home life was in turmoil. This reordering of priorities and restructuring of relationships came to be reflected in TV shows aimed at Generation X; the sitcoms *Friends* and *Living Single* are quintessential examples. When a nuclear family is featured, there's nothing *Father Knows Best* about it.

"Shows like *Roseanne, My So-called Life,* and *Party of Five* tend to do more realistic families," said Jennifer Elise Cox, the 22-year-old actress who played Jan Brady in *The Brady Bunch Movie* and its sequel. "I think people crave to have a family, you aspire to have one, you create one in any way you can, and I think [GenX] can relate to dysfunctional families because I think everyone's in a dysfunctional family. I don't really know a functional one." Kimberly Costello, a Boomer who's a producer on Fox's *Melrose Place*, has a theory about how day care has shaped the *Friends* generation: "This generation has the ability to socialize in packs, which is incredibly interesting to someone like me who didn't," Costello said. "At age two they were taught how to get along with others [in day care] and what it means to respect others and somebody's space. So they value those friendships more than family because they spend so much time with them."

Photo Courtesy of Andrew Eccles/ABC
Photo © 1997 copyright ABC, Inc.

DEBBIE MATENOPOULOS
The View *on ABC*

TALK SHOW HOST

At 23, Debbie Matenopoulos is on one of America's top-rated talk shows—ABC's *The View*. *The View* is Barbara Walters's latest idea in programming—a kind of mid-morning "coffee talk" geared toward women of all generations. By hiring a fresh face, Barbara Walters was trying to appeal to jaded younger viewers. "We thought a lot of young people could relate to her, and older ones would be as fond of her as I am," said Walters. Still, Matenopoulos is reluctant to be the spokeswoman for Generation X. "I don't think anyone can speak for an entire generation. I certainly can't."

Doing things in groups also applies to viewing specific TV shows, especially *Friends*, *Melrose Place*, and *Beverly Hills 90210*. These shows have become a reason to watch with other people and socialize as the show is taking place, Larry Gianinno, vice president of program research for ABC, said. "When *90210* or *Melrose Place* is on, we've heard in various forms of qualitative research that people are talking about those as appointment shows, not only in terms of watching them but also in terms of having the gang over."

Prior to the 1980s, TV shows almost always wrapped up a story line within an episode, unless it was a two-part story that would be concluded the next week. That's not the case in nineties TV. Thanks to the quality drama genre (which borrowed serialized story lines from daytime soaps), almost all GenX TV shows, as well as others, are serialized.

Music also plays a much more important role in GenX TV than it ever has before. How could it not after MTV? First, music-video styling crept into prime time in *Miami Vice*. Now it's the quick-cut look of *ER* and *NYPD Blue*. Even if the look of TV isn't always MTV, the sound frequently is. With the onset of the Seattle grunge scene in the early 1990s, TV quickly got behind this music trend. First, Fox tried it by depicting a grunge band in *The Heights*. When that proved too blatant, *Melrose Place* started slipping alternative rock music into its opening guest credits.

MTV: So what of MTV? Yes, we are called the MTV generation, and for good reason. MTV, with its combination of music videos and lifestyle shows, is enormously popular with the 18- to 34-year-olds who are early in their careers as consumers—so popular that MTV's ad revenues have tripled in the last five years, to $600 million, and have provided much comfort to the otherwise sorely afflicted Sumner Redstone and his Viacom. Unlike most TV, where talent costs are high, MTV gets its music programming relatively cheap. MTV has pretax margins of close to 50 percent, compared with CNN's 25 percent or so.

MTV has made a business of keeping up with us. In fact, MTV has grown up with us as much as we have grown up with it. We remember when the first Madonna, Journey, and Duran Duran videos were released, with their grainy film and now-laughable special effects. Today MTV has given us a wide range of programs, from *Beavis and Butthead* to *The Real World*, evolving to match our tastes. President Judith McGrath explains that MTV gets a lot of its feedback from its sixty interns a year, aged 18 to 22. "The place is like a laboratory of tastes and styles: One year they all look like hippies. The next year they're wearing black, the next nobody has any hair, and the next you can't tell the genders apart." McGrath says that she is there not to judge but to learn. "My job is not to be the taste police. I make an environment where the interns feel welcome." Then she watches and listens as if her livelihood depends upon it—which it does. "If we lose them, we have nothing," she says.

A recent MTV poll found that one of every eight persons between 18 and 29 has surfed to an Internet political site. Another study, by the Computer Research Center, found that increasing numbers of young people were not tuning in to network nightly news, complaining of a lack of time. Viewership in the age group dropped from 36 percent to 22 percent in the past year. Researchers said the most likely reason was the increasing use of personal computers.

Ty Wenger is editor of *Link* magazine, a national campus magazine that is read by about a million students. He claims that young people really are concerned about the nation's problems, which they will inherit. He says, "Some days it seems like the news is dominated by stories about whose wife is going to be less offensive to the American public or this week's brushfire. It really doesn't count in the end. When you are twenty years old you care a lot about issues because you don't quite have to deal with reality yet."

GenXers complain that when the mainstream media do focus on issues, the story isn't reported from their point of view. It is geared to older generations, completely out of touch with Generation X. "The news talks about good economic times but young people are living with their parents and marrying later, and no one is buying a house or investing in a 401(K)," said Lou Penrose, a twenty-something radio talk-show host in Southern California whose market focus is young audiences. Meagen Liberman, executive editor of *Swing*, says, "Most of the stories in the mainstream media are still framed for an older audience. They don't talk about Social Security as something that is going to bankrupt the country, only how the elderly are upset that the benefits are being cut."

Others argue that the media are racially biased. In *Race, Multiculturalism, and the Media*, authors Clint Wilson II and Felix Gutierrez

present the notion of information "gatekeepers." Because of the infi-
nite amount of events occurring in the world each day, gatekeepers
are necessary to select which news is relevant and worthy of coverage. Historically, these news selectors have been whites. Consequently, say Wilson and Gutierrez, "The frequency and nature of the
coverage of nonwhites in news media . . . reveal the attitudes of
the majority population throughout American History." Farai Chideya, author of *Don't Believe the Hype*, found that only 5 percent of
the reporters in the United States are black—which may partly explain the overabundance of black violence stories in the press. "The
media's constant attention to certain stories—like crime—in the
black community borders on obsession," she writes. "The trend of ignoring others—like black community watch groups and self-help—
borders on true pathology."

But the mainstream media are starting to catch on as they see their
ratings drop. Advertisers want anchors who appeal to 18-to-49-year-
olds. TV networks and cable channels earn about $46 billion in an-
nual advertising, revenues that are directly linked to the number of
viewers. The headhunter Dawn Fitzpatrick says, "From 1994 till now
has been the largest hiring surge I have seen in my twenty-five years
in the business. The need for younger-looking people is growing. Stations are being Foxified, reaching out to younger viewers trying to be
hipper with more graphics and taking their cues from MTV." Even
such traditional providers as CNN and ABC are giving airtime to hipper, younger reporters, who are given much more leeway in terms of
visuals and writing.

"Political coverage in general tends to be pretty straightforward,
pretty conservative in style," said Jonathan Karl, a Washington correspondent who covers the issues and concerns of Generation X for
CNN. Karl says, "We are trying to have a different style by putting
less emphasis on talking heads and experts, we are trying to use all
fresh footage, jazzing it up and taking some creative risks." Karl was
told he wouldn't get training or even be given guidelines on his
appearance, so he often appears in jeans and without a tie. They

Photo Courtesy of Steve Rosenbaum

STEVE ROSENBAUM
President, Broadcast News Network

PRODUCER, NEWS-GATHERER

Steve Rosenbaum has been with Broadcast News Network since its birth more than fifteen years ago. Steve has produced shows for A&E, VH1, and Disney, and he created and launched MTV's News Unfiltered. His vision? To bring viewers closer to the news by having the general public do the news gathering. Many of his shows are based on the concept of small-format cameras and viewer/storytellers.

Participation in news gathering will make people trust the news again. "There are few organizations or authorities that we trust, and the result is a kind of overarching paranoia. We need to set goals that balance our personal needs and the sense of what is right for our society, and that means redefining our society." Steve's latest move was into the Internet with the launch of I-Media, a Web-based production company.

said they wanted to get away from a slick delivery and blow-dry presentation.

MSNBC is a $500 million venture launched by Microsoft and NBC/GE that promises to be the future of news. Its tag line is "It's time to get connected." From its debut in July 1996, MSNBC has promoted itself as a younger, hipper CNN. The network was launched with a companion Internet news service staffed by more than 100 journalists. The traditional anchorperson's set has been abandoned for a funky chrome-and-brick work space where casually dressed anchors schmooze several times daily with MSNBC contributors, a diverse set of young talking heads.

Mark Harrington, MSNBC's vice president and general manager, describes the network as an on-air experiment. "There are plenty of people who give speeches about what will happen in the future. The fact is, we are doing it on cable and the Internet every day," he says. "Computer and TV are coming together somehow, and we are wrestling with that editorially now." What's unclear is exactly how Generation X stands to gain from this supposedly revolutionary union of computers and TV. Talk to people at MSNBC and you will hear the postmodern vocabulary of re-purposing journalism and extending the brand name of NBC onto new platforms. The high-tech minds of Generation X will be watching this development and will participate when they see advantages.

The New Filmmakers

Last year, the Hollywood entertainment complex employed more Californians than all the giants of Cold War aerospace combined, and exported more goods than any other American industry with the exception of defense. Twenty-somethings are a predominant force in the film industry.

Young stars like Uma Thurman, Ethan Hawke, Winona Ryder, Gwyneth Paltrow, Leonardo DiCaprio, Matt Damon, and Ben Affleck have taken their place on the silver screen and are bringing in hundreds of millions for Hollywood studios. But what is most unusual is not the age of the actors. Indeed, actors are most often young and beautiful. What is extraordinary, says Stanley Kauffman of the *New*

Republic, is that "Films about young people—say those under 30— are being made by people under 30."

These twenty-somethings are bringing something new to Hollywood: an independent flair, which is reinvigorating the industry. Entertainment news is littered with stories of moviemakers like Kevin Smith, 26, who financed his first movie, *Clerks*, on his credit cards and then went on to make *Chasing Amy*. Now he has won the respect of the mainstream movie houses. He has been hired to write the script for a new Superman movie to star Nicholas Cage.

And then there is Ed Burns who won the Grand Jury Prize at Robert Redford's Sundance Film Festival with his low budget tale of young Irish-American men in New York, *The Brothers McMullen*. Ted Hope, a producer of Burns's films remarked, "*McMullen* has definitely helped young filmmakers find investors. Before, people used to look at investing in indie films and think there was no way that they'd make money, let alone recoup it. But *McMullen* raised people's expectations . . . for young filmmakers."

According to the American Film Marketing Association, independent film is a budding market. In Los Angeles alone, indie films (movies not made by the big movie houses) employ about 131,000 people, with a total payroll of $2.1 billion. Of the approximately 400 films produced in 1997, over sixty percent were produced by independents.

And that is just in Los Angeles. More and more young filmmakers are also producing outside Hollywood. Dozens now work out of New York led by producers like Hal Hartley and Spike Lee. Richard Linklater, director of *Slackers*, *Dazed and Confused*, *Before Sunrise*, and *SubUrbia* works out of Austin, Texas. Kevin Smith stays close to home in New Jersey. "There are too many filmmakers [in Los Angeles]," Smith says. "Go home and make a movie in Nebraska."

And Hollywood isn't just drawing the creative types. There are the young hopefuls who want to be the financiers, the lawyers, and the agents of tomorrow. David Samuels of the *Weekly Standard* writes, "If Hollywood is the Wall Street of the 1990s, then the talent agencies are its investment banks—entrepreneurial centers that trade access to multi-million-dollar properties like Sylvester Stallone and Jim Carrey—the stocks and bonds of the movie business—to institutional investors like Universal Studios in exchange for a 10 to 15 percent cut." Jeff Berg of International Creative Management, one of Hollywood's three major talent agencies, says his industry is hiring some of the best and brightest recent graduates in the country. "We can really recruit and draw from the best graduate students and undergrads in the country who would ordinarily go to work for Paul Weiss or Morgan Stanley," he says. "And that is because there's a career path now and a terrific financial upside if they get it right."

Next-Generation Media: Computers and the Internet

We, the most frequent buyers and users of personal computers, have led the nation into new realms of games, amusement, and information that the corporate computer age of the sixties never imagined. Some can vaguely recall times without the computer and wonder how we managed things. The computer is the single most monumental product of the electronic age. Many of my generation make their livings using computers, generating billions of dollars in new businesses. The computer will continue to revolutionize the workforce, industry, and communications. It is dramatically altering buildings and their uses as we move offices home, buy directly from warehouses, increase global trade, and buy, sell, and communicate through electronic means.

The Internet.   No one knows the full, awesome potential of the Internet, but one thing is certain: Generation X will write the first chapters of the story because we are into it like no other generation. We'll set the tone for generations to come because we are in touch with the technology. More than 30 million people now regularly use the Internet. Jupiter Communications predicts that college students will purchase $2.6 billion worth of products on-line by 2002. Fifty-seven percent own a personal computer; 83 percent accessed the Internet at least once last semester, and of those, 38 percent used it at least once a day. The most popular activity is e-mail, followed by Web surfing related to school research and then general personal interest.

Jupiter Communications says that 4 million Americans under 18 had access to the Internet by the end of 1996, twice as many as a year earlier. The firm predicts that by the year 2002 more than 20 million kids will have access to the Internet from their homes and 90 percent will have access from schools. Kids' favorite Net activities are much the same as adults'. They like to play games, chat electronically, and browse for interesting information. The most popular Web sites for kids include lego.com, disney.com, and spicegirls.com.

Not everyone is excited about the Internet's potential. *The Economist* points out that "surfing the net, with its boring corporate promotion sites, its dire webzines straining to be trendy and its 20 million answers to your one simple question, is less 'Endless Summer' than chronic wipe-out. However, it stretches the imagination not to be excited by a technology that can stretch the imagination into a billion tangents—as a starter."

Multimedia. GenXers will be the first generation to realize the potential marriage of TV and the computer. The next step is interactive TV, which will bring together TV, the telephone, and the personal computer. Interactivity will put control into the hands of the consumer to a greater degree than was ever possible with broadcast TV alone.

For example, since huge databases can be stored it would be possible to digitize full-length motion pictures to make them available on demand. The same principle will allow personal communication between households with interactive sets as part of an interactive TV hookup. Baking, shopping, budget programs, educational software, video games and the like will eventually reside in the single commu-nications device. This isn't science fiction. The technology is avail-able today. Practical applications will be disproportionately adopted by Generation X. We, not Boomers, will be the ones furnishing new households. We will be the primary purchasers of new electronic sys-tems in the twenty-first century.

Interactivity and multimedia mean consumers have more control. The more control that rests in the hands of the consumer, the more difficult it will be to expose that consumer to a traditional advertising message. Remote control and channel surfing interrupt commercial viewing. Pay-per-view premium cable networks and most home video already allow the viewer to completely bypass commercial in-terruptions. Whenever the least hint of commercialism has intruded upon the Internet, the reaction has been extremely negative—now *that's* a calming thought in the midst of the daily media barrage on our senses.

Books on the Internet.   Many observers say that the Internet is reviving reading. There are sites where you can order books, down-load electronic books, post your own work to be critiqued by Web surfers, sell your own material, or play an electronic game of "refrig-erator poetry or prose."

Books are now sold frequently over the Internet. The Internet book business began in 1995 when Geoff Bozes created an on-line book-store with the Web site amazon.com, whose stock featured a million titles consumers could research by subject, title, and author. The site let shoppers order with a few clicks of a computer mouse and get book reviews by other readers, and it encouraged them to submit their own. Amazon can offer 40 percent discounts because it doesn't have the overheads of spacious rental outlets, warehouses for stock, or truck deliveries. The early success of the venture is best judged by the fact that major book retailers like Barnes & Noble and Borders are rushing to create their own on-line bookstores.

Some sites offer electronic books. Steve Potash is the president of OverDrive Systems, whose Electronic Book Aisle is an on-line service that sells electronic books or books in which the full text is available on the Internet and one can pay per page to read. The site has become a profit center for booksellers. One benefit of the service is that the customer has a powerful instrument to preview material, and can buy an entire electronic book or purchase by the chapter or page. Darcy Critchfield, the sales and marketing manager at Zane Publishing, a digital publisher, noted that print-on-demand will become the norm within ten years. Objective Software or Tale.com are fiction factories where readers are treated to a few pages of a story, usually of the fantasy type, and if they like it they can purchase the rest of the story with a credit card.

Tomorrow's Media

What is Generation X's media formula for the near future? For this generation, the media have been the most important industry in our nation—not only because of our intimate relationship with the media (it was our source of knowledge, our teacher, our baby-sitter, our parent), but also because the media are, and will likely continue to be, one of America's biggest exports. And what an export it is, with its ability to disseminate news and entertainment that change and alter perceptions and lifestyles. America's ability to influence the world may well come primarily from our ability to communicate and entertain the world.

This generation is uniquely placed to participate in and mold that influence. We are the first generation to fully realize the power of interactive media with computers and the Internet. And we will be the first true multimedia generation, from music television to Web TV to books on-line. Our challenge will be to stay at the forefront of this media technology and to be responsible while we produce the content the rest of the world will watch.

CHAPTER 12

A Window to the Future

Peering into the Third Millennium

"Each of us is all the sums he has not counted. . . . Each moment is the fruit of forty thousand years . . . and every moment is a window on all time." —Thomas Wolfe

In the story of his youth, *Look Homeward Angel*, Thomas Wolfe tells us, "Every moment is a window on all time." Examining a single slice in human time gives you insight into everything that has come before and everything that is to be. Add this generation up and we are the sums of the past. We are each, with all our frailties, faults, and insecurities, the great product of centuries of human time, and we are the forecast of the future. Our generation of Americans does not yet view itself as this crucial link in history. "As a generation I think our greatest weakness is not taking things seriously, whether it be education, a job, death, or a relationship," says political activist Heather Lamm. "I think we have a tendency to gloss over a lot of life." We have tremendous untapped assets, but, as a generation, we have yet to act. "We have a tendency toward self-indulgence," said Bobby Jindal. "We naturally look inward at the risk of ignoring everything that does not affect us or is not derived from our personal experience."

Other generations viewed themselves as having a mission, a greater good. John F. Kennedy expressed that feeling in his State of the Union address when he said the torch was passed to a new generation of Americans. Our grandparents, too, understood their place in history. They brought us through the Depression, carried us through a world war. And whether or not we agree with former generations' decisions, we must realize that their strength to weather obstacles came from a profound understanding and acceptance of the mission that fate dealt them. Perhaps their destinies were more clearly defined, imposed on them by outside pressures such as financial ruin, Hitler, the Cold War. In some ways our challenge is tougher. More fortunately, though, we can choose our battles instead of having them thrust upon us. But what battles will we choose to fight? Which ones will we leave for future generations? Can we carry America to new heights?

Many of us understand the challenges ahead. They have to do with reinvigorating America, building confidence in a nation whose institutions have been thrown into question. It is our generation's mission to restore the faith—in government, business, religion, and family. If it was our parents' duty to challenge and dismantle the old, it is our duty to rebuild the pieces they left in their wake. The dismantling of our modern institutions in our parents' time has been a painful process. Now, in the absence of external conflict, the fog has cleared and we can see what we have devised.

Economics, rationality, practicality, are the new lenses through which we see the world. It is a system based not on ideology or religion, although certainly it has aspects rooted in both. Nevertheless we have entered upon a new era of logic and numbers. And given our deep cultural and religious differences both in America and with other countries, economics provides the one universal language. It is the opening ground for bridging international differences with nations like China, Iran, India, and Cuba. And it is the coming-together point on domestic issues like Social Security, Medicare, education, and the environment.

Economics is not just about statistics and equations, supply-and-demand charts. It is a way of thinking, of weighing interests, and indeed, a system predicated on our own morality. Most important, it allows us to see beyond the "rhetoric," to ground our statements in fact, in proof, in numbers. At last, in providing true justice to our world we have developed a scale. As John Kenneth Galbraith reminds us, "In the good and intelligent society policy and action are not subordinate to ideology, to doctrine. Action must be based on the ruling facts of the specific." Using our scale, our new ways of seeing, we can identify our obstacles and chart the road ahead.

Perhaps our greatest challenge will be battling economic inequalities both between generations and, now, increasingly between the educated and uneducated. Those inequalities threaten to fragment us into the have and have-nots, the old and the young, the media and the audience, the politicians and the common man, the gold-collar worker and the blue. As the industrialized nation with the highest level of inequality, we are now on a road which could divide America so thoroughly that our nation would cease to exist.

Restoring equality will not be easy, nor is it a commonly declared goal. The redistribution efforts of the welfare state offered little solution. Social Security and Medicare, designed to provide equitable relief for America's older generations, are now economically unstable. Despite the crumbling of those programs, there is still a desire to create a society in which all members share in progress. Perhaps our common ground can be in education. Education is the most important determining factor of a person's wealth. If we are committed to equality, then we must be willing to give the tools to the impoverished by first providing real education at the grade school and high school levels, by making college more affordable, and by teaching people to invest wisely for themselves. Yes, there will always have to be fallbacks for those who slip through the cracks, but the basic do-it-yourself incentives have to be there. That is something this generation is well poised to implement.

To do the job, this generation has to become politically engaged. And the basics is voting. "As a group, we need to vote more and make ourselves more of a presence in the political arena," says Beth Kobliner of *Money* magazine. "That is the only way to ensure the

Photo Courtesy/© of Arturo Patten

EDWIDGE DANTICAT
Author, **Breath, Eyes, Memory** *and* **Krik? Krak!: Stories**

FOLK WRITER, VISIONARY

Edwidge Danticat published her first writings at the age of 14, just two years after she came to the U.S. from Haiti. Since then she has appeared in over 20 periodicals and has won high praise for her first novel, *Breath, Eyes, Memory* about a young girl's journey, exile, and return to Haiti. She says of her American experience, "We live in a smaller world than we think. Migration continues to happen in great numbers all over the world. I think people will continue to have transnational ties. Thus we'll be forced, whether we like it or not, to continue to share ideas and learn about other people's cultures." Her take on her generation? "I think Generation X will be a very memorable generation. Fifty years from now, people will say, 'Imagine, in the beginning, they thought these people were slackers.'" In 1998, Edwidge is coming out with her second novel, *The Farming of Bones.*

passage of the kind of economics policies that will help further our long-term goals." If we don't vote, there is very little we can expect from Washington. We have shown our enthusiasm in the private sector, becoming the most entrepreneurial generation in American history. We must apply the same energy that we have for starting our own businesses into making the business of government better.

The pundits and cynics of politics say that good intentions quickly become compromised in city halls, state capitals, and Washington. Each generation sends its idealists, optimists, and go-getters to the various legislative bodies, only to see them turned into fatalists and pessimists. Perhaps this generation will be different. Already inculcated by scandal after scandal, we come to the process with what presidential speech writer Jeff Shesol calls a "healthy cynicism." We can use our knowledge to cut through the rhetoric and get to the heart of the matter. Maybe we can even be the generation that is not controlled or fragmented by special interests—but think on our own terms—not on the socioeconomic, ethnic, generational, or cultural lines that pollsters draw.

To overcome our differences and move forward as a nation, this generation has to determine what it now means to be an American. Defining America has always been a difficult problem. Unlike most other nations we have no common ethnic or cultural background. Being an American means holding a set of beliefs—it is demanding to have a voice in your government, loving liberty, and wanting a better way of life for the next generation. For America that belief is critical to our survival. For our generation we must enliven that message, redefine if we have to and make it ours.

Finally, we say to those older generations who have, to this point, labeled us: Give us the chance to write a story that proves the soothsayers wrong. We will bring more to the table than the generations before us, not less, for we are the generation without wars, without the tears of assassination, without the hunger of depression, without the fear of atomic destruction. We can make this land safer and richer and freer for all the right, positive motivations. We begin our journey not fueled by fear or rage or want, but with the precious luxury of peace, the priceless gift of knowledge, the wealth of lessons learned and corrected.

"Something will ultimately test [Generation X]," reported *Newsweek* in January 1997. Indeed, something will and is challenging us.

But don't expect that test to be a flashy event. It is only in today's myopic media that disasters have to be quick and numerous—not in history. Our biggest danger is that our problems, not offering high ratings, will go undetected. After all, many empires lasted centuries before decay or conquest wiped them out. Would TV have kept our interest in the Thirty Years War, the Crusades, or the centuries-long decline of the Roman empire? The disaster we face, the war we must win, may be decades in the making. It is no less real than short-term wars. And it won't be solved as fast as Desert Storm. It is about changing the direction of America—back to a course of equality, fair play, good education, and honest politics—in short, to bring America home.

SELECTED READINGS AND RESOURCES

Chideya, Farai. *Don't Believe the Hype: Fighting Cultural Misinformation about African-Americans.* New York: Penguin Books, 1995.

Dunn, William. *The Baby Bust: A Generation Comes of Age.* New York: American Demographics Books, 1993.

Foot, David K. *Boom, Bust, and Echo.* Toronto: Macfarlane, Walter, and Ross, 1996.

Fukuyama, Francis. *Trust.* New York: Simon and Schuster, 1995.

Galbraith, John Kenneth. *The Good Society.* New York: Houghton Mifflin Company, 1996.

Heflin, Jay S. and Richard Thau. *Generations Apart: Xers vs. Boomers vs. The Elderly.* Amherst: Prometheus Books, 1997.

Howe, Neil and William Strauss. *13th Generation: Abort, Retry, Ignore, Fail?* New York: Random House, 1993.

Howe, Neil and William Strauss. *The Fourth Turning: What Cycles of History Tell Us About America's Next Rendezvous with Destiny.* New York: Bantam Doubleday Dell, 1997.

Huntington, Samuel P. *The Clash of Civilization and the Remaking of the World Order.* New York: Simon and Schuster, 1996.

Kobliner, Beth. *Get a Financial Life: Personal Finance in Your Twenties and Thirties.* New York: Simon and Schuster, 1996.

Levi, Giovanni and Jean-Claude Schmitt. *A History of Young People: Volume One and Two.* Cambridge: Harvard University Press, 1997.

Peterson, Peter G. *Will America Grow Up Before It Grows Old? How the Coming Security Crisis Threatens You, Your Family, and Your Country.* New York: Random House, 1996.

Schor, Juliet B. *The Overworked American: The Unexpected Decline of Leisure.* New York: HarperCollins, 1992.

Tulgan, Bruce. *Managing Generation X.* Santa Monica, California: Merritt Publishing, 1995.

Reich, Robert B. *The Work of Nations.* New York: Random House, 1992.

Ritchie, Karen. *Marketing to Generation X.* New York: The Free Press, 1995.

Rushkoff, Douglas. *The Generation X Reader.* New York: Ballantine Books, 1994.

———. *Playing the Future.* New York: HarperCollins, 1996.